CYCLE TOURING IN FRANCE

by

Stephen Fox

2 POLICE SQUARE, MILNTHORPE, CUMBRIA LA7 7PY
www.cicerone.co.uk

ISBN-13 978 1 85284 432 5
ISBN-10 1 85284 432 9

© Stephen Fox 2006
Reprinted with updates 2007

A catalogue record for this book is available from the British Library.

All photographs by the author and Roan Fair.

ACKNOWLEDGEMENTS

First and foremost I must thank Roan Fair, who accompanied me on seven of the eight routes and was always so patient whenever I had to stop to write notes or take photographs. Many thanks also to Ian Uren who cycled with me on the Auvergne and Languedoc tour, and to Monique Cousquer, Gilles Rigole, Marie Sorin and Boris Wahl for their help and guidance. Last but not least, this guide would not have been possible without the wonderful support of my wife, Ilaria.

ADVICE TO READERS

Readers are advised that while every effort is taken by the author to ensure the accuracy of this guidebook, changes can occur which may affect the contents. It is advisable to check locally on roads, transport, accommodation and shops. Please advise the publishers of any changes: info@cicerone.co.uk.

Front cover: Pierrefonds (Route 2)

CYCLE TOURING IN FRANCE

About the Author

A couple of muddy mountain-biking weekends in Wales (with the evenings spent reading Robin Neilland's *Walking through France* whilst wet gear dried in front of a crackling fire) – followed by daily doses of Channel 4's coverage of the Tour de France in July 1989 – inspired Stephen Fox to attempt his first bicycle tour a month later, a 600-mile coast-to-coast charity ride across France from Caen to Montpellier.

Smitten ever since, he has cycled extensively in France and also central Italy, where he lived for several years. In 2001 he completed a challenging and exhilarating cycle tour of Norway's spectacular Lofoten Islands, situated 150 miles north of the Arctic Circle.

He now lives in southern England with his wife and daughter, and works in the photographic industry, as well as being a freelance writer and photographer.

CONTENTS

MAP SYMBOLS

Tour road	═══
Motorway or dual carriageway	═══
Other roads	═══
Town or village	▢
Airport	
Interesting place	
Forest or woods	
Hilly terrain	
Mountainous terrain	
Mountain col	
Vineyards	
Lighthouse	

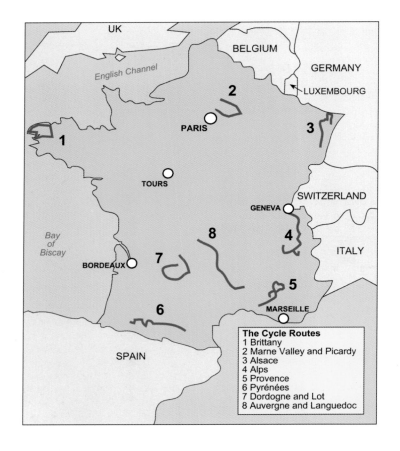

The Cycle Routes
1 Brittany
2 Marne Valley and Picardy
3 Alsace
4 Alps
5 Provence
6 Pyrénées
7 Dordogne and Lot
8 Auvergne and Languedoc

INTRODUCTION

Twice as big as the United Kingdom and four-fifths the size of Texas, France is a country rich in diverse landscapes and beautiful scenery, offering some of the best cycle touring in the world.

The routes in this guidebook have been specifically selected to give cycle tourists a taste of eight individual areas of France. Whether you want to tackle some of the steep mountain climbs of the Tour de France, or simply cycle alongside meandering rivers overlooked by hill villages and châteaux in the Dordogne and Lot, there is something here for everyone. The rugged, rocky coastline of Finistère and the magical, mythical woods near Huelgoat in Brittany; the vineyards and battlefields of the Marne, and beautiful forests of Retz and Compiègne in Picardy; the lavender fields and olive groves of Provence; the Route des Vins d'Alsace near the border with Germany; the volcanic Auvergne and wild Cévennes in the Massif Central – there is wonderful cycling country wherever you decide to go.

The eight routes – ranging from 209km (131 miles) to 354km (221 miles) in length – have been divided into several stages. Newcomers to cycle touring or cycling in France may wish to consider Routes 1, 2, 3, 5 (excluding the optional climb of Mont Ventoux) and 7, since none exceeds 2000m in total ascent, and all offer a splendid introduction to the country. Routes 6 and 8 (and the climb to Mont Ventoux in Route 5) will appeal to cycle tourists who are looking for more challenging rides in more remote or mountainous parts of France. Route 4 is reserved for those who want to attempt some of the classic Alpine climbs of the Tour de France, involving nearly 6000m of ascent between Geneva and Grenoble with some steep inclines at altitude.

WHICH ROUTE AND WHEN TO GO

Route 1 Finistère, 'the End of the World': Brittany
Character and terrain This circular tour starts in Morlaix and heads north to Carantec and the Ile Callot (an island that can only be reached during low tides) before veering west across undulating farmland to Le Folgoët, which has one of the finest Gothic basilica in Brittany. The route then follows the rugged, rocky coastline of northwest Finistère down to the most westerly point of France, the Pointe de Corsen, crossing steep-sided, narrow

ROUTE SUMMARY

Route	Location	Start point	Total Distance	Number of Stages	Stage Distances (km)	Total Climb
1 Finistère, 'the End of the World'	Brittany, Northwest France	Morlaix	277km (173 miles)	6	54/64/52/35/42/30	1750m
2 Champagne and The Kings' Forest	The Marne Valley and Picardy, Northern France	Paris CDG	226km (141 miles)	5	67/40/56/25/38	1040m
3 The Wine Road and Bas-Rhin	Alsace, Northeast France	Colmar	209km (131 miles)	4	50/62/37/60	1495m
4 An Alpine Experience	French Alps	Geneva	308km (192.5 miles)	6	53/51/73/68/14/49	5950m
5 The Land of Lavender	Provence, Southern France	Arles	283km (177 miles)	6	46/50/34/37/52/64	3082m*
6 Meadows and Mountains	French Pyrénées	Foix	313km (196 miles)	6	54/56/41/38/49/75	3581m
7 Rivers and Castles	Dordogne and Lot, Southwest France	Brive-la-Gaillarde	344km (215 miles)	6	61/40/90/69/46/38	1980m
8 Rugged and Remote	Massif Central, Auvergne and Languedoc, Central to Southern France	Meymac	354km (221 miles)	5	73/65/70/63/83	3330m

* (1850m excluding Mont Ventoux)

WHICH ROUTE AND WHEN TO GO

estuaries, known locally as Les Abers. Follow the coast road round to Brest, cross the Rade de Brest by ferry to Le Fret and cycle the length of the Crozon peninsula to Le Faou. The route then becomes fairly hilly as it continues east across the Parc Naturel Régional d'Armorique to Huelgoat and its fascinating forest. From Huelgoat head north to return to Morlaix.

Best time to visit Spring and summer.

Northwest France suffers more rain than anywhere else in the country because of the proximity of the Atlantic Ocean. The blustery weather that whips its way up the English Channel separating France from the UK has shaped the rugged Breton coastline. On a fine day (and there are many in Brittany!) this is an enchanting corner of the country. Spring and summer are generally mild, despite the occasional downpour, and some Summers can get unusually hot. July is usually the driest month, followed by June and August. It is often damp, misty and rainy from October through to March. Coastal campsites can get quite full from mid-July to mid-August.

Route 2 Champagne and The Kings' Forest: the Marne Valley and Picardy

Character and terrain Leaving from Paris CDG airport you immediately cycle across undulating farmland to Vareddes and the tranquil Canal de l'Ourcq. Once Charly-sur-Marne is reached you are on the Route Touristique du Champagne, following the wide Marne Valley with its vineyard-covered slopes all the way to Dormans. Here you will find the magnificent Mémorial des Deux Batailles de la Marne, a huge memorial chapel dedicated to the war dead on the battlefields of the Marne.

From Dormans head north across more undulating farmland to visit the Oise-Aisne American Cemetery, the second largest World War I American military cemetery in Europe. The route soon turns west towards the beautiful Retz Forest, home to a wonderful variety of fauna including deer, rabbits, hares, foxes, pheasants and even wild boar. Some historic buildings follow: the house in Villers-Cotterêts where Alexandre Dumas, author of *The Three Musketeers*, was born; the Donjon de Vez and the Abbaye de Lieu-Restauré in the Automne Valley; the Notre Dame church of Morienval, one of the earliest and finest Gothic churches in France; and finally the immense château of Pierrefonds.

The route then follows a splendid cycle path through the Forest of Compiègne to Compiègne itself, then runs on to the Clairière de l'Armistice site where the World War I Armistice was signed, before returning through the forest to Pierrefonds.

Best time to visit Late spring, summer, and harvest time in autumn.

Driest months are normally April and August. Winters are cold, and

Above Celliers Dessus on the climb to the Col de la Madeleine (Route 4)

night temperatures stay low until late April. If you plan on camping it might be better to visit in spring or late summer/early autumn as there are few campsites in this part of France – otherwise book in advance for summer.

Route 3 The Wine Road and Bas-Rhin: Alsace

Character and terrain Setting off from the city of Colmar, you soon cycle along the celebrated Route des Vins d'Alsace – the Alsace Wine Road – to Barr, passing through typically quaint Alsatian villages surrounded by vineyards. From Barr the route passes through beautiful woods and climbs up through the Forêt de Haslach to Wangenbourg before a long descent to Saverne. Once more the countryside opens up as you follow the Marne–Rhine Canal from Saverne,

then cross flat farmland via a charming cycle path and skirt the southern edge of the forested Vosges du Nord Regional Natural Park all the way to Niederbronn-les-Bains. A wonderful ride up into the Forêt de Niederbronn follows with a visit to the ruined Château de Fleckenstein, situated literally a stone's throw from Germany. Another cycle path, this time through pretty woodland, leads from Lembach to Woerth, after which the path crosses open countryside before a pleasant ride through another forest to Haguenau.

Best time to visit Summer, and harvest time in autumn.

May and June are normally the wettest months. Winters are cold, and it quite often snows until early spring in the high, forested hills of the Vosges, situated to the west of Colmar and Strasbourg.

Route 4 An Alpine Experience

Character and terrain Starting in Geneva and finishing in Grenoble, this route crosses Haute-Savoie with a gradual ascent up the Gorge des Eveaux and scenic climbs to the Col du Marais and Col de Tamié before reaching Albertville, home to the Winter Olympics in 1992. The first of three tough climbs encountered on the Tour de France awaits you, to the Col de la Madeleine (2000m above sea level). A giant descent to the Arc Valley is then followed by another magnificent climb to the Col de la Croix de Fer (2067m) with splendid mountain views. The third and final climb is the unforgiving l'Alpe d'Huez (with 21 hairpin bends). As a reward there is a refreshing 25km descent to Vizille with a visit to its grand château, and from there on to Grenoble.

Best time to visit Summer.

Snow lingers above 3000m throughout the year, and late snow-falls often block high mountain passes well into June. If attempting this route in June, find out whether the passes are open by visiting the local infor-mation offices. The valleys are often hot in July and August, while up in the mountains it is noticeably cooler. As with all high mountain ranges the weather in the French Alps can be quite changeable in summer, so be prepared for the occasional thunder-storm. September is normally drier than June, July or August.

Route 5 The Land of Lavender: Provence

Character and terrain Provence is a colourful patchwork of lavender fields, olive groves, cherry orchards and vineyards, a fabulous part of France for cycle touring. Starting in the historic city of Arles this route visits Alphonse Daudet's windmill and Les Baux-de-Provence before heading east to the spectacular hill village of Gordes and the Abbaye de Sénanque. A tour around Mont Ventoux and the option of cycling up to its summit follows, then a scenic 20km descent down the Gorges de la Nesque to Villes-sur-Auzon and thereafter to L'Isle-sur-la-Sorgue.

Best time to visit Late spring to early July, then September to mid-October.

Arles (Route 5)

The south of France, protected by the Pyrénées, is hot in summer and mild in winter. Inland temperatures often reach the mid-30s in summer, so most tourists head for the cooling waters of the Mediterranean. June and July are normally the driest months. Provence often experiences a strong wind, the Mistral, which blows from north to south along the Rhône Valley and is responsible for the 'lunar' landscape of the summit slopes of Mont Ventoux, the Windy Mountain.

Route 6 Meadows and Mountains: Pyrénées

Character and terrain Crossing the heart of the French Pyrénées from east to west, this route starts in Foix, dominated by its imposing château ruins. From here cycle across lush, quiet countryside and through the giant cave known as Grotte du Mas d'Azil to St Girons. High, rolling hills follow as you continue west to St Bertrand-de-Comminges with its landmark cathedral dominating the valley down which the River Garonne flows north from the high Pyrénées. A gradual ascent to Arreau up the Vallée d'Aure is followed by a climb to the Col d'Aspin (1489m) before a long descent to Bagnères-de-Bigorre and on to Lourdes. Follow the long cyclepath that runs from Lourdes to Pierrefitte-Nestalas, 'La Voie Verte des Gaves'. If you want to try one of the big Tour de France climbs the optional Stage 6 up the scenic Val d'Azun to the Col d'Aubisque provides a spectacular finale.

Best time to visit June to September.

The mountainous Pyrénées, although not as high as the Alps, can also experience fickle weather conditions in summer, so be prepared for the odd afternoon thunderstorm in July and August. High mountain passes are often not open until late May/early June due to late snowfalls in the spring. July is normally the driest month.

Route 7 Rivers and Castles: Dordogne and Lot

Character and terrain This circular tour starts in Brive-la-Gaillarde and heads south, crossing the River Dordogne to the charming villages of Carennac and Autoire with their clusters of typically medieval Quercynois houses with brown-tiled turreted roofs, dovecots and towers. The castles of Castelnau-Bretenoux and Montal are visited before an ascent through lovely woods to Figeac.

From Figeac cycle alongside the unspoilt River Célé for almost 50km to its meeting with the River Lot and the magnificent hill village of St Cirq-Lapopie. Follow the Lot west through Cahors and Luzech with vineyards bordering the river, then cycle across hilly country to the massive castle of Bonaguil and the *bastide* town of Monpazier before once again crossing the Dordogne. Travelling east along its northern bank you encounter yet more impressive castles and some of the most beautiful villages in France, before eventually reaching Souillac and taking a short train ride back to Brive-la-Gaillarde.

Best time to visit Spring, or late summer to autumn.

The Dordogne and Lot are very popular areas for summer holidays with both French and foreign tourists, so book accommodation in advance if visiting in July or August. Spring and autumn are generally mild seasons for cycle touring in southwest France, but winters can be quite cold. June and July are normally the driest months.

Route 8 Rugged and Remote: Auvergne and Languedoc

Character and terrain Starting from Meymac, on the edge of the high Plateau des Millevaches in the *département* of Corrèze, ride southeast, crossing the River Dordogne and cycling up into the Parc Naturel Régional des Volcans d'Auvergne.

This is the largest Nature Park in France: a vast, open, rugged landscape of high, rolling hills and extinct volcanoes. Continuing southeast to the hill town of St Flour cross the Truyère river below the immense Viaduc de Garabit railway viaduct and cycle into Lozère, the least populated of France's 96 *départements*. Here you leave one region for another, the Auvergne for Languedoc. Cycle down the remote Vallée d'Enfer and pass through Marvejols, crossing another of France's great rivers, the Lot, before climbing to the barren plateau known as the Causse de Sauveterre. A descent into the spectacular Gorges du Tarn, one of the most beautiful canyons in Europe, is followed by another climb to the Corniche des Cévennes which grants splendid panoramas of the surrounding Parc National des Cévennes – wild and remote, rich in

Parc National des Cévennes (Route 8)

flora and fauna. This marks the southern end of the great Massif Central, and the route ends with a long descent to St Jean-du-Gard and then on to Alès.

Best time to visit Late summer and early autumn.

The weather can be changeable, with some summers decidedly hotter or wetter than others. Driest months are normally July and August. Winters are usually long and very cold, with snow lingering on higher ground until the spring.

The following table gives average monthly temperatures in degrees Centigrade for each of the routes.

AVERAGE MONTHLY MAXIMUM AND MINIMUM TEMPERATURES

		J	F	M	A	M	J	J	A	S	O	N	D
Route 1	max	9	10	11	12	16	18	20	21	18	16	12	10
Brest	min	3	4	5	5	8	10	12	12	11	9	6	4
Route 2	max	6	7	10	13	18	20	23	24	19	15	10	7
Compiègne	min	1	2	3	5	8	10	13	13	10	7	4	2
Route 3	max	4	7	11	15	21	23	25	26	20	16	8	5
Strasbourg	min	-1	0	2	4	9	12	13	13	10	7	2	0
Route 4	max	3	4	8	10	15	19	22	23	18	12	8	4
Albertville	min	-2	-1	0	2	7	9	12	12	9	6	1	-1
Route 5	max	12	13	16	19	22	25	29	29	24	20	15	12
Arles	min	4	5	7	9	12	16	19	18	15	12	7	4
Route 6	max	8	10	13	15	19	23	26	26	23	18	11	9
Foix	min	1	2	4	6	9	12	15	15	11	8	4	2
Route 7	max	8	10	13	16	19	23	26	25	23	18	12	9
Souillac	min	1	2	3	6	9	11	14	13	12	9	4	2
Route 8	max	6	8	10	14	18	22	24	24	20	16	8	6
Murat	min	0	0	2	4	6	10	12	12	10	8	2	0

A SHORT HISTORY

Major evidence of human settlement in France dates from around 25000BC, most noticeably traces of the Cro-Magnon people (as they became known) who lived from the Upper Palaeolithic to the Neolithic Age. Their cave paintings were discovered in Périgord, those in the Grotte de Lascaux being perhaps the most famous. The first Megalithic sites appeared in Brittany – a region peppered with dolmens and menhirs – around 5700BC. From about 1200BC several peoples – including the Celts from Britain and Ireland – came and settled in what is now known as France.

Gaul (as the Romans called it) became part of Julius Caesar's Roman Empire in the 1st century BC and remained so for 500 years until the Franks, a Germanic tribe led by Clovis I, conquered the fertile land between the Loire and the Somme in AD486. Clovis chose Paris (just another little town on the map at that time) as his capital at the turn of the 6th century. Roman Catholicism became the main religion, with Clovis declaring himself a Christian. Frankish society was subsequently converted, with the Franks (from whom 'France' derives) pushing southwards through Aquitaine as far as the Pyrénées.

In the mid-8th century the Carolingian dynasty came to power, with Pepin the Short being crowned king by the Pope. It was his successor, Charlemagne, who reunited the Frankish domains of Roman Gaul of old in 771. Charlemagne was crowned Emperor of the Roman Empire by Pope Leo III in 800. In 843 this empire was divided between his grandsons into the West Frankish Kingdom, the Middle Frankish Empire and the East Frankish Kingdom. During the 9th century France was often attacked by Norsemen (from Scandinavia) who eventually settled in Normandy; two centuries later, in 1066, William the Conqueror, Duke of Normandy, conquered England.

In 987, when the last Carolingian successor died, Hugues Capet was elected as the first of 13 kings of France by a select group of powerful provincial governors. This Capetian dynasty lasted until 1328, nine years before the start of the Hundred Years' War between France and England. However, large parts of France were under English rule from the second half of the 12th century, as a result of Eleanor of Aquitaine divorcing Louis VII of France and marrying Henry Plantagenet of Normandy, who soon became Henry II of England.

A significant battle during the Hundred Years' War took place in 1415 when Henry V of England defeated the French at Agincourt. The tides turned 14 years later when that celebrated leader of the French armies, Jeanne d'Arc (Joan of Arc), defeated the English at Orléans, leading to the coronation of Charles VII at Reims. Unfortunately Jeanne d'Arc fell into the hands of the

Ossuaire du Vieux Bourg de Quimerc'h (Route 1)

Burgundians (allies of the English), and she was burnt at the stake by the English in 1431. News of her martyrdom spread, however, and inspired the French to fight on, resulting in the English finally being driven out of France in 1453.

The War of Religions between Protestants and Catholics in France started in 1562 and lasted for more than 30 years. During this war Henri III was assassinated and France saw her first Bourbon king, Henri IV, who helped bring about reconciliation and played an important role in the Edict of Nantes (which formalised the tolerance of Protestantism) in 1598.

France was ruled by just two kings for nine-tenths of the 17th century, Louis XIII and Louis XIV, the latter ascending the throne at the very early age of five and ruling for 72 years until 1715. Cardinals served both kings, Cardinal Richelieu for Louis XIII being the best known. France became a powerful state during this century (despite costly wars and deteriorating home economic conditions), mostly due to gaining territory overseas, thereby opening up profitable trading routes. However, in the Seven Years' War (1752–63) France lost most of her colonies to the English, and monarchy and parliament became increasingly divided. On 14 July 1789 the Bastille was stormed; the French Revolutionaries toppled the king, Louis XVI, and the Ancien Régime was destroyed. The unfortunate Louis

XVI and his queen, Marie Antoinette, were executed in 1793, the year after the monarchy was abolished and the First Republic established.

In 1804 Napoleon Bonaparte had himself crowned Emperor of France, 19 years after becoming an officer of the French army. His own armies conquered most of Europe by 1810, but two years later, hoping to extend his control of territory to Russia and beyond, his forces reached Moscow. A harsh winter forced them to retreat. A vast number of troops died on the long, cold return home, resulting in Napoleon Bonaparte's abdication in 1814. Twice exiled, he eventually died on the South Atlantic island of St Helena in 1821.

Ironically it was to be his nephew, Louis-Napoleon, who led a coup in 1851 and proclaimed himself Emperor Napoleon III after the establishment of the Second Republic. During the 1850s France prospered both economically and industrially, but the Franco-Prussian War in 1870 was Napoleon III's downfall and he was defeated, resulting in a Third Republic. France also lost Alsace and most of Lorraine to Germany as a result of this war, only regaining them at the end of World War I (1914–18). A Fourth Republic began in 1946 after World War II (1939–45), and women were finally given the vote. The Fifth Republic was formed in 1958 under the leadership of President Charles De Gaulle who remained in power until 1969, the year before his death. François Mitterrand,

The château of Foix (Route 6)

leader of the Socialist Party, won the presidential election in 1981 and stayed in power for 14 years, thus becoming the longest-serving president in France's history to date. In 1993 France, together with 11 other members of the European Community, ratified the Treaty on European Union and so became one of the EU countries. A year later the Channel Tunnel was completed, linking France with England.

GETTING THERE

From the UK and Ireland

Flying to France is much cheaper now than a decade ago. The number of budget airlines has grown at such a rate that the major airlines have found it hard to compete and have reduced their fares accordingly. Budget airlines include:

* Ryanair (**www.ryanair.com**)
* Easyjet (**www.easyjet.com**)
* Flybe (**www.flybe.com**)
* Thomsonfly (**www.thomsonfly.com**)
* Aer Lingus (**www.aerlingus.com**)
* bmi/British Midland (**www.flybmi.com**)

The major airlines include British Airways (**www.ba.com**) and Air France (**www.airfrance.com**).

The following table indicates the start points of the eight routes, the nearest airport to each, and which airlines fly there from the UK.

If flying to the nearest airport to the start of a route is not feasible, another option is to fly to Paris and travel on to your destination from the capital. The journey onward from Paris airports to central Paris is described below. From here you can take a train to your final destination.

Further information regarding travel to the start points is given at the beginning of each route description,

Route	Start point	Nearest airport	Airline
1	Morlaix	Brest	Flybe
2	Paris CDG	Paris CDG	Easyjet, BA, Air France
3	Colmar	Strasbourg	Air France
4	Geneva	Geneva	Easyjet
5	Arles	Marseille Nîmes Montpellier Avignon	Easyjet, BA Ryanair Ryanair Flybe
6	Foix	Toulouse	Easyjet, BA
7	Brive-la-Gaillarde	Limoges	Ryanair & Flybe
8	Meymac	Limoges	Ryanair & Flybe

Val d'Azun (Route 6)

as well as a few alternative airports located further away than those listed above.

Most airlines now stipulate that your bike goes in a bike bag, and UK airlines may charge £15–£20 for a bike on a single flight. They will want the tyres fully deflated, pedals removed, and handlebars turned so that they are parallel with the top tube. I recommend bubble-wrapping the derailleurs and any other parts of the bike you cherish, and removing the rear rack which can be used to further protect the rear derailleurs inside the bike bag. You can buy bags through most reputable bike shops in the UK.

If you don't like flying, there are other options. From Ireland, Brittany Ferries (**www.brittanyferries.co.uk**) operate one weekly crossing from

Cork to Roscoff between April and October, and Irish Ferries (**www.irish-ferries.ie**) operate up to three crossings between Rosslare and Roscoff from mid-April to October. These are convenient for those wanting to tackle the Brittany tour (Route 1). Irish Ferries also operate a route between Rosslare and Cherbourg three times a week. Ferry crossings from Ireland take anything from 12–20 hours.

Crossings from England are much shorter. From the south coast Brittany Ferries operate four routes (Portsmouth to St Malo, Portsmouth to Caen-Ouistreham, Poole to Cherbourg and Plymouth to Roscoff) and Condor Ferries (**www.condorferries.com**) operate two (Poole to St Malo and Weymouth to St Malo). The Condor ferries are fast, reaching St Malo in five hours. Hoverspeed (**www.hoverspeed.co.uk**), Sea France (**www.seafrance.com**) and P&O Ferries (**www.poferries.com**) operate ferry crossings between Dover to Calais. Foot passengers can take bicycles on all of these (£5–£10 charge). A useful website for information is **www.aferry.co.uk**.

There are regular train services to Paris from all the French ports mentioned (although some, such as Caen-Ouistreham, require a ride into town to the main station).

Cyclists can also reach France by train from England. The regular Eurostar service (**www.eurostar.com**) via Ashford International in Kent and the Channel Tunnel departs from London Waterloo International and takes about 3 hours to Paris Gare du Nord. Trains run every hour during the week from 5.30am to 7.40pm. You can also get off at Lille (2 hours from London Waterloo) and take a high speed TGV (Train à Grande Vitesse) to the Paris airport CDG where the Marne and Picardy tour (Route 2) begins. This TGV line bypasses Paris and continues on to the south of France.

It is also possible to travel direct to Avignon (Route 5) in the south of France from London Waterloo International by Eurostar on Saturdays from the end of May to mid-October, but you need to book well in advance. The direct services operate from London Waterloo and Ashford in Kent to and from Avignon Centre station and the journey time is only 6 hours 15 minutes (an hour less from/to Ashford). Tickets can be purchased through the Eurostar contact centre in the UK on 08705 186 186, online at **www.eurostar.com**, at Waterloo and Ashford International Terminals or through registered agents. Check in at least 1 hour before departure. If you want to travel on other days of the week, you can use Eurostar and connecting TGV services in Paris or Lille to travel to or from Avignon ('Eurostar Plus' services). Lille is probably preferable to Paris since you have to get across the centre of Paris for your TGV connection.

You can take your bicycle with you on the Eurostar in a bike bag as long as its dimensions do not exceed 120cm x 90cm together with your panniers, otherwise they advise you to use the registered baggage service which operates between London, Paris, Lille and Brussels Eurostar Terminals. Registered items will be ready for collection within 24 hours of registering them. The charge for a bicycle (tandems not accepted) is £20, and £12 for all baggage up to 30kg. For more information call 08705 850 850 (in the UK). If 10 or more of you travel together a special group luggage service operates between London Waterloo International, Paris Gard du Nord and Brussels Midi with all your luggage loaded up in a secure compartment on the train that can be collected at your destination. Call 08705 850 850 for more information, or email group.baggage@eurostar.com.

The onward journey from Paris train stations is described below, and information given on taking bicycles on trains in France.

From the United States and Canada

It is possible to fly direct to Paris from about 30 cities in the United States, and from Toronto and Montreal in Canada. Major airlines serving Paris include:

- Air Canada (**www.aircanada.ca**)
- Air France (**www.airfrance.com**)
- American Airlines (**www.aa.com**)
- British Airways (**www.ba.com**)
- Continental Airlines (**www.continental.com**)
- Delta Airlines (**www.delta.com**)
- Lufthansa (**www.lufthansa.com**)
- United Airlines (**www.ual.com**)

Delta and Air France also fly direct from JFK to Nice, which would be useful for those wanting to do the Provence tour (Route 5). It is also worth considering flying to other European cities from the US or Canada from where you can easily get connecting flights or trains – London or Frankfurt, for example. Visit **www.travelzoo.com** for good value flights available from the US and outside Europe.

From Australia and New Zealand

Although it is possible to fly direct to Paris from Sydney and other major cities in Australia, and Auckland in New Zealand, most people prefer to fly to London via Southeast Asia and from there to Paris. It is also possible to fly via the United States, but this is usually more expensive and the journey time is longer.

Getting from Paris airports to central Paris

Cycling into Paris from either of her two airports is not recommended. To reach central Paris it would be best to leave your bike in its bag and make use of the regular transport services mentioned below. Once in central Paris, you can then either reach the relevant railway station for your onward journey by taxi or on your bike. Air France buses go to Gare Montparnasse in central Paris from both airports.

Paris is served by two airports: Charles de Gaulle (CDG) and Orly. The majority of international flights arrive at CDG, situated 23km northeast of the capital. It has two main terminals: CDG1 and CDG2, the latter split into five halls (2A, 2B, 2C, 2D and 2F). The much smaller terminal 3 (formerly T9) is used for seasonal charter flights only. All Air France flights arrive at CDG2, as well as some international flights including Air Canada and Delta, but the majority of international flights arrive at CDG1. The two main terminals are linked by a free bus shuttle service, and there is a train station at CDG2 with an RER line to central Paris. There is also a TGV station at CDG2, enabling you to bypass Paris altogether if you want to go to Lille, Lyon or Avignon. For TGV departures from the Gare Montparnasse in Paris you can take an Air France bus from CDG (1 hour), or for central Paris jump on a Roissybus (RATP service); buses leave from both terminals. Taxis cost about 40 euros to central Paris from either terminal. Air France operates a bus service between CDG and Orly airports.

Orly airport is situated 15km south of Paris and has two terminals, Sud and Ouest. Air France's domestic flights go to most French cities from Orly, with fewer routes from CDG. Some international and charter flights arrive at Orly Sud from where there are several options to reach central Paris. Air France buses (Door K) stop at Montparnasse en route to central Paris, and Orlybus (Door H) will take you to the metro/RER station of Denfert-Rochereau not far from Montparnasse. Buses leave every 15 minutes and the journey takes about 30 minutes. There are also shuttle buses (*navettes*) to the RER (suburban railway) station of Pont de Rungis (line C) from where you can take a train to Gare d'Austerlitz, or a shuttle train (Orlyval) which connects the two terminals with the RER station of Antony (line B) from where you can take a train to central Paris. Taxis cost about 35 euros. It is possible to walk from Orly Sud to Ouest if you are taking a domestic flight from the latter. Air France also operates a bus service between Orly and CDG. Visit

www.adp.fr for more information about both airports.

Getting from Paris train stations to your destination

There are six principal train stations in Paris:

* Gare du Nord: TGV Nord trains, and trains for northern France
* Gare Montparnasse: TGV Atlantique trains, and trains heading west
* Gare de Lyon: TGV Sud-Est trains, and trains heading south-east
* Gare St Lazare: trains for Normandy
* Gare de l'Est: trains for the east
* Gare d'Austerlitz: trains for the southwest.

A TGV Est line is under construction. The whole railway network in France is run by the SNCF (Société Nationale des Chemins de Fer).

If you have taken the Eurostar to Gare du Nord and you need to reach one of the other main stations in Paris you will either have to carry your bike in its bag and panniers on the Métro, or assemble your bike and cycle across the capital's centre. The latter option is far more interesting as you get to see some of Paris and don't have to worry about turnstiles, escalators and stairs. If, however, you need to get across Paris quickly to catch your next train, take a taxi that will accommodate you and all your gear.

Route	Station	Destination
1	Gare Montparnasse	Morlaix
2	Gare du Nord	CDG airport
3	Gare de l'Est	Strasbourg, then change for Colmar
4	Gare de Lyon	Geneva
5	Gare de Lyon	Avignon TGV station, then shuttle bus to Arles or train from Avignon Centre station to Arles
6	Gare Montparnasse or Gare d'Austerlitz	Toulouse, then change for Foix
7	Gare d'Austerlitz	Limoges, then to Brive-la-Gaillarde
8	Gare d'Austerlitz	Limoges, then change for Meymac

The table above indicates which train station in Paris you need for the onward train journey to the start point of a given route. Further information regarding travel to the start points is also given at the beginning of each route description.

BICYCLES ON TRAINS IN FRANCE

You can put your bicycle on most TER (regional trains), Corail and Transilien trains, without charge. There will either be a specific carriage/luggage van (*fourgon à bagages*) or a compartment with a designated area for three or four bikes (*éspace vélo*). The latter may involve hanging your bike from a hook in the ceiling. They are usually to be found near the end of the train, if not the last carriage itself. Double-decker trains usually do not have a designated compartment for bicycles, and you can just wheel them into any 2nd class carriage at the platform conductor's discretion. On older trains you need to look out for the luggage van with the metal roller shutter door which may be locked from the inside, so make sure you've introduced yourself to the platform conductor beforehand who should assist in getting it opened. I recommend taking the rear panniers off, as you may either have to get the bike through a narrow doorway or lift it up into the luggage van. If there are two of you, it's easier if one gets in the van and pulls the bikes up. Some trains have a bicycle symbol painted on the outer door of the designated carriage. Contacting the platform conductor is important as he or she often allows you to take your bike on a slow train that stops at every station but does not have a bike carriage or designated area.

If you pick up the relevant timetable leaflet at the station, check the top/bottom of each regional train column for the little bicycle symbol which indicates that you can take your bike on certain trains free of charge without having to dismantle it (*transport de vélo gratuit*). On some trains you may have to pay a *réservation supplémentaire* of 10 euros and travel in 2nd class, but still not have to dismantle the bike. This is the case with TGV Lyria trains between Lausanne, Zurich and Paris, as well as most Corail Lunéa and Corail Téoz trains between Paris and Clermont-Ferrand, Paris and Strasbourg, and Paris and Toulouse. Occasionally, in rural areas, a bus service (*autocar*) is used to connect certain stations at certain times – look for the bus symbol on the train timetable.

For TGV (Train à Grande Vitesse) trains in general, and many daytime trains (especially between 7am and 9am) run by Corail, you will have to dismantle your bike and put it in a bike bag (*housse à vélo*) no bigger than 120cm x 90cm. There are designated luggage holds or racks on these trains, but it is a good idea to get on before everyone else, as there is nothing short of a rugby scrum as people try to get their luggage in the designated area before departure.

You could, alternatively, send your bike on ahead by going to a SERNAM depot, which may or may not be located near a French railway station. SERNAM is the trucking company associated with the French railway system that will box your bike and deliver it to your chosen depot for about 40 euros within 48 hours. You can phone 08 25 84 58 45 to locate your nearest depot, for other

Trains and bicycles

information, and to pay the delivery charge by credit card. You can also pay for this service when you buy your train ticket at the station, or at a SERNAM depot. However, it is important to bear in mind that the depots are usually only open from 8am to 5pm, Monday to Friday, with only major depots open on Saturday mornings. They are closed Sundays and public holidays. As some depots are situated some distance from a town's railway station you will have to take alternative transport to reach the station.

I prefer to be on the same train as my bike and keep an eye on it whenever the train stops – that way it will reach your destination when you do, and you are ready to start your tour without any hitches.

For timetables and further information visit **www.ter-sncf.com** for regional networks, or **www.voyages-sncf.com** for train journeys from one region to another.

ROADS

The condition of French roads varies considerably. One moment you may be cycling along a recently resurfaced road with a cycle lane – the next you are avoiding potholes on a bumpy stretch of cracked asphalt! The reason for this is usually a régional, départmentale or communale one. In effect, there are three levels of local government.

France is divided into 22 regions, sub-divided into 96 *départments*, and these are, in turn, sub-divided into about 36,000 local *communes* – the equivalent of a parish or borough. The regional councils are responsible for Autoroutes (motorways) and Routes Nationales (main trunk roads), often marked on maps and road signs as 'N' or 'RN' roads. Bicycles are not allowed on Autoroutes, which are marked as 'A' roads and their road signs are blue. 'D' roads are the responsibility of the *départmentale*

Near Gabre (Route 6)

councils and are quieter secondary roads, while 'C' roads are rural roads that the local *commune* looks after (or not, depending on funding). Most of the roads covered in this guidebook are in good condition or have recently been resurfaced, many with cycle lanes or paths running alongside them. It is also not uncommon to discover, for example, that the D77 (that you have been cycling along) suddenly becomes the D52 for no apparent reason. This is probably due to you having crossed the boundary line between *départements*.

Apart from always remembering to cycle on the right side of the road, it is important to take care at roundabouts which come in all shapes and sizes and spring up all over the place. Do not be surprised to find that a junction mentioned in this guidebook is now a mini roundabout – the French love building them. Traffic already on a roundabout has the right of way. You will often see signs indicating that you do not have right of way (*vous n'avez pas la priorité*) or that you must give way (*cédez le passage*). At junctions, traffic coming from the right has right of way (*priorité à droite*), even if they are on a minor road. Traffic on these roads, however, must give way to you if they have a stop sign. You know you have right of way if you see the sign with a yellow diamond inside a white one.

If a road has a cycle lane or path, you must use it. Drivers do not take kindly to cyclists who ignore a cycle path and hold up traffic on a narrow stretch of road. A cycle path (*piste cyclable*) is usually indicated by a white bicycle symbol on a blue background, or could be a narrow green track with a white bicycle symbol painted on it. A cycle lane (usually about a metre wide) will run along the extreme right of the road and also has a bicycle symbol painted on it.

As cycling is a national sport in France, the vast majority of drivers are very considerate, will give you a wide berth and may honk to let you know they are coming up behind. Strangely, I have discovered that in some parts of France you can cycle for days without anyone honking you, but in other parts nearly every car or truck will hit the horn. Don't get the hump if they do – they mean well. Many disused railway lines have now been turned into well-surfaced cycle paths and I have included several of them in the tours.

MAPS

The blue IGN (Institut Geographic National) 1:100,000 Carte Topographique Top 100 maps are highly recommended for the tours in this guide. There are 74 in all, covering the whole of France. They are detailed maps complete with contour lines, aimed especially at cyclists and walkers. Most good bookshops can order them in, or you can buy them online at **www.stanfords.co.uk** or **www.mapsworldwide.com**.

This is a list of the relevant map numbers for the tours in this guidebook:

- **Brittany tour** 13 (Brest/Quimper), 14 (St Brieuc/Morlaix)
- **Marne Valley and Picardy tour** 09 (Paris/Laon)
- **Alsace tour** 12 (Strasbourg/Forbach), 31 (St Dié/Mulhouse/Basle)
- **Alps tour** 45 (Annecy/Lausanne), 53 (Grenoble/Mont Blanc), 54 (Grenoble/Gap)
- **Provence tour** 60 (Cavaillon/Digne les Bains), 66 (Avignon/Montpellier), 67 (Marseille/Carpentras)
- **Pyrénées tour** 70 (Pau/Bagnères de Luchon), 71 (St Gaudens/Andorre)
- **Dordogne and Lot tour** 48 (Périgueux/Tulle), 57 (Cahors/Montauban)
- **Auvergne and Languedoc tour** 49 (Clermont-Ferrand/Aurillac), 58 (Rodez/Mende), 59 (Privas/Alès)

Michelin publish the very useful France 1:200,000 *Motorist and Motoring Atlas*, updated annually. It covers the whole of France, indicates most recommended campsites, and includes some city and town maps. The campsites in this atlas are described in detail in Michelin's *Camping Caravaning le guide*, which is also updated annually.

PASSPORTS, VISAS, HEALTH AND INSURANCE

At present, citizens of the United States, Canada, Australia and New Zealand do not need an entry visa for France for stays up to 90 days, only a full passport. If you intend to stay longer than three months you need to apply for a visa in your home country before reaching France. Citizens from European Union countries can travel freely in France (passport, or identity card, depending on issuing country) for up to three months, but should officially apply for a *carte de séjour* if wishing to stay any longer than this. South African citizens need to apply for a short-stay visa up to three months. For information regarding visa requirements for entering France from any country in the world visit **www.diplomatie.gouv.fr**. For Embassy and Consulate addresses, websites and relevant information regarding visas, passports, emergencies and so on see Appendix F.

Citizens of all European Union and Scandinavian countries are entitled to take advantage of French health services under the same terms as residents, providing they have the correct documentation. British citizens need to have a European Health Insurance Card (EHIC); apply online via the Department of Health website, or call 0845 606 2030 for an application form. You can also pick one up at major post offices. North American and other non-European Union citizens have to pay for most medical

The Donjon de Vez (Route 2)

attention, so it would be prudent to consider travel insurance.

Any hospital visit, doctor's consultation and prescribed medicine incur a charge, which could be expensive. If you are unwell you can visit a local GP/doctor (*un médecin*) who nearly always speaks some English and charges about 25 euros, regardless of nationality. Most pharmacies (look for a blinking green neon cross above a shop) can give you the name and address of a GP nearby, or look under *Médecins Qualifiés* in the local Yellow Pages. To see a GP outside business hours or at weekends you will have to locate the doctor on call (*médecin de garde*) in the immediate area. Either dial the number 15 (*SAMU* – French Emergency Health Service/ Paramedics number) and await the operator, or check in the local newspaper, which should list the doctor on call and out-of-hours pharmacy (*pharmacie de garde*) for that given week. A closed pharmacy will display the address of the nearest open pharmacy, daytime or evening. In serious emergencies you will always be admitted to the nearest hospital. The local fire brigade is not averse to helping out in an emergency either, so remember the phone number 18. Dialling 15 or 18 are free of charge, as is 17 for the police.

French pharmacies do not stock most medicines on shelves accessible to the general public (as is the case in the United States); you have to ask for a specific medicine at the counter. It would be wise to write down particulars of any prescription medication you take on a daily basis before leaving for France, in case of any unforeseen emergency while you are there. If you pick up a mystery illness or suffer badly from an allergy while in France, try to explain the symptoms as best you can to a pharmacist who will recommend a medication.

Travel insurance is an important consideration even if you are a citizen of a European Union country. Apart from medical problems other ugly things can spoil your holiday such as theft, loss of baggage and other items, and serious injury causing a long spell in hospital (to name but three). Check your home insurance cover before splashing on another policy – some will cover loss of possessions abroad. Often, policies can be tailor-made to suit your trip. If you do take full medical coverage, it is worth checking if any treatment received would be paid for during your stay or only after returning home. As regards baggage cover, check that the maximum payout per item lost or stolen is more than your most valuable possession. You must obtain an official statement from the police should you be unfortunate enough to have anything stolen; if you need to make a claim you should keep receipts for any medicines and medical treatment. Similarly, American and Canadian citizens should also check to see that they're not already covered, so study the small print in home health plans. Students and teachers visiting France may often be entitled to certain health benefits.

MONEY, BANKS AND PAYPHONES

The euro is the only currency in France now, having replaced the French franc in 2002. Banknotes come in 5, 10, 20, 50, 100, 200 and 500 euro denominations and coins in 1 and 2 euro denominations, as well as 1, 2, 5, 10, 20 and 50 cent denominations (1 euro = 100 cents).

Banks are generally open from 9am to 4pm or 5pm from Monday to Friday, but some close for lunch, typically from midday to 2pm, especially in southern France where they may also be closed on Monday. Some banks open Saturday morning, especially if they are closed Monday. No bank is open on Sunday and they all close early the day before a holiday, often as early as midday.

French ATMs/cashpoints can be found outside and sometimes inside banks: look for the sign of a hand holding a card. In France there are now ATMs that let you select your language, but the code pads are numeric only. Most credit and debit cards are accepted, but you will probably be charged interest from the moment you withdraw cash using a credit card, while with a debit card you will be charged about 2 percent of the total withdrawn. Taking travellers' cheques with you to France is another option. These can be cashed in banks, but you will need your passport for identification purposes.

You need a phonecard (*télécarte*) to make a call from a payphone (*cabine téléphonique*). Phonecards, in 50 or 120 units, can be purchased at a *tabac* shop or post office (*la poste*), and some other places which display a sign '*télécarte en vente ici*'. The top left button on the payphone (usually two flags and an arrow) allows you to choose between five languages in the LCD display: French (*Décrochez*), English (*Please lift receiver*), German (*Bitte abheben*), Spanish (*Descuelgue*) and Italian (*Sganciare*). Lift the receiver and wait for a dialling tone, then insert the phonecard with the chip and arrow topside and front of the card, and dial the required number when instructed. The units on the card will count down in the LCD once you are connected. Replace the receiver at the end of your call and remove the phonecard. Some payphones may also allow you to use a credit card. To phone the UK, call 00 44 (the IDD and country code), then the area code without the first zero, and then the local number. For the US and Canada call 001 + area code + number; for Australia call 0061 + area code minus zero + number.

PUBLIC HOLIDAYS

New Year's Day (1 January)
Easter Sunday and Monday
Ascension Day (40 days after Easter)
Whitsun (seventh Sunday after Easter)
    and Whit Monday
Labour Day (1 May)
VE Day (8 May)
Bastille Day (14 July)
Assumption Day (15 August)
All Saints' Day (1 November)
Armistice Day (11 November)
Christmas Day (25 December)

Banks, shops, museums and so on are closed for these public holidays. It is not uncommon for Ascension Day and Whitsun/Whit Monday to be in May, meaning four public holidays in this month alone. The French generally take their summer holiday in the first two weeks of August.

FRENCH FOOD AND WINE

For a diversity of delicious dishes and wonderful, world-renowned wines, look no further than France. Each region can proudly profess to be able to rustle up a wide variety of culinary delights, be they based around shellfish in Brittany, truffles and foie gras in Dordogne, or olives and aubergines in Provence. Bordeaux, Burgundy and Champagne immediately spring to mind when we think of French wine, but there are several other excellent wine-growing areas such as Alsace, the Loire and Rhône Valleys, Provence, the southwest of France and Languedoc-Roussillon, even Jura and Savoie. All large supermarkets stock a wide range of French wines and there is always a good choice to be found on restaurant menus, but why not sample the local wine if you're cycling past all those vineyards? Look out for roadside signs with the word *dégustation* (wine tasting) on them. It's not obligatory to buy a bottle after sampling the wine produced by a small *cave* or château, but it you would be putting money into the local community, even if it's only a few euros. And if one of the bottle cages on your bike frame is empty...

If you want to sample and buy some local produce the best place to go is the local market (*marché*) which usually happens on one particular

Violet Provençal garlic

Along the Route des Vins d'Alsace (Route 3)

morning each week. Local traders set up their stalls and sell anything from cheese and meat and fruit to cooking utensils and clothing, but look out for the local speciality foods. There will usually be a van or stall offering hot food, often a regional dish.

If you are not fortunate enough to be in a village or town on market day, then head for the *boulangerie*, the baker's shop. Every sizeable village has one selling bread rolls and *baguettes*, long thin loaves that the French buy daily to accompany their meals. You can also buy sweet breakfast rolls like *croissants, brioches* and *pains au chocolat*, as well as cakes, flans, pizza slices and quiches in some *boulangerie* shops. On Mondays this may well be the only shop open in a village. Buy a *baguette*

or two and then pop over to the *charcuterie*, which sells cooked meats, pâtés and sausages. Follow this with a visit to the *alimentation* or *épicerie* for cheeses and salad (there may even be a *fromagerie*, a cheese shop, if you are in a larger settlement), and you have all the ingredients for a cheap, delicious picnic at a roadside *aire* (a grassy or wooded area with picnic tables) after your morning's cycling. Otherwise, lunch can be taken in a village café or brasserie fairly cheaply; the *croque monsieur* (toasted cheese and ham sandwich) is nearly always on the menu, as is *steak haché avec frites* (steak and chips), served with salad or vegetables. There is usually a vegetarian dish or two, and *crêpes* (rolled pancakes with a choice of fillings) may also be on offer.

35

A buckwheat variety of *crêpe* called *galette* is very tasty and is particularly popular in Brittany. The *plat du jour* (dish of the day) or *menu touristique* are set meals that can be tasty or bland depending on the establishment or the chef's imagination, and usually appear on a restaurant's menu too. If you decide to eat lunch at a restaurant why not be a little more adventurous and choose something with a local twist. Restaurants are only open for lunch or dinner, whereas cafés, brasseries and bars are open all day and will normally serve food throughout the afternoon. If you are running low on water and the shops are shut you can buy bottled water here too, but it won't be cheap.

Supermarkets are plentiful. In towns and villages you will find a *Casino, Huit-à-huit* or *Coccinelle,* mini-supermarkets selling fruit, vegetables, salad, tinned food, water, wine, beer, soft drinks and packaged meat slices and cheese. Unlike bigger supermarkets there are no cheese or meat counters, only shelf items. *Intermarché* and *Ecomarché* supermarkets are larger and are usually found in the suburbs of towns or on a main road just outside big villages; they have bread, meat and cheese counters that also offer local produce. Some also sell maps, CDs and other such items. Bigger still are the hypermarkets such as *LeClerc* found on the outskirts of large towns and in cities which sell everything imaginable, most importantly basic bicycle accessories, tools, inner tubes, and so on. Most supermarkets, regardless of size, are open from 8.30am to 12.30pm and 3pm to 7.30pm, Monday to Saturday (although some are not open on Monday mornings, or not at all on Mondays). Many are open on Sundays from 8.30am to 12 noon. Many big supermarkets, on the whole, do not close for lunch.

Small villages may just have an *alimentation* which caters for all basic needs regarding food and drink. Although most items are a little more expensive than in supermarkets, these tiny shops are very useful when you might be camping in the middle of nowhere, or need to pick up something for lunch on the road. Generally speaking, if a village has a church it will invariably have an *alimentation*, *boulangerie* and probably a *boucherie* (butcher's shop).

Finally, if you have a sweet tooth or are feeling 'bonky' (when blood-sugar levels fall too low and you feel weak and wobbly), there's the *pâtisserie* shop that sells a delicious, colourful array of cakes, flans and tarts. I will never forget feeling bonky once in the Limousin region and finding a *pâtisserie* open in Bourganeuf – on a Sunday afternoon! Marvellous.

See the maps marking several regional specialities and major wine regions of mainland France in Appendix D. A brief description of each speciality and wine region is also given.

Greg Lemond and Rob Harmeling (TVM/143), Tour de France 1991

THE TOUR DE FRANCE

The first Tour de France – the world's greatest bicycle race – took place in 1903. Created by Henri Desgrange, the editor of *L'Auto*, and George Lefèvre, the rugby and cycling reporter, to help publicise and improve circulation of this sports newspaper, the first event was a six-stage race covering 2428km. The riders left Paris for Lyon, then cycled on to Marseille, Toulouse, Bordeaux, Nantes, and finally back to Paris. The average stage distance was 405km, which meant the competitors had to cycle nights as well as days! They also had to carry out their own repairs if necessary.

Maurice Garin won that first Tour in front of 20,000 Parisiens, and *L'Auto*'s circulation quadrupled,

heralding the birth of something very special. Yet the following year's Tour was almost the last, with many riders cheating by catching trains on occasion and even sabotaging each other's bicycles. Fortunately the organisers decided to stage the race again in 1905 with more concrete rules and they introduced the first mountain stage, the Ballon d'Alsace. Desgrange added a stage through the Pyrénées in 1910, and one in the Alps a year later. By now the Tour had more than doubled in overall distance and number of stages, but the average stage distance was still frighteningly long at 356km.

Immediately after World War I Desgrange introduced the yellow jersey (*maillot jaune*). He chose this colour for two reasons: the roadside

Laurent Fignon in the Tour de France 1991

spectators could pick out the race leader easily and, perhaps more significantly, L'Auto was printed on yellow paper. Eugene Christophe was the first man to don the yellow jersey on 18 July 1919. The first Italian to win the Tour – previously dominated by the French and Belgians – was Ottavio Bottecchia in 1924. He notched up another victory the following year. The longest-ever race in Tour history took place in 1926, covering a total distance of 5745km. Such monstrous rides had become a thing of the past by the early 1930s when the Tour was opened to other advertisers, coverage was broad-casted live on the radio, and French riders won the race six years in a row.

In 1937 the first derailleurs were allowed in the Tour de France. A year later the Italian cyclist Gino Bartali won the Tour, then won it again 10 years later in 1948 at the age of 34. Bartali was physically assaulted on the Col d'Aspin in the Tour of 1950, but went on to win the stage before he and his Italian team-mates (including Fausto Coppi, the 1949 victor) with-drew in protest.

Two of the toughest climbs of the Tour de France were introduced in the early 1950s: Mont Ventoux in 1951 and l'Alpe d'Huez in 1952. Coppi won the first historic stage of l'Alpe d'Huez, and then went on to win the Tour that year. French riders, including Louison Bobet and Jacques Anquetil, dominated the next five Tours, and the great Spanish climber

Federico Bahamontes won the 1959 event. Anquetil went on to win four consecutive Tours between 1961 and 1964, becoming the first of only five riders to notch up more than three victories to date. The Tour's second tragic fatality occurred in 1967 when Tom Simpson collapsed near the summit of Mont Ventoux; Francesco Capeda had died on the Galibier in 1935.

The Belgian Eddy Merckx became the second man to win five Tours (1969, 1970, 1971, 1972 and 1974), subsequently matched by Bernard Hinault (1978, 1979, 1981, 1982 and 1985). Laurent Fignon, winner of two Tours, and Greg Lemond, the first American to win a Tour in 1986, battled against each other for victory in Paris in 1989. It came down to the final time-trial in the capital, which Lemond famously won by the slimmest of margins in the history of the Tour de France: 8 seconds!

The early 1990s belonged to one man in particular, Miguel Indurain. He won five Tours in a row from 1991 and 1995 and, like Lemond, was strong in all disciplines. During his reign another American was emerging; Lance Armstrong won a stage in the 1993 and 1995 Tours. Diagnosed with testicular cancer in 1996, Armstrong was given a slim chance of living, since it had also spread to various parts of his body and brain. Following an operation and painful chemotherapy, he fought back with a vengeance and won the 1999 Tour de France. He never looked back, joined the élite club of Anquetil, Merckx, Hinault and Induráin by winning five Tours… and then went two better.

ABOUT THE BIKE

Which bicycle is best for touring?

A touring bike is the obvious answer as it is built specifically for carrying heavy panniers and granting a comfortable ride over long distances with good steering. It has drop handlebars (like a racing bike), but they are set in a more upright position, 700c wheels, and usually a steel frame, mudguards and a triple chain-ring.

Although lighter, a racing bike is not really suited to cycle touring as the frame geometry is more severe and most racing bikes do not come with seatstay lugs for the rear pannier rack (although there are ways of overcoming this). It also does not respond too well to hairpin descents when fully laden with panniers. Having said this, I have done three mountain cycling tours on a bicycle made up of racing bike and hybrid bike components to good effect. The hybrid bike is something between a touring bike and a mountain bike in that it offers the relaxed frame geometry and larger 700c wheels of the touring bike, but has straight or rising handlebars like

the mountain bike, at least 21 gears, and a sloping top tube. Cycle tourists who suffer from back or neck pains should definitely 'test drive' a hybrid if they are not sure which type of bicycle to choose.

Mountain bikes are robust, affordable and often surprisingly suitable for cycle touring. They usually come with chunky, knobbly tyres which are great for all-terrain adventures, but not suitable for cycle touring on roads. Replace them with slicker, thinner tyres that will reduce the effort you have to exert on paved roads; 26 x 1.5 or 1.75 tyres with good tread are recommended. For mountainous terrain, a triple chain-ring (30/42/52 teeth) together with a Mega-range freewheel/sprocket on the back wheel (11–34 teeth) will get you up the steepest hills imaginable, but smaller range sprockets are usually adequate for most rides.

Folding bikes are becoming increasingly popular for cycle touring, especially if you are also considering using public transport. Brompton and Dahon folding bikes with 20in wheels are sound choices, but make sure you buy one fit for touring (not commuting) and able to carry loaded panniers. There are also folding mountain bikes with 26in wheels. Visit **www.foldabikes.com**, **www.bromptonbicycle.co.uk** and **www.dahon.com**.

If you haven't already got a bicycle for touring, make sure you buy one from a reputable bike shop.

They can advise you on the correct frame size for your height. To determine the correct saddle height for a comfortable ride, sit on the bike saddle and line up one of the crankarms with the seat tube, then put your heel on the pedal and adjust the saddle height until your leg is almost straight.

If you plan to camp you will probably need two rear pannier bags, a handlebar bag and a rear rack bag. The rear rack bag is not essential as you can strap gear onto the top of the pannier rack itself (rolled up bike bag and so on), but I find it useful for carrying food, cooking gear, repair kit, spare bike bits and the like. Clothes, tent, sleeping bag and mat can then be put in the rear panniers, leaving the handlebar bag free for valuables. Always line your panniers with durable bin liners to keep everything dry when the heavens open. If these four bags do not suffice, you either need to trim your gear down, or consider front bags, which many cyclists like because they counterbalance the rear panniers.

Make sure you buy a strong, good quality rear rack to take the weight of heavy panniers. Altura make some great bags and their Arran handlebar bag (5 litre) clicks into the Rixen and Kaul quick-release support that can be left permanently attached to the handlebars.

Finally, a frame with two water-bottle carriers is better than a frame that only has one. You can buy still mineral water in 1½ litre plastic bottles at any supermarket or *alimentation* shop (2 litre bottles are too fat) on a daily basis, rather than having to keep topping up those non-transparent bike bottles which soon make the water taste of plastic.

Repairs
Knowing your bicycle and how to carry out repairs, sometimes in the middle of nowhere, are important considerations in cycle touring. *The Bicycling Guide to Complete Bicycle Maintenance and Repair for Road and Mountain Bikes* by Todd Downs gives detailed descriptions with photographs covering bicycle basics, maintenance, and all repairs imaginable, and there are many other good, detailed books on the market. Serious repairs, or perhaps the replacement of a component, will inevitably mean visiting the nearest bicycle shop on a tour, but you can usually carry out common repairs yourself on the road. Two of the most common hiccups on a tour are punctures (flats) and broken spokes. Read up on and practise how to remove the freewheel/cassette on your rear wheel before a tour in case you have to replace a broken spoke behind the rear cogs.

Puncture (flat tyre)
If you complete a cycling tour without suffering a single puncture then consider yourself lucky! Since the rear wheel takes most of your weight and the rear pannier weight, it is usually

this wheel's inner tube that punctures (and is also the more complicated of the two because of the rear derailleur and chain).

If it's raining, try to find some shelter. Deflate the punctured tyre completely, and if it's a rear tyre puncture turn the bicycle upside down with the saddle on the ground, having removed the panniers. This also protects the rear derailleur from getting damaged.

To remove the rear wheel, shift the derailleur to the smallest cog on the freewheel/cassette and innermost front chain ring. Remember where the axle sits in the dropouts. Release the wheel's quick-release (if your bicycle has them), otherwise loosen both nuts either side of the dropouts. Pull the rear derailleur back to allow the cogs to clear the chain. Lift the wheel (you may have to pinch the tyre either side of the brake pads to slip the tyre

Puncture repair, Gorges du Tarn (Route 8)

between them) and pull it forwards to clear the chain and derailleur. If tyres are fat you will probably have to release cantilever brakes or V brakes in order to pull the tyre past the brake pads.

For a front wheel puncture simply deflate the inner tube fully and pull the wheel out between the brake shoes after releasing the quick release or loosening the nuts either side of the dropouts.

Removing the tyre and inner tube: start tyre removal directly opposite the valve area, squeezing the sides of the tyre towards the centre and inserting a tyre lever under the lip of the tyre. Lift this up and over the edge of the wheel's rim, then insert another tyre lever under the edge of the tyre about 3in from the other lever and lift the tyre edge over the rim here too. By sliding and lifting one of the levers sideways, thus releasing more of the tyre's edge, you should soon be able to lift the whole edge of the tyre clear of the wheel's rim on one side.

Pull the inner tube out from inside the tyre, starting opposite the valve area. With most of the tube out now unscrew the nut on the valve and lift the valve out of the valve hole to completely remove the tube from the tyre. Depending on your circumstances, you may now either simply opt to replace the punctured tube with a new one and repair the punctured tube later on at the next campsite or hotel stop, or patch the puncture if you do not have a spare

inner tube. Visually check the inside of the tyre and run a thin cloth around its interior, just to be sure there are no sharp objects inside or protruding through the wall that will simply cause another puncture.

If you plan to repair the inner tube, chalk or mark around the hole area after inflating the tube and locating the puncture hole. Next deflate the tube, place it on a flat, clean surface and roughen the puncture area with some sandpaper. Apply a smooth layer of glue around the hole, just slightly bigger in circumference than the repair patch you will attach to it after a few minutes (once the glue has dried and become tacky). Firmly apply a patch that will substantially cover the hole (it will expand when the tube has been inflated) and make sure there are no air bubbles or folds in the patch before inflating the tube. If you suffer a blow out, the hole will usually be too large to repair, so your only option is replacing the inner tube with a spare one.

Happy that the puncture is repaired, deflate the tube and put one side of the tyre's edge inside the wheel's rim, then push the valve back through the valve hole and work the inner tube back inside the tyre. Inflate the inner tube a little and make sure you do not pinch it under the other edge of the tyre when you lift this back over the rim by hand. The final section may require the use of the tyre levers to help flip the remaining tyre edge back inside the wheel's rim;

once again, check the tube isn't pinching here before reinflating it. Finally, screw the nut back onto the valve and return the wheel to the dropouts.

Replacing a spoke

If a spoke breaks, try to repair it as soon as possible. Strip the wheel down as described above, so that the rubber strip that runs around the wheel trough is exposed. If the broken spoke's pinhead sits in an eyelet on the hub flange directly behind the freewheel/cassette on the rear wheel, you will have to remove the latter. Remove the nipple of the broken spoke beneath the rubber strip and the spoke itself, paying attention to the way the old spoke is aligned (under or over other spokes). Replace the spoke, threading a new one through the eyelet on the hub flange up to the new nipple, repeating the correct alignment of the old spoke. The pinhead of the curved end of the spoke should sit well in the eyelet. Use a spoke wrench or flathead screwdriver (depending on the nipple head) to tighten the nipple onto the spoke thread. Do not overtighten – the new spoke should 'ring' the same as the other spokes when you pluck it.

Occasionally you may not be able to carry out roadside repairs, or need to replace a broken or damaged component, *and* be a long way from the nearest bicycle shop. If it happens, stand back and review the situation and work out how you can **adapt**,

improvise, **overcome**. On the Marne and Picardy tour one of my pedals sheared off because I had misthreaded it onto the crankarm before leaving the airport. As I was only a kilometre away from the village of Montreuil-aux-Lions I wheeled my bicycle there in pouring rain and found a garage. I asked the mechanic if he had a long bolt with two locking nuts that could act as a temporary pedal until I reached a good bike shop. He came up trumps, and although it didn't rotate as a pedal does this bolt got me to Château-Thierry, some 30km away, where there was a good bicycle shop. My cycling companion on the Alps tour suffered a stripped thread in the steerer tube resulting in a total loss of steering, but managed three cols before reaching a good bicycle shop in Albertville. He overcame the problem by tightly tying two webbing straps from his handlebars to the fork crown, thereby being able to control front-wheel direction. Whatever the dilemma, there is always a temporary solution.

Appendix A covers most French vocabulary for bicycle parts.

WHAT TO TAKE

When flying to France your hold luggage allowance is generally 20–25kg, and hand luggage is 5–10kg. Your bicycle is accepted as 'sporting equipment' and you may be charged for it. A group with four or more bicycles should notify the airline in advance. I've found that the airline check-in staff are somewhat more lenient with the luggage allowance if you check in early for your flight. A few kilograms over the limit might be tolerated, but they can charge you for excess weight. Unless it is too hot to do so, or the flight too long, I recommend wearing any heavy clothes rather than packing them, and putting all valuables in your handlebar bag (if you take one) which can be your hand luggage.

Typical clothing list
- Waterproof and windproof, breathable jacket, preferably with pit-zips (for example Gill).
- Waterproof and breathable overtrousers (both jacket and overtrousers should be lightweight and compact when stored away).
- Warm fleece/mid-layer fleece (depending on climate and tour; Berghaus).
- Fast-wicking cycling tops (Altura; white or light-coloured tops absorb less heat).
- Cycling shorts with chamois insert, or lightweight trousers that have 360° zips around the thighs so that they become shorts in hot weather (North Face).
- Comfortable cycling shoes, trainers or lightweight hiking boots with low-cut heel. I found the latter excellent in the Alps and Pyrénées (Hi-Tec), especially during mountain storms and trudging across wet campsites. On the other hand, in temperatures reaching 35ºC without a cloud in the sky, I did the Brittany tour in yachting deck-shoe style trainers with a high rubber rand above the sole.
- Arm socks. Suffering from sunburn high in the Alps once, I cut the 'toes' off a pair of thin socks which protected my arms on a couple of climbs that offered little shade.
- Cap/sunhat. Again, very useful on hot, sunny days in the saddle. Some caps also have neckerchiefs attached to Velcro strips inside the cap to protect the back of the head/neck. You may look like Lawrence of Arabia. but who cares if the sun is beating down on you on a relentless climb!
- Neck gear (for cold descents).
- Gloves (for cold descents and nights at altitude).
- Cycling mitts. Some people like them, some don't.
- Helmet. Again, a personal choice. On long, hard, hot climbs your head can get really hot… but then on long, snaking, slippery descents I was glad I brought it on the tour.
- Sunglasses, or surround sunglasses if you wear spectacles (bowls retailers often stock them).
- Fibre-pile hat (for cold nights).
- Spare clothing.

Sundries

- Suncream and lipbalm.
- Small first aid kit including painkillers for headaches and so on.
- Pack-towel and shower gel.
- Toothbrush and paste.
- Small torch (for example Maglite).
- Camera, films/memory card and spare batteries.
- Pen and notebook.
- Swiss Army knife (cannot go in hand luggage on flights).
- Pocket phrase book/dictionary.

Important documents

- Passport/Visa.
- Money/travellers' cheques/credit card.
- EHIC (UK).

Note Photocopy all important documents and keep the photocopies separate from the originals. Make a note of credit card details.

Bicycle accessories

- Compact bike pump.
- Bike lock (cable locks are compact).
- Front and rear lights.
- Multi-tool kit. There are many good, compact kits on the market today. I always carry a Canyon Super Multi Tool kit which comprises 6 x Allen keys, 1 x small Philips/cross-head screwdriver, 1 x small flat blade screwdriver, 3 x socket set, 1 x multi spanner, 1 x spoke adjuster, 2 x tyre levers, tube repair patches/adhesive and file. This all fits in a compact pouch (with a belt loop) about the size of a pack of playing cards. Check the sizes of all Allen key bolts and other nuts and the like on your bicycle to determine the best multi-tool kit for you.
- Spare inner tube.
- Freewheel tool (for freewheel blocks if you need to replace spokes on freewheel side of back wheel). Most bicycles now have cassette blocks, which are easier to remove.
- Two or three spare spokes with nipples (buy the right length, usually gauged in millimetres; tape these to the rear pannier rack where they won't get bent or damaged).
- Spanner for wheel nuts, or adjustable spanner. Quick releases save time, but you will still need a spanner to hold the opposite nut if you have to remove a freewheel.
- Spare gear and brake cable.
- Chain tool.
- 'Third hand' chain hook to hold the chain taut if you need to carry out repairs on it. You can make one out of a 10cm length of coat hanger wire; bend the ends so that they face each other, forming a U at each end.
- Spare washers and spring washers.
- Spare Allen key bolt.

- Spare wheel nuts, nylstop nuts and valve nut.
- Spare chain links.
- Nylon cord (useful for all sorts of emergencies, and as a washing line!)
- Swarfega wipes or solvent-free hand-cleaning cream for removing chain oil from hands. Transparent gloves, often freely available at petrol stations, can also be donned during messy repairs.
- Gaffer/duct tape.

Camping kit list
- Sleeping bag. I would recommend a 4-season sleeping bag for the Alps and Pyrénées tours. Although heavier and bulkier than a 2- or 3-season bag, you will definitely benefit from the extra warmth should the weather turn nasty and cold in the mountains. I took a 3-season bag on the other tours in late spring or autumn, and a 2-season bag plus liner for those in the summer. For some people a liner is often sufficient on its own if it's a hot night; put together with the 2-season bag it can make the difference between a comfortable night and a sleepless one if it turns chilly.
- Self-inflating mattress or sleeping mat. Thermarest or similar makes of self-inflating mattresses pack down smaller than sleeping mats and are more comfortable on stony ground. However, the latter will never puncture!

- Tent. There are some very good, lightweight tents on the market – too many to mention. A 2-person tent should weigh no more than 3kg as a rule. I slept in a Coleman 2-RS tent (2.78kg) on most of the tours, including the Alps and Pyrénées. Both the inner tent and outer sheet pack down into separate compact bags and the two poles are made of light but robust duraluminium. It also only took a few minutes to put up, which was certainly good news halfway up the Madeleine climb during a relentless mountain storm.
- Cooking gear. An MSR petrol stove was used on most of these tours. You cannot carry fuel on any flight so you will have to buy it from a petrol station when you arrive; a full MSR canister of fuel should cost about 1 euro and be enough for 5–7 nights' cooking. Gas canisters are an option but most small town and village shops do not stock them, and again you cannot take them on aircraft.
- Cooking pans, sieve, cutlery, cup, biodegradable washing-up liquid and brush. Salt and cooking oil in small, plastic containers/bottles.

HOW TO USE THIS GUIDE

There are eight routes in this guide-book, each divided into several stages that start and finish in towns or villages that offer accommodation. Each stage can be cycled in a day (most average between 45 and 52km), but because unforeseen things can occur (bad weather, bicycle repairs, sickness), additional accommodation possibilities along or near each route are also given. These are useful for those who may want to spend more time exploring villages and historic sites along the way and are not intent on completing the stages on a daily basis, perhaps preferring to dedicate 10 days or even two weeks to fully appreciate what a particular region has to offer. On the other hand, some cyclists may want to cover more distance than that of a recommended stage, or are not that keen on stopping and exploring. Such cyclists could feasibly complete two routes in a fortnight, especially if they are close geographically. A few stages are extremely short, but this may be because there is much to see and explore, or perhaps a ferry crossing or train journey/transfer has to be taken into account.

Although the stages start and finish in towns or villages, your preferred accommodation may occasionally be located several kilometres before or beyond the end of a stage (a campsite, for example). It would be wise to study the selected accommodation lists given at the end of each route (but remember that these lists are not exhaustive).

If you are touring during the peak summer months, it might be better to book a room in an hotel or bed and breakfast well in advance, and even a pitch at small campsites in areas popular with tourists. Remember, too, that the French also like to get away from it all (especially the cities), so accommodation soon gets booked up in advance for public holidays, or for Saturday nights near cities and big towns.

Coloured bicycle symbols on the sketch maps give an idea of the severity of a significant hill climb on any given stage, and the total ascent in metres within each stage can be found at the beginning of each stage description (Climb). The 'Climb Difficulties' table (right) indicates the coloured bicycle symbols used, and their corresponding degree of difficulty.

The sketch maps give an overview of the stages of each route, and ascent profiles of the major climbs are also included, with the steeper parts indicated.

All towns and most large villages have very good information centres (*offices de tourisme* and *syndicats d'initiative*), well stocked with informative, up-to-date brochures and glossy leaflets (often with English translations), and helpful, knowledgeable staff who usually speak English very well. Principal information centres for each route can be found in Appendix E.

There are several abbreviations in the route descriptions. North, south, east and west are abbreviated to N, S, E and W; NE therefore stands for northeast, SW for southwest, and so on. Similarly, L and R stand for left and right, and a roundabout is abbreviated to rdbt.

CLIMB DIFFICULTIES

 Easy climb, sometimes short and punchy.

 Gradual climb. Occasionally steep.

 Moderate climb. Some steep sections.

 Hard climb. Several steep sections.
Tour de France Grade 1 difficulty.

 Very hard climb that can be classified as
extremely hard in adverse weather conditions.
Tour de France *hors categorie* difficulty.

ROUTE 1

FINISTÈRE, 'THE END OF THE WORLD': BRITTANY

ROUTE SUMMARY

From	To	Km	Terrain
Morlaix	Le Folgoët/ Lesneven	54	Fairly flat; coastal, farmland
Le Folgoët/ Lesneven	Lanildut	64	Occasionally hilly
Lanildut	Brest	52	Occasionally hilly; coastal
Brest	Le Faou	35	Fairly hilly
Le Faou	Huelgoat	42	Hilly; woods
Huelgoat	Morlaix	30	Hilly then river valley

Stage 1 Morlaix to Le Folgoët/Lesneven

Distance	54km/34 miles
Terrain	Fairly flat; coastal, then farmland
Climb	200m

How to get to Morlaix

You can now fly to Brest with Flybe from Southampton, Exeter or Birmingham in the UK, or with Air France from Paris. A bus (*navette*) service operates between Brest Bretagne airport and the SNCF railway station in Brest, costing about 5 euros (single) and taking 20min. You can

Morlaix

then take the train to Morlaix or, since this is a circular tour, you may prefer to start it from Brest (see Stage 4) if you are flying there. Roscoff (north of Morlaix) can be reached by ferry from Plymouth in the UK or from Rosslare in Ireland. Again, you may prefer to start the tour from some point N of Morlaix if you are catching a ferry to Roscoff. You can reach Morlaix by train from Paris Montparnasse.

Ryanair fly to Dinard near St Malo from East Midlands (Nottingham), London Luton and London Stansted. A 20km cycle ride from Dinard airport to either Dinan (S) or Plancoët (SW) railway stations enables you to reach Morlaix by train from the E. St Malo is another ferry port which can be reached from the UK (see Getting There in the Introduction). Flybe also fly to Rennes from Southampton, then you can catch a train from Rennes railway station to Morlaix (TGV) which takes 1hr 40min. Morlaix's SNCF station is situated at the western end of the railway viaduct up on the hill. You can either go S down Rue Hippolyte Vigleau and Rue Gambetta to reach the Rue de Brest and go L (W) along here to reach Place des Otages below the viaduct, or via some steep steps (Venelle de la Roche) directly down to the town centre.

Morlaix is dominated by its enormous viaduct, built in 1861 for the Paris–Brest railway. The old town beneath it is interesting, its narrow streets and steep alleyways lined with half-timbered houses. The Maison de la Duchesse Anne in rue du Mur dates back to the 16th century. Open daily to the public in summer, except Sun.

The route

Starting from below the viaduct in Morlaix town centre take the D769 N past the moored sailing boats (Quai de Léon) towards St Pol-de-Léon/Roscoff, along the wooded W bank of the River Morlaix. Bear R after 3km for Kerdanet and Carantec on the D73 where the river widens and then opens out into the Rade de Morlaix. There is a good view across the bay of the quaint village

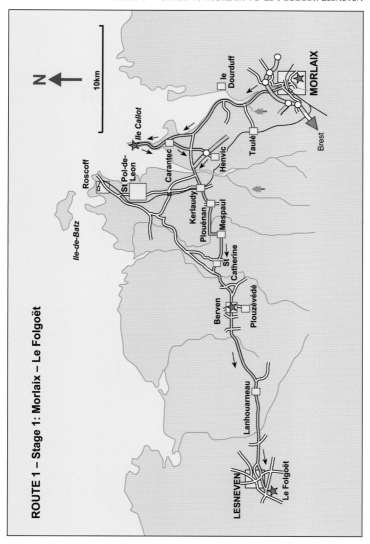

ROUTE 1 – Stage 1: Morlaix – Le Folgoët

of le Dourduff en Mer. Continue straight on at Kerdanet towards **Carantec** (still the D73) and cycle through this small resort to reach the *Chaussée Submersible*, a bumpy road (only viable during low tides) that connects Carantec with the **Ile Callot**. The Chapelle Notre Dame de Callot, situated on the highest part of the island, was erected on the site of a primitive oratory thought to have been founded in the 6th century. This ancient chapel was ruined during the Revolution and rebuilt at the beginning of the 19th century. The wonderful belfry dates from 1672.

Return to **Carantec** and cycle S past a supermarket on your L to the D173 and take the country road opposite to Kermen. Keep straight on at a minor crossroads and past artichoke fields on your R before cycling under the D58 to **Henvic**.

Henvic is a quiet little village that has a small campsite, and a very interesting belfry dating from the late 16th/early 17th century. This was famously used as a landmark for boats entering the bay far off to the north. Take the D58 down to the Pont de la Corde, and having crossed this bridge over the Penzé river turn immediately L (C25) to **Kerlaudy** then **Plouénan** on the D65 where the farmland begins to flatten out to the west. Here continue straight at the rdbt for **Mespaul**, past a supermarket on your R and at the rdbt on the D69 go straight on (C2) for **Ste Catherine**. From this village continue W to the D788 and take this L to **Berven**, an important stopover for pilgrims with a very interesting church dating from 1573, with a peaceful parish enclosure that has a sacred fountain on the south side. In the choir there is a beautiful 17th-century retable (decorated panels above and behind the altar) of carved wood that depicts the Trinity. The Renaissance belfry (1576) had a strong influence on Breton art. Follow the D788 W again across mostly flat farmland to **Lanhouarneau**, after which the road dips and climbs to **Lesneven**. Before reaching this town look out for signs L to **Le Folgoët** which has one of the finest Gothic basilica in Brittany and an interesting museum close by.

Inside the church of Berven

Le Folgoët literally means *fou du bois* in the local tongue, which translates as 'madman of the wood'. The madman in question was the legendary Solomon, a local lad in the 14th century. After his death, legend has it that a magnificent white lily grew from the earth of his burial place. The impressive church of Notre Dame was built soon after on this very site. It has a grand façade with two towers; the north tower is 56m high, but the south tower was never finished. On the east side of the church there is a fountain whose source is supposedly under the basilica's altar. Musée Notre Dame (open Mon–Sat, 10am–12.30pm and 2.30–6.30pm, Sun 2.30–6.30pm).

Stage 2 Le Folgoët/Lesneven to Lanildut

Distance	64km/40 miles
Terrain	Occasionally hilly
Climb	260m

The route

Return to the main road from the basilica and take the C5 to the R side of the cemetery and L of an intriguing monument that loosely resembles an old decorative bandstand. Take next R to a rdbt and then the D28 towards Lannilis. After 1km take the D32 R to Plouguerneau, stopping off en route after 9km to visit the neatly restored church of Notre Dame de Grouannec that boasts an ossuary (charnel house), tiny cloister and fountain. Reaching **Plouguerneau** – a large, vibrant village whose claim to fame is that of having been awarded the Prix de l'Europe in 1990 by the Council of Europe for developing strong ties with the German town of Edingen Neckerhausen, thereby resulting in a great number of Franco-German marriages (!) – take the D71 W towards Lilia.

After passing a land lighthouse on your L the road descends. On this descent take the turning R for Kelerdut. Go L at an island junction signposted Kelerdut after 1km round a small cove. Ignore the first L for Kelerdut and take the second L which leads to a campsite (Camping Meledan) and a promontory from which there is an excellent view of the **Vierge** lighthouse, especially at sunset. There is also a good view of this lighthouse from the coastline beyond Lilia.

L'Aber Wrac'h is one of three steep-sided, narrow estuaries in northwest Brittany, l'Aber Benoît and l'Aber Ildut being the other two.

Returning to Plouguerneau take the D113 for Les Abers and Lannilis past a quaint church on your R, then a snaking descent to Aberhtach (viewpoint) and a bridge over l'Aber Wrac'h followed by a punchy climb to **Lannilis**. ◄

Continue S from Lannilis, crossing l'Aber Benoît and bearing R along the D28. After approximately 3km look

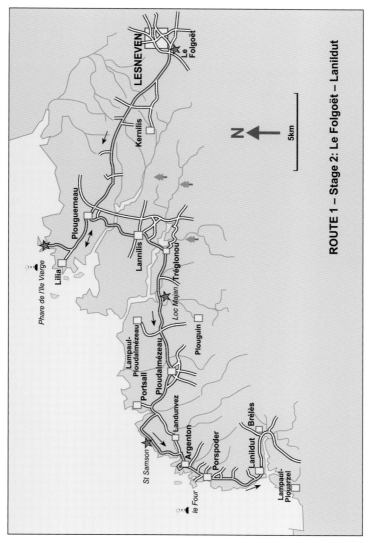

ROUTE 1 – Stage 2: Le Folgoët – Lanildut

The coastal village of **Portsall**, 1km N of here, is home to the giant anchor of the *Amoco Cadiz* oil tanker which was wrecked 1km off this rugged Breton shoreline in 1978, causing one of the worst oil spills in history.

out for the **Chapelle de Loc Majan** on the grassy hillside L which overlooks l'Aber Benoît. This tiny chapel is dedicated to Saint Majan who, legend has it, sailed all the way here from Great Britain in a stone trough! Having discovered a spring near l'Aber Benoît he built a hermitage and chapel here around AD620.

Continue on the D28 past a turning L to the Menhir of Loc Majan (worth a quick detour) uphill to the sprawling village of **Ploudalmézeau** and from here follow the D168 W to Kersaint. ◄

Take the narrow, winding coastal road (D127) W to Trémazan, whose overgrown castle ruins stand on the hillside looking down on the beach below. The landscape opens up after this; the undulating road faithfully following the rocky coastline, crossing barren slopes of grass and heather that offer little shelter to the scattered farmsteads and cottages hereabouts. Remember that this is, appropriately, Finistère, literally translated 'the End of the World'.

The miniscule chapel of **St Samson**, situated a stone's throw from the sea beside the road, is named after St Samson from Wales who landed in Cancale about AD548 and built many monasteries around which villages developed. Numerous chapels throughout Brittany were dedicated to him, and this one is set in a particularly romantic and remote corner. There is just enough space inside to house the altar and four pews.

The chapel of St Samson

The coast road gently climbs and falls S from St Samson for a few kilometres, after which turn R at a junction for Argenton (D27) and take a R (Hent aod Penfoul) for St Gonveld chapel and a view of the rocky coastline and the Phare le Four lighthouse in the distance. Continue round back to the main road past a large campsite for **Argenton**. Continue on the D27 S to **Posporder** and then on to **Lanildut** overlooking the Aber Ildut estuary.

The rocky coastline near Argenton

Stage 3 Lanildut to Brest

Distance	52km/32 miles
Terrain	Occasionally hilly; coastal
Climb	240m

The route

From Lanildut continue E on the D27, soon skirting **Brélès** and turning R soon afterwards uphill to **Plouarzel** (D28). Take the D28 towards Ploumaguer and turn

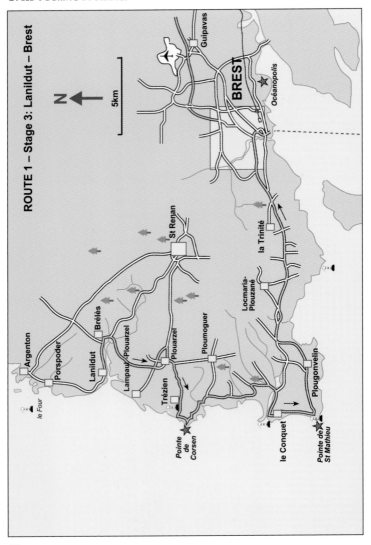

ROUTE 1 – Stage 3: Lanildut – Brest

immediately R for Trezien past five wind turbines on your R. Descend to the coast, turning L uphill and stopping at the second parking area where you can cycle L along a track/path to the **Pointe de Corsen** where there is a monument dedicated to sailors who have lost their lives at sea near the rocky coastline. ▸

Take the road that climbs the hill from the rough ground/parking area near the monument up to a coast-guard surveillance centre (radio mast) and turn R, then R again, followed by a 14% hill climb to a junction. Go L towards Ploumoguer, then R after 100m to Illien/Plage d'Illien and a steep descent to Illien cove, a popular little beach. Take the rough track in front of the beach to the other side where a steep road leads to a viewpoint over-looking the Plage des Blanc Sablons. Go L at the junction then R (signposted Brest) to Lanfeust and a wooded descent to the D789. Bear R here for **le Conquet**.

Cycle through this busy coastal place past the church and follow the road to Lochrist and St Mathieu (not Brest), and R at Rue Dr Laennec signposted 'Route Touristique'. Follow these signs down to the D85, turning L at the bottom to the **Pointe de St Mathieu** with its inter-esting combination of abbey ruins and giant lighthouse. Continue on the D85 E (cycle lane alongside it) to **Plougonvelin**. From here N to the main road (D789) and

The Pointe de Corsen, a 50m-high cliff, is the most westerly point in France, excluding islands. A short walk down the path N leads to a splendid view of jagged rocky outcrops sheltering clean sandy beaches.

View from the Pointe de Corsen

follow this E to Brest. The road can be busy – it is the trunk road that connects le Conquet with **Brest –** but there is at least a cycle lane running alongside on the descent into this big, bustling city port.

After the quiet and remoteness of the rugged west coast you may well want to cycle straight down to the Port de Commerce by following signs for *centre ville* on the long descent, then signs for Port de Commerce. Turn R when you arrive at this harbour for the Le Fret ferry (Societé Maritime Azenor) which currently makes four crossings a day Mon–Sat in summer (8.30am, 10am, 12.30pm, 5.45pm) and two crossings (10am, 5.45pm) Sun and holiday days. Visit **www.azenor.com** for more information. The crossing takes 25min and bicycles are accepted. Not operational between October and March. ◄

If you have to wait a while for the next ferry then visit **Océanopolis** between the Port de Commerce and Port de Plaisance, one of the world's biggest and most impressive aquaria (**www. oceanopolis.com**).

Should you be doing this tour out of season, or the ferry from Brest to Le Fret is not operational for whatever reason, there is a bus service from Brest railway station to Le Faou around the Rade de Brest which takes about 45min.

Stage 4 Brest to Le Faou

Distance	35km/22 miles
Terrain	Fairly hilly
Climb	250m

The route

Having crossed the Rade de Brest by ferry to the Crozon peninsula and the picturesque village of **Le Fret**, take the D55 R towards Crozon and turn L at the rdbt for **Lanvéoc** (*alimentation*). A hill climb follows to the D63, then

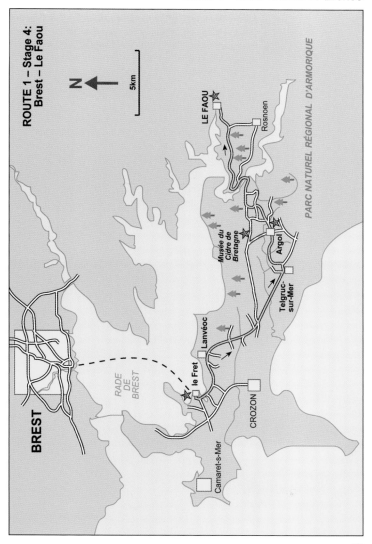

ROUTE 1 – Stage 4:
Brest – Le Faou

N

5km

BREST

RADE
DE
BREST

Camaret-s-Mer

le Fret

CROZON

Lanvéoc

Telgruc-
sur-Mer

Argol

Musée du
Cidre de Bretagne

Rosnoen

LE FAOU

PARC NATUREL RÉGIONAL D'ARMORIQUE

63

follow this road to Taul Ar Groaz. Take the D887 down-hill towards **Telgruc-sur-Mer**; near the top of an ascent after 5km take the L turn for Kernon/Kergonan and L again after 200m, following a country road past an old *crêperie* to **Argol**.

Argol is a vibrant little village with an interesting church and even more attractive cider museum N, the Musée du Cidre de Bretagne (Route de Brest – Ferme de Kermarzin, 29560 Argol, ☎ 02 98 27 35 85, **www.musee-cidre-bretagne.com**). The farm has an organic cider apple orchard covering 21 hectares from which you can sample and purchase the bottled product (10am–1pm, 2–7pm July and August, 10am–12pm, 2–7pm April–September). To reach the museum from Argol, take the D60 NW to the D791 (2km) and turn R here for 1km, then L for the museum and farm. Return to the D791 and continue L along this main road for Le Faou, crossing the Térénez suspension bridge over the Aulne after 3.5km.

Le Fret

If the cider museum is not for you, follow the D60 E out of Argol towards Tregervan bearing L after 200m for la Fontaine Blanche and R at the next junction. Climb to la Fontaine Blanche and bear L here before a descent to reach the D791. Go R here to cross the Térénez suspension bridge, the undulating D791 (cycle track in parts) bringing you into **Le Faou** (9km from the bridge).

At one time **Le Faou** was, like Morlaix, a prosperous port situated at the head of an estuary. Several houses from the 16th century still remain, and the 16th-century church with its ornate belltower is picturesquely situated on the S bank of the Rivière du Faou. The main tourist information centre for the Parc Naturel Régional d'Armorique is located in Le Faou.

Stage 5 Le Faou to Huelgoat

Distance	42km/26 miles
Terrain	Hilly
Climb	600m

The route
From Le Faou take the D770 SE for Brasparts, a long climb with good views NW across the rolling countryside of Finistère just before reaching the village of **Quimerc'h**. Turn L soon after the viewpoint (D21), and after 4km look out for interesting church ruins on a grassy hillside on your L. This is the **Ossuaire du Vieux Bourg de Quimerc'h**, an historic monument of 1579 comprising the ruins of a church, a chapel and *les trois ifs* – three yew trees that are over 400 years old (beware, wasps' nest in summer!). There are lovely views from here S over the Breton countryside.

65

ROUTE 1 – Stage 5: Le Faou – Huelgoat

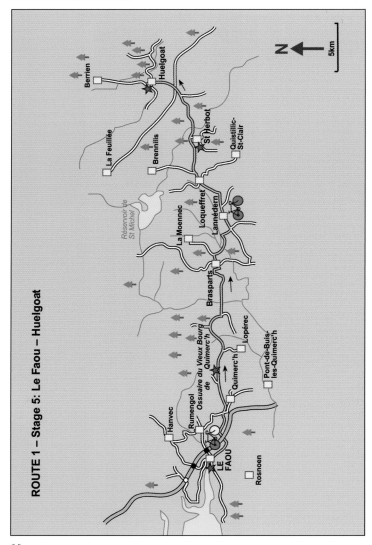

Ossuaire du Vieux Bourg de Quimerc'h

Continue E on the D21 to Brasparts, which descends past a viewpoint for 3km to Kervez. At the junction with the D121 that follows, keep L on the D21, crossing the St Rivoal stream (56m) and then up to **Brasparts**. This village has a very interesting church with a fine calvary, reminiscent of the two more famous parish closes of St Thégonnec and Guimiliau on the other side of the Monts d'Arrée, some 25km N. A descent E out of Brasparts on the D21 towards Huelgoat is followed by a climb past woods and fields to a crossroads (4km). Go L here up the D14, a gradual ascent through the village of **Lannedérn** which then steepens through **Loqueffret**. ▸

Just beyond Loqueffret and the turning L for Brennilis, a brown sign indicates there is a viewpoint in the trees R as the road climbs to 270m. It is worth climbing up onto the rock known locally as the Roc'h Bégheor to appreciate the splendid view.

Lannedérn also has an interesting church, hidden away from the main road on your L on the hillside.

A refreshing descent in woodland and brushwood follows to a junction R for **St Herbot**. The village is tiny, its Gothic church is not. A dark, sombre interior houses a finely carved oak screen (on a hot summer's day it certainly provides some cool respite; if this doesn't suffice have a cold drink at the café next to the church).

Return to the D14 which climbs NE to **Huelgoat**, crossing over the D764 before a steep, short descent into this vibrant little town by a lake.

Stage 6 Huelgoat to Morlaix

Distance	30km/19 miles
Terrain	Hilly
Climb	200m

Huelgoat is popular with tourists due to the wonderful forest to the east and lake to the west. Until the tremendous hurricane of October 1987 the Forêt de Huelgoat was dark and mysterious, with tangled trees and dense thickets surrounding giant granite boulders. Much of the forest and many of the village buildings did not survive that incredible storm. Near the information office in Huelgoat, the Grotte du Diable (Devil's Cave) and the Roche Tremblante (Trembling Rock) can be found on the edge of the forest. The Trembling Rock does not tremble at all, however – just another local legendary tale. By following a network of paths into the forest you can reach the Camp d'Arthus, a Gallo-Roman oppidum much like the fictional village that was home to Astérix the Gaul and his portly companion Obélix in the cartoon masterpieces of Goscinny and Uderzo.

The route
Cross the Argent river at the eastern end of the lake, following the D14 N out of Huelgoat through the wooded, western fringe of the Forêt de Huelgoat and on up to the village of Berrien (5km). Take the D42 E for 0.5km before turning L along the D769 (NW) and crossing the Monts d'Arrée – high, open country, a mixture of grazing land and moorland. A descent to **le Plessis** (177m) is then followed by a charming, gradual 13km descent down the wooded Queffleuth Valley, running alongside its babbling stream all the way into **Morlaix**, the start and end of this tour.

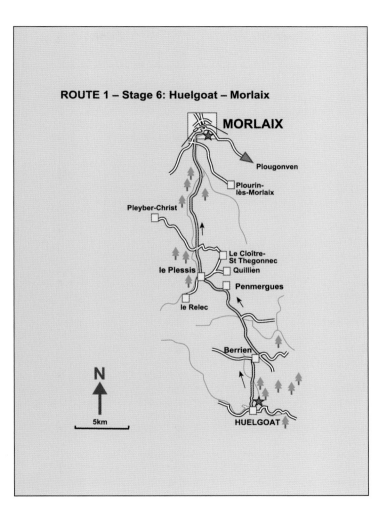

SELECTED ACCOMMODATION
ROUTE 1

STAGE 1 MORLAIX TO LE FOLGOËT/LESNEVEN

Campsites
Carantec
Camping Les Mouettes ★★★★

Henvic
Camping Municipal de Kerilis ★★

Roscoff
Camping Municipal de Perharidy ★★
Camping Manoir de Kerestat ★★

Santec
Camping Municipal ★★ (W of Roscoff)

St Pol-de-Léon
Camping Ar Kleguer ★★★
☎ 02 98 69 18 81
Camping Le Trologot ★★★

Plouénan
Camping Tal Ar Mor ★★

Plounevez Lochrist (5.5km N of Lanhouarneau)
Camping Municipal ★★

Lesneven
Camping Municipal 29260 Lesneven
☎ 02 98 21 07 01

B&Bs
St Martin-des-Champs (W of Morlaix)
Keréliza, 29600 St Martin-des-Champs
☎ 02 98 88 27 18

Kermen (S of Carantec)
Tanguy
Kermen, 29660 Carantec
☎ 02 98 67 00 41

Santec (W of Roscoff)
183 route du Dossen, 29250 Santec
☎ 02 98 29 70 65
mariepierre.rivoallon@wanadoo.fr
**www.perso.wanadoo.fr/mariepierre.riv
oallon**

Sibiril (W of St Pol-de-Léon)
Kermenguy, 29250 Sibiril
☎ 02 98 29 95 12

St Pol-de-Léon
Cardinal
11 rue Goarem-Veguen, 29250 St Pol-de-Léon
☎ 02 98 29 09 02

Plouénan
Cazuc
Lopreden, 29420 Plouénan
☎ 02 98 69 50 62
allain.cazuc@wanadoo.fr

Mespaul
Lehmann
La Garenne, 29420 Mespaul
☎ 02 98 61 59 72

Moal
Kertanguy, 29420 Mespaul
☎ 02 98 61 57 77
mickael.moal@wanadoo.fr

Lanhouarneau
Queguineur
Kergollay, 29430 Lanhouarneau
☎ 02 98 61 47 35

Lesneven
Le Hir
Pen-ar-C'hoat, 29260 Lesneven
☎ 02 98 83 19 18

Bodennec
La Garenne Gouer Ven, 29260 Lesneven
☎ 02 98 83 24 85
abodennec@tiscali.fr

Plouider (N of Lesneven)
Kermabon, 29260 Plouider
☎ 02 98 25 40 41
claudine.Roue@wanadoo.fr

Kernilis (W of Lesneven)
Route de Kerbrat, 29260 Kernilis
☎ 02 98 25 54 02

Loc-Brevalaire (W of Lesneven)
Pencreach, 29260 Loc-Brevalaire
☎ 02 98 25 50 99

Hotels
Morlaix
Hotel du Port, 3, Quai de Léon, 29600 Morlaix
☎ 02 98 88 07 54

Hotel de l'Europe, 1, rue d'Aiguillon, 29600 Morlaix
☎ 02 98 62 11 99
www.hotel-europe-com.fr

Roscoff
Les Chardons Bleues, 4, rue Amiral Reveillère, 29680 Roscoff
☎ 02 98 69 72 03

Pont du Châtel (NE of Lesneven on D110)
Le Week-end, Pont du Châtel (Plouider) 29260 Lesneven
☎ 02 98 25 40 57

**STAGE 2
LE FOLGOËT/LESNEVEN
TO LANILDUT**

Campsites
Plouguerneau
Camping La Grève Blanche ★★
Camping Curnic Vougot ★★
Camping Meledan ★★

Laneda (W of Lannilis)
Camping Les Abers ★★★
Camping Municipal Pen Enez ★
Camping Fort Cezon ★

Saint Pabu
Camping Municipal ★★
Lampaul Ploudalmezeau
Camping Municipal des Dunes ★★

Ploudalmezeau
Camping Familial de Tréompan ★★
Camping Municipal de Tréompan ★★

Argenton/Landunvez
Camping Municipal Saint-Gonvel ★

Porspoder
Camping Municipal Les Dunes ★

Lanildut
Camping Municipal Le Tromeur ★★
☎ 02 98 04 31 13

B&Bs
Kernilis (W of Lesneven)
Route de Kerbrat, 29260 Kernilis
☎ 02 98 25 54 02

Loc-Brevalaire (W of Lesneven)
Pencreach, 29260 Loc-Brevalaire
☎ 02 98 25 50 99

Lannilis
Saint Alphonse, 29870 Lannilis
Tel. 02 98 04 14 13

Mingant
Pellan, 29870 Lannilis
☎ 02 98 04 01 55

Portsall
Cabon
La Demeure Océane
20 rue Bar ar Lan, 29830 Portsall –

Ploudalmézeau
☎ 02 98 48 77 42
www.demeure-oceane.fr

Lanildut
13 route de Mézancou, 29840 Lanildut
☎ 02 98 04 43 02
mfgourm@hotmail.com
www.leclosdildut.free.fr

4 Hent Kergaradoc, 29840 Lanildut
☎ 02 98 04 38 41
dominique.le.tarnec.menezhom@megalis.org
www.domletarnec.free.fr

4 Hent Mez ar Goff, 29840 Lanildut
☎ 02 98 04 37 46
guy.perrot7@wanadoo.fr

Prigent
2 chemin de Kerambellec, 29840 Lanildut
☎ 02 98 04 42 41

STAGE 3 LANILDUT TO BREST

Campsites
Plouarzel
Camping Municipal de Porstevigne ★★
Camping Municipal Porscuidic ★★
Camping Municipal Ruscumunoc ★★

Lampaul Plouarzel
Camping Municipal Porspaul ★★

Ploumoguer
Camping Kerebel Kerhornou ★

le Conquet
Camping Municipal Le Theven ★★
Camping Quere ★★

Plougonvelin
Camping de Bertheaume ★★
Camping Municipal Saint-Yves ★
Camping l'Iroise ★

Locmaria Plouzané
Camping Municipal de Portez ★★

Brest
Camping Municipal de Saint-Marc ★★
Camping du Goulet ★★

B&Bs
Plouarzel
L'Hostis
Graeoc, 29810 Plouarzel
☎ 02 98 89 60 42

le Conquet
Pillain
Rue Surcouf, 29217 le Conquet
☎ 02 98 89 15 16
py.pillain@wanadoo.fr

Vaillant
3 chemin des Dames, 29217 le Conquet
☎ 02 98 89 14 67

Kerneis
Kérinou, 29217 le Conquet
☎ 02 98 89 13 97

murielle.kerneis@wanadoo.fr

Plougonvelin
Keryel
29217 Plougonvelin
☎ 02 98 48 33 35
saliou.monique@wanadoo.fr

Le Mouillour
53 rue du Perzel, 29217 Plougonvelin
☎ 02 98 48 00 29
brigittelemouillour@wanadoo.fr

Locmaria-Plouzané
Benard
126 route de Kerfily, 29280 Locmaria-Plouzané
☎ 02 98 48 54 14
did.benard@wanadoo.fr

Plouzané
Lannevel Vras, 29280 Plouzané
☎ 02 98 05 94 60

Lézavarn
29280 Plouzané
☎ 02 98 48 41 28
christiane.philipot@wanadoo.fr

Hotels
Brest
Hotel de la Corniche, 1 rue Amiral Nicol, 29200 Brest
☎ 02 98 45 12 42
hotel@hotel-la-corniche.com

Center Interhotel, 4, Boulevard Léon Blum, 29200 Brest
☎ 02 98 80 78 00
www.hotelcenter.com

Hotel Kyriad, 157 rue J. Jaurès, 29200
Brest
Tel. 02 98 43 58 58
www.kyriadbrest.com

STAGE 4 BREST TO LE FAOU

Campsites
Crozon
Camping La Plage de Goulien ★★★
Camping Les Pieds dans l'Eau Saint-
Fiacre ★★★
Camping Les Pins ★★★
Camping Le Bouis Morgat ★★
Camping l'Aber
Camping Pen Ar Menez ★★
Camping Renouveau-Kernaou ★★

Lanvéoc
Camping Municipal ★★
Camping Gwel Kaer ★★

Telgruc-sur-Mer
Camping Le Panoramic ★★★★
Camping Armorique ★★★
Camping Les Mimosas ★★
Camping Pen Bellec ★★

Argol
Camping Ar Menez ★★

Rosnoen
Camping Le Seillou ★★

Le Faou
Camping Municipal ★★

B&Bs
Crozon (S of Le Fret)
28 rue de Goulien, 29160 Crozon
☎ 02 98 27 07 35

Argol
La Ferme Hizou
Trovéoc, 29560 Argol
☎ 02 98 27 74 49
accueil.bolndeau@tiscali.fr
www.la-ferme-hizou.fr.fm

Lanvily (1.5km NW of Argol)
Malcom Rider
29560 Lanvily
☎ 02 98 27 38 87
malcom.rider@tiscali.fr
www.lanvily.com

Rosnoën (S of Le Faou)
Le Seillou
29590 Rosnoën
☎ 02 98 81 92 21
le-pape-herve@wanadoo.fr
www.gites-finistere.com/gites/seillou

Hotels
Le Fret
Hostellerie de la Mer
29160 Le Fret
☎ 02 98 27 61 90
hostellerie.de.la.mer@wanadoo.fr

Le Faou
La Vieille Renommee Hotel de
Beauvoir, 11 place aux Foires, 29590
Le Faou
☎ 02 98 81 90 31
la-vieille-renommee@wanadoo.fr

STAGE 5 LE FAOU TO HUELGOAT

Campsites
Brasparts
Camping Tuchennou ★★

Brennilis (N of Loqueffret)
Camping Municipal ★★

Huelgoat
Camping La Rivière d'Argent ★★
Camping Le Lac ★★

B&Bs
Brasparts
Chaussy Romy
Domaine de Rugornou Vras, 29190 Brasparts
☎ 02 98 81 46 27
romy.chaussy@wanadoo.fr

Huelgoat
O'Brien
4 route de Berrien, 29690 Huelgoat
☎ 02 98 99 82 73
www.chateaubrien.com

Berrien (N of Huelgoat)
Callec
Le Bourg, 29690 Berrien
☎ 02 98 99 01 17

Hotels
Huelgoat
Hotel du Lac
12 rue du Général de Gaulle, 29690 Huelgoat
☎ 02 98 99 71 14

STAGE 6 HUELGOAT TO MORLAIX

B&Bs
Berrien (N of Huelgoat)
Callec
Le Bourg, 29690 Berrien
☎ 02 98 99 01 17

Plourin-les-Morlaix (SE of Morlaix)
Lestrezec, 29600 Plourin-les-Morlaix
☎ 02 98 72 53 55
phelary@yahoo.fr

St Martin-des-Champs (W of Morlaix)
Keréliza, 29600 St Martin-des-Champs
☎ 02 98 88 27 18

Hotels
Morlaix
Hotel du Port, 3, Quai de Léon, 29600 Morlaix
☎ 02 98 88 07 54

Hotel de l'Europe, 1, rue d'Aiguillon, 29600 Morlaix
☎ 02 98 62 11 99
www.hotel-europe-com.fr

For further information on accommodation, see Appendix B

ROUTE 2

CHAMPAGNE AND THE KINGS' FOREST: THE MARNE VALLEY AND PICARDY

ROUTE SUMMARY

From	To	Km	Terrain
Paris CDG	Charly-sur-Marne	67	Fairly hilly; farmland
Charly-sur-Marne	Dormans	40	River valley; vineyards
Dormans	Villers-Cotterêts	56	Hilly; farmland, forest
Villers-Cotterêts	Pierrefonds	25	Occasionally hilly
Pierrefonds and back	Compiègne	38	Mostly flat; forest

Stage 1 Aeroport Paris CDG to Charly-sur-Marne

Distance	67km/42 miles
Terrain	Fairly hilly; farmland
Climb	350m

How to get to Paris CDG

This tour starts from Paris Charles de Gaulle airport Terminal 1 (CDG1) which handles most international flights to and from Paris (except Air France flights which arrive at CDG2 terminal). A shuttle bus service connects

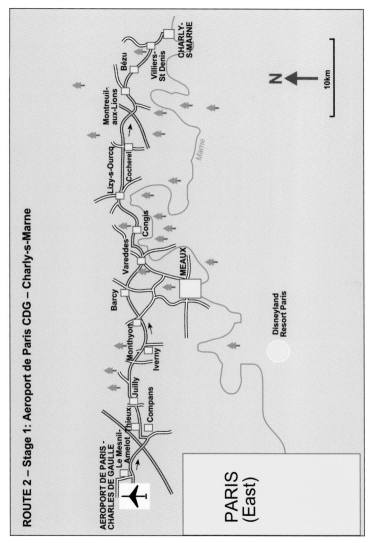

ROUTE 2 – Stage 1: Aeroport de Paris CDG – Charly-s-Marne

CDG1 with CDG2. See Getting There in the Introduction.

Charles de Gaulle airport can also be reached from central Paris using the regular RATP bus services – Roissybus which leaves from 9, rue Scribe near the Opéra Garnier (every 20min), taxis, or by RER B trains from Gare du Nord station, which is also a regular service.

The route

After Customs at Arrivals head straight ahead to the exit and cycle off L (take care, traffic from R) down a long ramp road leading away from the terminal. Bear L at first junction signposted *Autres Directions* then filter L again for Roissypole and Zone Centrale Est, just beyond a plant with eight tall chimneys on your L. Continue straight at traffic lights, following signs to Zone Centrale Est past the vast Hilton, Novotel and Ibis Hotel complex on your L. Filter R again for Zone Centrale Est and Marne la Vallée, then ignore sign for Zone Centrale Est after 400m, continuing straight for Marne la Vallée and **Le Mesnil-Amelot**.

Take R turn (D212) at rdbt signposted Meaux/Soissons/Marne la Vallée. Shortly after crossing over the N2 take second exit at rdbt for Thieux (D83), uphill through **Thieux**, then to **Juilly** (straight ahead at junction 'Rue de la Rochelle' through village). Exiting **Iverny**, turn L for **Monthyon** (D97) then straight over at crossroads to **Barcy**. ◄

From Juilly onwards the countryside is mostly gently undulating arable land, here and there stretching for several miles in all directions.

Notre Dame de la Marne, a large war memorial, appears on your R, followed soon after by a tiny war cemetery L before a hairpin descent through woods to the Canal de l'Ourcq and Vareddes. Go through **Vareddes** and take the D121 for Congis-sur-Therouanne, which follows the canal (no cycling allowed along this stretch of the track beside the canal).

Cycle through **Congis-sur-Therouanne** to reach **Lizy-sur-Ourcq** and take the D401 for Château-Thierry past a supermarket on your L (*not open Mon mornings*). Cross the Canal de l'Ourcq again, after which the D401 climbs

up to a plateau of vast stretches of farmland either side of the road before joining the N3. Go L here (descent) to **Montreuil-aux-Lions** and take the turning R (D16) before the long climb out of this village, towards **Bézu**. After Bézu there is a long descent through woods with wild flowers to **Villiers St Denis** (twinned with Aldborough in the UK). This is one of many villages that form part of the long 'Route Touristique du Champagne', a signposted wine route along the Marne Valley from Crouttes-sur-Marne to Trélou-sur-Marne in the *département* of Aisne. The road descends into the Marne Valley to the village of **Charly-sur-Marne**.

The Canal de l'Ourcq near Vareddes

Stage 2 Charly-sur-Marne to Dormans

Distance	40km/25 miles
Terrain	River valley; vineyards
Climb	60m

The route

From Charly-sur-Marne, cycle E through the village of **Saulchery**, vineyards stretching up the hillside L and the River Marne R. Passing through woods known locally as the Bois de Romeny, the Marne Valley opens up again before reaching **Azy-sur-Marne** with fields stretching to the banks of the Marne R and vineyard slopes L. **Essômes-sur-Marne** has an impressive 13th-century church, St Ferréol, but the village unfortunately suffers a lot of traffic, most of it heading for Château-Thierry nearby.

Each village on the 'Route Touristique du Champagne' proudly promotes its own homegrown establishments of Champagne, sign after sign hanging either side of the road or the name painted on a wall or arched above iron gates.

Château-Thierry, a bustling town on the Marne, is renowned as the birth-place of the French poet and writer of fables, Jean de la Fontaine (1621–95). A huge war monument overlooks the town on a hill to the W, which can be reached via the N3. It is one of 11 battlefield monuments built by the American Battle Monuments Commission after World War I to remember the soldiers who gave their lives on the battlefields of the Marne and surrounding areas.

From the centre of Château-Thierry do not cross the bridge over the Marne, but go straight (E) on the D3 staying on the N side of the river to **Brasles** (*which has a*

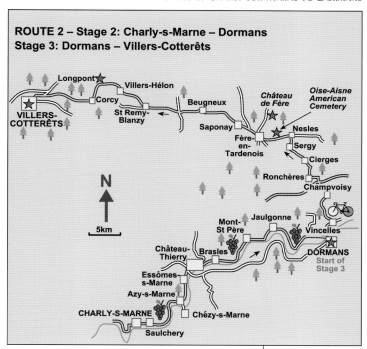

**ROUTE 2 – Stage 2: Charly-s-Marne – Dormans
Stage 3: Dormans – Villers-Cotterêts**

good bicycle shop – 'Sport Passion' – for parts or repairs 0.3km on the L after the village sign). The countryside opens up again after Brasles as the D3 follows the Marne, vineyards covering the slopes L as you continue along the Route Touristique du Champagne, passing through Gland and **Mont St Père** where the painter Leon Lhermitte lived from 1844 to 1925. A statue dedicated to him stands besides the road. When you reach Chartèves, take the time to go down to the river just after the church; there are picnic tables here with a lovely view across the Marne of the Gothic 13th-century church of Mézy-Moulins between the trees. Continue to **Jaulgonne** *(mini-market on R)* and a short descent through the village to cross a stream, then a short ascent is followed

81

by yet more vineyard slopes after Rosay. There is an interesting old winepress beside the road R before reaching Passy-sur-Marne with good views S across the valley. Trélou-sur-Marne is the final village on the Route Touristique du Champagne within the *département* of Aisne, and is soon followed by a descent to a bridge over the Marne into Dormans.

Dormans, a small and pleasant town hugging the S bank of the Marne, is where you will find the magnificent Mémorial des Deux Batailles de la Marne. This is a huge memorial chapel dedicated to the war dead on the battlefields of the Marne, and over 1000 unknown soldiers are buried in its ossuary. Follow signs from the village centre and go through the large gates (cycles permitted) into the château grounds. A track leads up through a pleasant park past the château on your L to the memorial. There is a good view of it from the vineyard slopes beyond the outer wall.

Stage 3 Dormans to Villers-Cotterêts

Distance	56km/35 miles
Terrain	Hilly; farmland, forest
Climb	450m
Map	See Stage 2

The route

From Dormans return to the bridge over the Marne, and having crossed it turn immediately R towards Vincelles past the Municipal campsite. The road climbs gently to **Vincelles** past vineyards. Turn L in the village, signposted Champvoisy. A very steep climb follows (rough road to begin with; turn L at first junction) past a Madonna on your L in woods before a clearing where there is a good

The country road to Sergy

view of the Marne Valley and Dormans. The road soon flattens out passing through secluded birch woodland, then descends gradually past farmland to la Chapelle Hurlay and **Champvoisy**.

Fork R in Champvoisy before reaching the village centre for Ronchères, the road climbing out of the village through vast tracts of arable land, over the Autoroute de l'Est (A4) and TGV Est line (under construction). Hereabouts the road is very narrow and throws the occasional pothole at you before reaching a T-junction. Turn L here for **Ronchères** and in the village take the R turn just after passing the memorial and church on your R (Rue de Cierges) for Cierges and Sergy. Here there are extensive views L across farmland, stretching some 40km on a clear day. The road is once again very narrow and a little bumpy in places, but this only adds to the charm of the open, peaceful countryside. Reaching **Cierges** turn R (Rue de l'Eglise) round the church, then first R after 200m on the D14 for Coulonges-Cohan. Take the narrow country road that appears on your L very soon (not signposted) which cuts across open farmland (slight ascent) to reach **Sergy**; here turn R at the church for **Nesles**. Turn L at the junction (D2), passing the Ruines du Château de Nesles (feudal château of 13th/15th centuries) R, and continue on the D2 to the **Oise–Aisne American Cemetery**, also R.

The Oise–Aisne American Cemetery

The **Oise–Aisne American Cemetery** is the second largest American World War I military cemetery in Europe, where 6012 American soldiers who died hereabouts now rest. The 36.5-acre cemetery and its memorial are the responsibility of the American Battle Monuments Commission. After World War I this commission erected a memorial chapel in each of the eight American military cemeteries in Europe, as well as 11 battlefield monuments. The names of 241 Americans whose remains were never recovered or were unidentified are also inscribed on the walls of the chapel at this cemetery, and a bronze rosette indicates the names of those who were subsequently found.

About 1.5km from Fère-en-Tardenois along the D967 to Fismes stands the impressive **Château de Fère**, now a luxurious hotel, beside impressive castle ruins on the hill.

Continue to **Fère-en-Tardenois** (*cycle shop on L before reaching the centre of town*). From the 16th-century market place with its large tiled roof and timbered struts supported by stone pillars in Fère-en-Tardenois take the D2 (NW) for Villers-Cotterêts (descent from town past station on your R) to a rdbt. Take the third exit W on the D2 to **Saponay** (Rue de Fère) and continue straight to Cramaille. Go through this village (Rue des Sources) W to **Beugneux**. Go straight at the crossroads in the village along Rue Prinicipale, which bends L after 250m and leads to Grand-Rozoy. Continue W through this village along Rue de Montier to a crossroads with the busy D1. Cross over here to the D2 which continues W to le Plessier-Huleu and then **St Rémy-Blanzy**. Here bear L at a junction and at a crossroads after 150m turn R (Route de Soissons) on the D2 climbing out of the village (bear L at junction with D83) up to **Villers-Hélon** (keep L at a junction with the D172). Again on the D2 (Rue de l'Eglise), passing the church on your R before a descent and over a railway line into the village of **Longpont**.

The impressive ruins of the Cistercian abbey of Longpont which overlook the village date back to 1131 when it was founded by St Bernard. Unfortunately, very little remains of the great rose window on the grand west front of the church since most of the stone was removed and sold during the Revolution.

Take the D17 S from Longpont to Corcy alongside the eastern perimeter of the Retz Forest, the largest forest in Aisne, covering 13,000 hectares. This is a beautiful forest of predominantly beech, but hornbeam, oak, chesnut, cherry, maple and birch can also be found here. It is home to a wonderful variety of fauna, including deer, rabbits, hares, foxes, pheasants and even wild boar.

The road crosses over the railway line (Rue de l'Etang) and bears L by the lake to join the D80. Go R here (Rue de la Ramée) and follow the D80 into the Retz Forest to the lovely village of Fleury. Stay on the D80 for another 4km to where it meets up with the D231; go L here into **Villers-Cotterêts**.

Villers-Cotterêts was the birthplace of the famous writer Alexandre Dumas, who is best remembered for his celebrated work *The Three Musketeers*. He was born at 46 rue Alexandre Dumas, formerly rue du Lormet (now privately owned, exterior viewing only). Look out for the plaque above the garage door of the building on its left, which lists his most famous work. The Musée Alexandre Dumas at 24 rue Demoustier, dedicated to three generations of the Dumas family, and the Renaissance Château built by François I between 1532 and 1541 (N side of Place A. Briand opposite the *office du tourisme*), are also both worth visiting.

Stage 4 Villers-Cotterêts to Pierrefonds

Distance	25km/10 miles
Terrain	Occasionally hilly
Climb	130m

The route
Follow signs from the centre of Villers-Cotterêts for Compiègne (*bike shop at 69 rue Général Leclerc, Villers-Cotterêts as you leave town heading W and a LeClerc hypermarket which stocks bicycle parts/tyres on D936 S to la Ferté-Millon*) towards Largny. Continue straight at a junction after a sculpture fountain on your R, and out of

The **Donjon de Vez** (on your L before reaching the village) is worth visiting and is usually open every day from early July to late October and also Sun in March, April and May as well as holiday days from 2–6pm. This impressive medieval fortress with its imposing ramparts, lovely gardens and chapel dates back to 1214 and was built on a Gallo-Roman site, then subsequently seized and fortified by Louis d'Orléans in the 14th century.

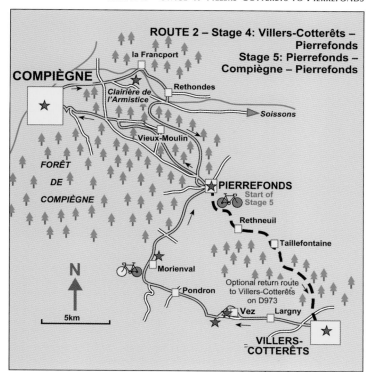

town across flat farmland with an impressive windmill on your L in the distance. There is a pleasant descent through woodland, the start of the Automne Valley, passing picturesque period properties after reaching **Largny**. Arriving at the village sign for Vez, turn R up a steep hill signposted 'Vez – centre bourg'.

Continue on up through the village and turn L (sign-posted 'Donjon de Vez') before reaching the walled cemetery at the top of the hill. Descend past the chateau and turn R to continue along the D32 to the **Abbaye de Lieu-Restauré** on your L, which has a magnificent rose window. Although only open to the public on Sat

Morienval

(10am–12pm and 2–6pm) and Sun (10am–12pm and 2–6pm) you can ☎ 01 43 29 93 55 for a private viewing. Continue along the flat D32 lined on the S side with birch trees, past the charming Château de Pondron on your R before reaching the pretty village of the same name. Continue straight here (D32) for Morienval past the church in **Pondron** (12–15th century, leaded glass windows sadly in a sorry state). After Fresnoy the road bears R (D335) uphill to **Morienval**.

The Notre Dame church of Morienval is one of the earliest Gothic churches in France and certainly one of the finest. Believed to have been founded by King Dagobert in the 7th century, the original abbey actually housed both monks and nuns together in the 9th century. Little has changed since a late 11th-century reconstruction apart from slight modification in the 17th century, then restoration. Of particular note is the very narrow ambulatory whose arches date back to early 12th century and were unique at this time. Continue uphill out of Morienval, after which the countryside flattens out into a high plateau of farmland before a descent through woods to Palesné and **Pierrefonds**.

Overlooking a lake, the village of **Pierrefonds** is dwarfed by its immense chateau that just has to be seen to be believed. Originally built in the late 14th and early 15th centuries, the château was dismantled in the 17th century and the ruins were purchased by Napoleon I in 1813. Napoleon III commissioned Viollet-le-Duc to restore it to its former glory. The exterior is a remarkable reconstruction with its double crowned colossal towers, drawbridge and moat, whilst inside are many Renaissance touches executed by the romantic architect. Open every day from 9.30am–6pm, 15 May–15 September and from 9.30am–12.30pm and 2–6pm, 16–30 September and 1 April–14 May. Open Sun from 9.30am–6pm. Same hours as Sun only closing at 5.30pm from 1 October–31 March.

Pierrefonds

Stage 5 Pierrefonds to Compiègne and back

Distance	38km/22.5 miles
Terrain	Mostly flat; forest
Climb	50m
Map	See Stage 4

The route

Follow the D973 NW towards Compiègne for 1km to the junction with the D547 (R for Clairière de l'Armistice) where you join the cycle path that cuts through the beautiful forest of Compiègne. You can also start this stage from Rue du Beaudon in Pierrefonds where the cycle path begins. The cycle path is flat as far as **Vieux Moulin** (do not turn R for the village, but cross the D602 to continue along the path through beech woods) but then descends through a mixture of beech and pine forest after 1km before flattening out again and meeting up with the D14. Although the path continues opposite, turn L here along the D14 to a rdbt that is visible from the cycle path. Take the second R for **Compiègne** (4km), then follow signs for Compiègne *centre ville*.

Head E out of Compiègne, following the N31 which skirts the Forêt de Compiègne to a major rdbt (R for Pierrefonds). Go straight here, then bear L after 200m, the D546 for Clairière de l'Armistice. After 1.5km the road curves N where there is a war memorial with a fallen eagle statue. Bear R here to reach the **Clairière de l'Armistice**.

Clairière de l'Armistice is where the Armistice of World War I was signed on 11 November 1918 and, symbolically, was the location chosen by Hitler for the signing of the French surrender in June 1940 during World War II. Railway trucks branching from the Compiègne-to-Soissons line were purposely put down to arrive at the clearing where this historic first meeting took place in 1918. Maréchal Foch, commander-in-chief of the Allied Forces, arrived here by private train on 7 November, followed a day later by the Germans on a train from Terguier. The Armistice was signed in Foch's carriage, which had also been converted into his personal office. In 1940 the Germans transported this carriage to Berlin, and it was subsequently destroyed in 1945.

Today, a replica carriage can be visited by tourists in the small Musée Wagon de l'Armistice situated beyond the memorial, which is flanked by railway lines. Nearby, a statue of Foch which the Germans left intact following the second historic meeting in 1940 watches over this clearing.

The museum is open daily (except Tues) from 10am–12pm and 2–5.15pm (last admissions at 11.30am and 4.45pm).

*The Hôtel de Ville,
Compiègne*

Compiègne is a town steeped in history and was a favourite residence of kings dating back to the 9th century, when Charles the Bald had a palace built here. The nearby Forêt de Compiègne was a popular royal hunting ground and is certainly one of the most beautiful forests in France today. Joan of Arc was captured here by the Burgundians in 1430.

The royal château of Charles V was demolished in the mid-18th century and a new triangular-shaped château completed during the reign of Louis XVI and restored by Napoleon I. It was later to become a favourite residence of Napoleon III and the Empress Eugenie.

In the town centre the flamboyantly restored Hôtel de Ville overlooks a pretty square and has a tall belfry upon which stand the three 'Picantans', colourful figures that strike the hours and quarter hours.

Continue on the D546 to **le Francport**, crossing the picturesque Aisne river with weeping willows lining its banks. From this pretty village follow the D81 to **Rethondes** (which boasts the Alain Blot restaurant) and cross the river again to reach the N31, turning R at this junction. Turn L after 0.5km for **Vieux Moulin**, cycling through the Forêt de Compiègne again. If you are lucky you may catch a glimpse of wild deer or a red squirrel or two. Stay on this scenic road (D547) through beech and oak woodland past the turning for Vieux Moulin and then the Etangs de St Pierre to arrive at the junction with the D973 again. Turn L to get back to the campsite, or keep straight over to the cycle path that leads back to **Pierrefonds**.

How to get back to Paris or CDG

There are rail connections from Compiègne to Gare du Nord in Paris, and from Villers-Cotterêts to Paris. If you want to return to CDG, but don't want to go into Paris, there is a train service from Villers-Cotterêts to Danmartin – Juilly – St Mard from where you can cycle to the airport. A pleasant cycle ride on the D973 from Pierrefonds to Villers-Cotterêts (15km) involves three climbs, with a good view of the immense château of Pierrefonds from the first ascent and welcome shade on a hot day courtesy of the beech forest of Retz up the third. Allow 1½hr for this ride.

The train ride to Danmartin – Juilly – St Mard takes ½hr and costs 8 euros. It would be advisable to pick up a free mini timetable booklet at Villers-Cotterêts station the first time you visit this town en route to Morienval and Pierrefonds for train times.

From Danmartin station turn R, signposted Rouvres, and then L at the next junction (*boulangerie* on corner). Cycle through the village; the road descends and passes under the busy N2, followed by a short punchy climb into Danmartin-en-Goele. Turn L at the top of the hill to get on the D401, which descends to Villeneuve before a ride across flat countryside to Le Mesnil Amelot. From here follow signs for Charles de Gaulle airport (15km from Danmartin to CDG airport; allow 1½hr).

SELECTED ACCOMMODATION
ROUTE 2

STAGE 1 AEROPORT DE PARIS CDG TO CHARLY-SUR-MARNE

Campsites
Vareddes
Le Village Parisien ★★★★ (0.5km NE, route de Congis)
☎ 01 64 34 80 80
leslie@villageparisien.com
www.villageparisien.com

Charly-sur-Marne
Camping Municipal Des Illettes ★★★ (S, route de Pavant)
☎ 03 23 82 12 11
Open 1 April–30 September

B&Bs
Charly-sur-Marne
Charpentier
Le Havre des Blanches Vignes,
11 route de Paris, 02310 Charly-sur-Marne
☎ 03 23 82 10 72
jean-marc@champagne-charpentier.com

Remiot
11 rue du Pâtis, 02310 Charly-sur-Marne
☎ 03 23 82 00 76

Hotels
Pavant (S of Charly-sur-Marne)
Le Toscane,
Place de la Marie, 02310 Pavant
☎ 03 23 70 87 85

STAGE 2 CHARLY-SUR-MARNE TO DORMANS

Campsites
Château-Thierry
Camping Municipal ★★ (Behind McDonalds, W end of town)
02400 Château-Thierry
☎ 03 23 83 48 23

Dormans
Camping Sous le Clocher ★★
Route de Vincelles 51700 Dormans
☎ 03 26 58 21 79

B&Bs
Château-Thierry
Maurice
10 rue du Château, 02400 Château-Thierry
☎ 03 23 83 17 63.
Mariechambres@aol.com

Mont St Père
Comyn
7bis rue Fontaine St Foy, 02400 Mont
St Père
☎ 03 23 70 28 79

Le Charmel
Assailly
6 route du Moulin, 02850 Le Charmel
☎ 03 23 70 31 27
www.assailly.site.voila.fr

Courtemont-Varennes
Adam
3 rue Vinot, 02850 Courtemont-
Varennes
☎ 03 23 70 92 20

Reuilly-Sauvigny
Sykes
Rue des Vaches, 02850 Reuilly-
Sauvigny
☎ 03 23 70 68 62
bgms@hexanet.fr
www.marneweb.com/bnb/indexeng.htm

Vincelles (N of Dormans)
Simon
3 rue Paul Chapelle – 51700
Vincelles
☎ 03 26 58 87 94

Hotels
Brasles (Château-Thierry)
Les Fabliaux
3 Ave de Château-Thierry, 02400
Brasles
☎ 03 23 83 23 14
contact@lesfabliaux.com
www.lesfabliaux.com

94

Reuilly-Sauvigny
Auberge Le Relais
☎ 03 23 70 35 36

Dormans
Hotel du Marché NC
Place du Luxembourg, 51700
Dormans
☎ 03 26 58 50 70

Le Champenois
14 rue de Châlons, 51700 Dormans
☎ 03 26 58 20 44

STAGE 3 DORMANS TO VILLERS-COTTERÊTS

Campsites
Fère-en-Tardenois
Camping Municipal des Bruyeres ★★
(0.5 km N, D967)
☎ 03 23 82 71 22

Villers-Hélon
Castel des Biches ★★★★
☎ 03 23 72 93 93

No campsite at Villers-Cotterêts.

B&Bs
Vincelles (N of Dormans)
Simon
3 rue Paul Chapelle – 51700
Vincelles
☎ 03 26 58 87 94

Fère-en-Tardenois
Chauvin (1km N, D967)
Clairbois, 7 Residence Charbois,

02130 Fère-en-Tardenois
☎ 03 23 82 21 72
chauvinfrancois@aol.com
www.clairbois.fr.fm

Longpont
De Frayssinet
3 place de l'Abbaye, 02600 Longpont
☎ 03 23 72 71 57

Haramont (NE of Villers-Cotterêts)
Eidelwein
37 route de Villers, 02600 Haramont
☎ 03 23 96 16 78
eidelwein.gabriel@tiscali.fr

Largny-sur-Automne (W of Villers-Cotterêts)
Dobbels
2 rue du Paty, 02600 Largny-sur-Automne
☎ 03 23 96 06 97

Hotels
Longpont
Hotel de l'Abbaye, 8 rue des Tourelles, 02600 Longpont
☎ 03 23 96 02 44
habbaye@wanadoo.fr   (Benoît Verdun)

Villers-Cotterêts
Hotel le Régent, 26 rue Général Mongin, 02600 Villers-Cotterêts
☎ 03 23 96 01 46
info@hotel-leregent.com

Hotel Restaurant Du Parc, 26 place Briand, 02600 Villers-Cotterêts
☎ 03 23 96 00 51

STAGE 4 VILLERS-COTTERÊTS TO PIERREFONDS

Campsites
Pierrefonds
Camping Municipal ★★ (D973 to Compiègne). Open April–October but not a big site; advance booking in summer recommended (☎ 03 44 42 80 83).

Compiègne
Camping Municipal de l'Hippodrome ★★

B&Bs
Largny-sur-Automne (W of Villers-Cotterêts)
Dobbels
2 rue du Paty, 02600 Largny-sur-Automne
☎ 03 23 96 06 97

Orrouy
Gage
60 rue de la Forêt, 60129 Orrouy
☎ 03 44 88 60 41
SCA.GAGE@wanadoo.fr

Pierrefonds
Bourne
Donjon House
10/12 rue Notre Dame, 60350 Pierrefonds
☎ 03 44 42 37 59
donjon.house@free.fr

Chelles (E of Pierrefonds)
Gras
9 rue du Priez, 60350 Pierrefonds
☎ 03 44 85 30
g.floroclam@aol.com
Hotels

Pierrefonds

Hotel des Etrangers, Rue du Beaudon
☎ 03 44 42 80 18

Hotel–Restaurant Auberge Aux Bles
D'Or
☎ 03 44 42 85 91

Compiègne
Hotel de Flandre, Quai de la
République – 60200 Compiègne

Hotel du Nord, Place de la Gare –
60200 Compiègne

STAGE 5 PIERREFONDS TO COMPIÈGNE AND BACK

B&Bs
Berneuil-sur-Aisne (E of Rethondes)
Abadie
Rochefort, 60350 Berneuil-sur-Aisne
☎ 03 44 85 81 78

See Pierrefonds in Stage 4 for other accommodation.

For further information on accommodation, see Appendix B

ROUTE 3

THE WINE ROAD AND
BAS-RHIN: ALSACE

ROUTE SUMMARY

From	To	Km	Terrain
Colmar	Barr	50	Mostly flat; vineyards
Barr	Saverne	62	Hilly; mostly forest
Saverne	Niederbronn-les-Bains	37	Occasionally hilly; canal, farmland
Niederbronn-les-Bains	Haguenau	60	Hilly, then mostly flat; forest

Stage 1 Colmar to Barr

Distance	50km/31 miles (or 65km including Haut-Koenigsbourg)
Terrain	Mostly flat; vineyards
Climb	130m (or 637m including Haut-Koenigsbourg)

How to get to Colmar
Strasbourg international airport to Strasbourg You can either take the shuttle to tram stop Baggersee, where there is a connection to tram line A for the city centre (every 20min from Arrivals/5 euros one-way), or by train

from Entzheim station into Strasbourg on weekdays. Entzheim station is 5min on foot from Arrivals, and trains leave every hour or so from 5.30am–7pm Mon–Fri. Unfortunately, few trains run on Sat and hardly any on Sun and holiday days.

Paris to Strasbourg Trains leave regularly from Paris Est for Strasbourg (Corail/Corail Téoz service); journey time is 4hr.

Strasbourg is a modern city where the European Parliament and Council are located. It is also a beautiful, cultural city that is typically Alsatian with an historic heart largely only accessible on foot, a picturesque island between two branches of the River Ill, at the centre of which stands the grand Gothic Cathédrale Notre-Dame. This spectacular cathedral was built with local sandstone from the Vosges, and dates back to the late 11th century. A walk along the Quai de la Petit France to see the old, half-timbered houses reflected in the canal waters is highly recommended, followed by the Ponts Couverts bridge nearby with its two striking medieval watchtowers.

Reaching Colmar from Strasbourg Trains run regularly to Colmar from Strasbourg, often Swiss SBB trains en route to Basle. The journey takes ½hr and there is a bicycle compartment, usually at the rear of the train.

Colmar is a beautiful town, typically Alsatian in character with its excellently restored half-timbered houses, its pretty 'Little Venice' canal quarter, as well as the Quartier des Tanneurs and other historic quarters. A walk along the Quai de la Poissonerie is a must.

The route
From Colmar station cycle N up the Avenue de la République past the Champ de Mars gardens R, and take the road L to a rdbt with a fountain. Bear R towards Turckheim and Ingersheim along Rue Stanislas before joining up with the D418, Route d'Ingersheim (tunnel

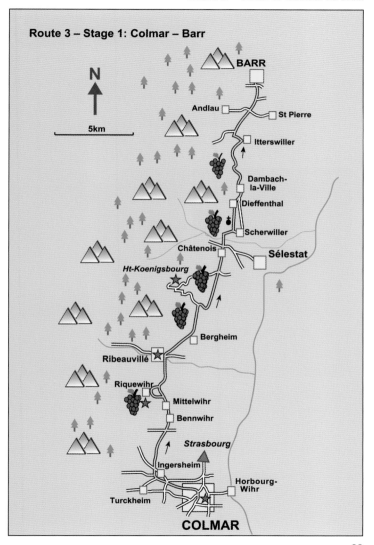

Route 3 – Stage 1: Colmar – Barr

N

5km

BARR

Andlau

St Pierre

Itterswiller

Dambach-la-Ville

Dieffenthal

Scherwiller

Châtenois

Sélestat

Ht-Koenigsbourg

Bergheim

Ribeauvillé

Riquewihr

Mittelwihr

Bennwihr

Strasbourg

Ingersheim

Horbourg-Wihr

Turckheim

COLMAR

under Colmar–Strasbourg railway line) that takes you W out of the town complete with cycle lane. Reaching **Ingersheim** (which boasts the Grand Cru Florimont and a baroque church) follow the D10 N to **Bennwihr** and **Mittelwihr** (6km), two of many vineyard villages dotted along the famous 'Route des Vins d'Alsace' – The Wine Road of Alsace. Both Bennwihr and Mittelwihr have Grand Cru wines, Marckrain and Mandelberg respectively, the former celebrated during the second weekend of August.

On the Route des Vins d'Alsace

Route des Vins d'Alsace Stretching some 170km from Marlenheim (W of Strasbourg) to Thann near Mulhouse, the Alsace Wine Route runs along the eastern foothills of the Vosges mostly between altitudes of 200 and 400m, with vineyards covering an area of 14,600 productive hectares. A combination of granite, limestone, gneiss, schist and sandstone and a warm, often dry climate provides ideal conditions for the cultivation of seven varieties of grape: Sylvaner, Pinot Blanc, Riesling, Muscat d'Alsace, Tokay Pinot Gris, Gewurztraminer and Pinot Noir. There are three appellations. The label of an A.O.C. Alsace wine will generally show the name of the grape variety used. It may also show a brand name or the word 'Edelzwicker' if the wine is made from more than one white grape variety. A.O.C. Alsace Grand Cru wines must come from specific vineyards, and must pass stringent tasting tests carried out by a panel of experts. The label must show the grape variety (only Riesling, Gewurztraminer, Tokay Pinot Gris and Muscat are permitted), the vintage and the name of one of the 50 defined vineyards that are entitled to Grand Cru status.

A.O.C. Crémant d'Alsace is the name given to the sparkling wines of Alsace. These are made by the traditional method (as in Champagne), mainly from Pinot Blanc, but also from Pinot Gris, Pinot Noir, Riesling or Chardonnay. All wines here must be bottled in the traditional slender Alsace bottle.

Now on the D1B, turn L 1km after Mittelwihr up the D3 to **Riquewihr**. Riquewihr boasts many beautifully preserved houses and fortifications from the 13th–17th centuries. Many of the balconies of these houses are decorated exuberantly with flowers, and plaques giving details of their history. The double ring of walls around this large village augments this example of constant preservation, surrounded in turn by the vineyards that have made Riquewihr prosperous over the centuries (Grands Crus Schoenenbourg and Sporen). Return to the D1B and continue N to Ribeauvillé.

Ribeauvillé – another picturesque little town full of traditional Alsatian houses decked in flowers – is a popular stop for tourists in summer due to its prominent location along the wine route. Visit some of the side streets where the houses have wine bottles as well as flowers decorating their façades. The town is dominated by the three châteaux of Ribeaupierre (Girsberg, Saint-Ulrich and Haut-Ribeaupierre – 12th–13th centuries) and is home to a number of storks that have taken residence on towers and chimneys! Expect a visit from one or more of them if staying at the Camping Municipal Pierre de Coubertin, E of Ribeauvillé. Wine festival during the penultimate weekend in July (Grands Crus Geisberg, Kirchberg and Osterberg).

Ribeauvillé

Continue on to the quaint, medieval, fortified village of **Bergheim** with its round towers, then N to Saint-Hippolyte (250m), another picturesque village renowned for its 'Rouge de St-Hippolyte' (Pinot Noir). High on the hill NW stands the impressive **Haut-Koenigsbourg** fortified château (757m), built by the Germans during their occupation of Alsace. Belonging to the Hohenstaufens in the 12th century and the Hapsburgs in the 15th century, the castle was rebuilt in 1479 to strengthen its defences. If you don't mind the climb this château is worth a visit (7.5km from Saint-Hippolyte) and there are splendid views en route.

From Saint-Hippolyte continue to Orschwiller on the D1B, now cycling into the *département* of Bas-Rhin, where the D1B becomes the D35 (*small campsite in the centre of Orschwiller – E side of D35*) and the charming village of **Châtenois**. The uninviting outskirts of Sélestat, 3km E (*supermarket on L after 2km*) stand in stark contrast to this town's beautiful interior of small squares and narrow streets; the churches of Sainte-Foy and Saint-Georges are both worth a visit.

Returning to Châtenois follow the D35 N, and just after it turns E towards Scherwiller take the cycle path L for Tannel Kreuz church. Beyond the vineyards L hereabouts stand the castle ruins of Ortenbourg on the hill. From the church the cycle path then becomes a rough track as it gradually climbs to **Dieffenthal** where you take the Rue Principale down to the main road again. Follow the D35 all the way to **Barr**, passing through the picturesque villages of **Dambach-la-Ville**, Blienschwiller, Nothalten, **Itterswiller** and Eichhoffen.

Stage 2 Barr to Saverne

Distance	62km/39 miles
Terrain	Hilly; mostly forest
Climb	815m

The route

From Barr the D35 climbs steeply to Heiligenstein with views E over the Alsace plains to Strasbourg, followed by a view of Mont-Sainte Odile in the wooded hills W before reaching **Ottrott**. Here the D35 and Route des Vins d'Alsace continue N to Rosheim and Molsheim. Instead turn L in Ottrott centre and cycle NW to **Klingenthal** through pleasant woodland past an aquarium that is home to some sharks and crocodiles!

There is a steep climb out of Klingenthal through woods to a crossroads (355m) after 3km. Leave the D204 here, going straight ahead for **Mollkirch** (D217), crossing the Magel stream. A descent from Mollkirch on the D704 leads down to the Bruche Valley and a roundabout on the busy N420. Continue straight here N past the 'Camping /Auberge des deux étangs' (D704 still), then turn L at the T-junction for 2km before turning R (D218) for **Niederhaslach** and its impressive Eglise St Florent Vitraux.

Note Few shops/bars between Niederhaslach and Saverne.

103

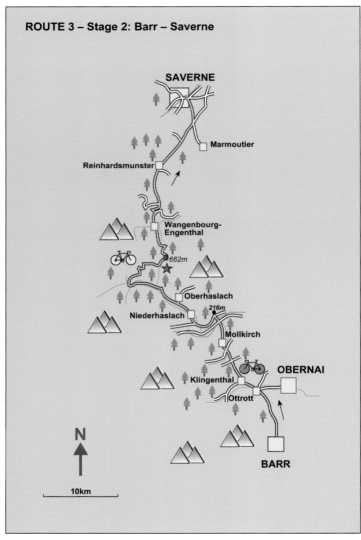

ROUTE 3 – Stage 2: Barr – Saverne

SAVERNE

Marmoutier

Reinhardsmunster

Wangenbourg-
Engenthal

662m

Oberhaslach

Niederhaslach

216m

Mollkirch

Klingenthal

OBERNAI

Ottrott

BARR

N

10km

Continue to **Oberhaslach** and stay on the D218 sign-posted 'Le Nideck' alongside the Hasel stream, cycling into the beautiful Forêt de Haslach.

Reaching 'Camping du Luttenbach' (about 3km after Oberhaslach), the road starts to climb up through the forest to a viewpoint of the ruins of Château Nideck tucked away in the woods (look out for a rock monument on R side of road approx 9km from Oberhaslach). The road climbs for another 3km to 662m, after which there is a refreshing descent to **Wangenbourg** village where the countryside opens out. Bearing L at the junction in the centre of Wangenbourg the D218 drops quickly to a narrow wooded valley before climbing again to a cross-roads with the D143 at 445m (L here for Obersteigen). Continue straight, still on the D218, which descends to **Reinhardsmunster** and offers views N to Saverne. Continue on the D218 all the way down to open coun-tryside where you join up with the busy N4 and tackle a steep, long climb into **Saverne**.

Stage 3 Saverne to Niederbronn-les-Bains

Distance	37km/23 miles
Terrain	Occasionally hilly; alongside a canal, then farmland
Climb	250m

Situated on the Marne–Rhine canal, **Saverne** is a pleasant town with an imposing red-sandstone château which overlooks the canal. Its north façade is very impressive and is about 150m long. The Maison Katz at 76 Grand Rue in the town centre is a remarkable example of many typical 17th-century half-timbered houses in Alsace.

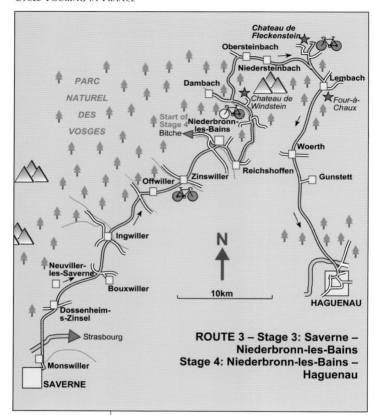

ROUTE 3 – Stage 3: Saverne –
Niederbronn-les-Bains
Stage 4: Niederbronn-les-Bains –
Haguenau

The route

From the Maison Katz cycle down to the canal and turn immediately R (do not cross the canal) where a signposted cycle path follows the canal out of town towards Monswiller. Approximately 0.5km after passing round the château follow the cycle path (signposted) under a bridge for 1.5km until you reach a road. Cross the bridge L here for **Monswiller** and then take the D219 to **Dossenheim-sur-Zinsel**.

In Dossenheim-sur-Zinsel take the road after the church towards **Neuviller les-Saverne**, then first R (cycle signpost) Rue de la Gare where the road becomes a tranquil cycle path through open countryside and farmland for 4.5km. When this meets up with the D17 (roundabout) take the road to Ingwiller and the C5 (Roman road) N at the next roundabout for Niedersoultzbach. Continue N here as the old road climbs before a short descent to **Ingwiller**. ▸

Take the undulating D28 to Rothbach and **Offwiller**, which offers lovely views SE, then on to **Zinswiller** (camping R after a descent soon after this village) and Oberbronn, before one final steep descent into **Niederbronn-les-Bains**, a prosperous spa town since Roman times because of its thermal springs.

The forested Vosges du Nord Regional Natural Park just N of Ingwiller covers some 1200sq km right up to the border with Germany, beyond which is the Pfälzerwald Natural Park.

Stage 4 Niederbronn-les-Bains to Haguenau

Distance	60km/37.5 miles
Terrain	Hilly, then mostly flat; mostly forest
Climb	300m
Map	See Stage 3

The route

From the centre of Niederbronn-les-Bains head SE on the D662 to **Reichshoffen** (3km) then N on the D53 to Jaegerthal past a lake R. This scenic road winds up into the northern part of the Forêt de Niederbronn, the ruined châteaux of **Windstein**, Wineck and Schoeneck hidden high above the road in the wooded hills. Just after Wineckerthal the D53 climbs into beautiful woodland where the latter two ruins can be found if you do not mind a hike, before joining up with the D3. Head E here through the pretty villages of **Obersteinbach** and

Note Few shops/bars between Niederbronn-les-Bains and Lembach.

The Château de Fleckenstein

The ruins of Château de Fleckenstein are only a stone's throw from Germany, perched precariously on a sandstone spur jutting out of a beautiful forest. The château was destroyed in 1680.

Niedersteinbach which lie below the craggy wooded slopes of the Forêt de Steinbach.

The road is mostly flat for 4.5km after Niedersteinbach with a view of the Château de Fleckenstein L high on the hill just before reaching the turning L for Schönau across the border in Germany. Take this road past a campsite and lake L, ignore the first road R which climbs to the Col de Litschhof, instead taking the second R which climbs through woods to the 12th-century **Château de Fleckenstein**. The final kilometre to these impressive ruins is closed to motorised traffic. ◄

Return to the D3 (after perhaps popping into Germany for lunch!) and continue SE to the picturesque village of **Lembach**.

The **Four-à-Chaux,** situated not far from Lembach, formed a small part of the incredible Maginot Line – a defence wall with underground fortifications and concrete infantry blocks built during the 1930s along the northeast border with Germany. This fort is still very much as it was before World War II with its barracks, telephone exchange and power station still in good order (guided tours). To reach it, cycle 1km S on the D27 from Lembach, then L along the D65 through woods for about 0.5km until you see a military tank on a bank on your L.

Just S of Lembach, look out for a narrow cycle path to the R of the D27 as you head S, which starts just after crossing the Schmelzbach stream and runs parallel with this road through pretty woods for approx 4.5km. Cross the D27 and follow a wide, rough cycle path (old road) S to some buildings below Liebfrauenberg. Bear R (W) here over the Sauer river, then L, and soon after the cycle path resumes alongside the D27 into **Woerth**. The cycle path continues to run parallel with the D27 towards Durrenbach, the countryside more open on this stretch and bordered by fields. When the cycle path reaches the D250 after 3.5km from Woerth go R here (L for Gunstett) and follow the D27 S through the Forêt de Haguenau to **Haguenau**. Although the cycle path does start again at Walbourg beyond Durrenbach, this section is often populated by roller skaters due to its close proximity to Haguenau.

How to get back to Strasbourg
There is a regular TER train service from Haguenau SNCF station into Strasbourg (45min).

Strasbourg

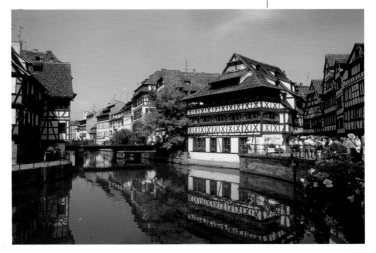

SELECTED ACCOMMODATION
ROUTE 3

STAGE 1 COLMAR TO BARR

Campsites
Strasbourg
Camping La Montagne Verte ★★★★

Colmar
Camping Intercommunal de l'ill ★★★

Riquewihr
Camping Intercommunal Riquewihr ★★★★

Ribeauvillé
Camping Municipal Base Pierre de Coubertin ★★★★

Selestat
Camping Municipal Les Cigognes ★★

Dambach-la-Ville
Camping Municipal ★★

St Pierre
Camping Municipal Beau Séjour ★★
☎ 03 88 08 52 24
Open mid-May–1 October

Barr
Camping Municipal Sainte-Odile ★★
Camping Saint-Martin ★★

B&Bs
Katzenthal (NW of Ingersheim)
Amrien
128 rue des Trois Epis, 68230 Katzenthal
☎ 06 82 21 76 31
sarl.amrien@wanadoo.fr

Mittelwihr
Edel
Domaine du Bouxhof, 68630 Mittelwihr
☎ 03 89 47 93 67

Beblenheim
Colaianni
41 rue de Hoen, 68980 Beblenheim
☎ 03 89 47 82 52

Hunawihr
Seiler
3 rue du Nord, 68150 Hunawihr
☎ 03 89 73 70 19

Rorschwihr
Meschberger
1 rue de la Forêt, 68750 Rorschwihr
☎ 03 89 73 77 32

St Hippolyte
Bleger
63 route du Vin, 68590 St Hippolyte
☎ 03 89 73 04 36

Orschwiller
Ehrhardt
6a route du Vin, Rose des Vignes,
67600 Orschwiller
☎ 03 89 92 82 29

Scherwiller
Sava
29 route des Romains, 67750
Scherwiller
☎ 03 88 92 84 74
4saisons.sava@wanadoo.fr

Dambach-la-Ville
Nartz
12 place du Marché, 67650
Dambach-la-Ville
☎ 03 88 92 41 11
nartz.michel@wanadoo.fr

Itterswiller
Kieffer
10 rue Viehweg, Rotland, 67140
Itterswiller
☎ 03 88 85 51 12

Eichhoffen
Kuss
Les Feuilles d'Or, 50/52 rue deu
Vignoble, 67140 Eichhoffen
☎ 03 88 08 49 80
kuss.francis@libertysurf.fr
www.lesfeuillesdor.fr.st

Heiligenstein (N of Barr)
Boch
6 rue Principale, 67140 Heiligenstein
☎ 03 88 08 41 26

Hotels
Strasbourg
Vendome, 9, place de la Gare. 67000
Strasbourg
☎ 03 88 32 45 23
hotel.vendome1@wanadoo.fr

Ribeauvillé
De la Tour, rue de la Mairie, 68150
Ribeauville
☎ 03 89 73 72 73
info@hotel-la-tour.com

Barr
Maison Rouge, 1, Ave de la Gare,
67140 Barr
☎ 03 88 08 90 40
maisonrouge@wanadoo.fr

Heiligenstein (N of Barr)
Relais du Klevener, 51, rue Principale,
67140 Heiligenstein
☎ 03 88 08 05 98
relaisduklevener@wanadoo.fr

STAGE 2 BARR TO SAVERNE

Campsites
Obernai
Camping Municipal 'Le Vallon de
l'Ehn' ★★★

Mollkirch
Camping Neuhiesel ★★
Camping Fischhutte ★

Oberhaslach
Camping du Luttenbach ★★

Wangenbourg
Camping Les Huttes ★

Saverne
Camping de Saverne ★★, 67700 Saverne (SW suburbs of Saverne)
☎ 03 88 91 35 65

B&Bs
Heiligenstein
Boch
6 rue Principale, 67140 Heiligenstein
☎ 03 88 08 41 26

Boersch
Taubert
Bienvenue Willkommen, 3 route de Rosheim, 67530 Boersch
☎ 03 88 95 93 06
alisnata@bienvenue-willkommen.com
www.bienvenue-willkommen.com

Hotels
Mollkirch
Fischhutte, Route de Grendelbruch, RD 204, 67190 Mollkirch
☎ 03 88 97 42 03
fischhutte@wanadoo.fr

Wangenbourg
Parc Hotel, 67710 Wangenbourg
☎ 03 88 87 31 72
parchotel@wanadoo.fr

Obersteigen
Hostellerie Belle Vue, 16, rte du Dabo. 67710 Obersteigen
☎ 03 88 87 32 39
hostellerie.belle-vue@wanadoo.fr

Saverne
Chez Jean et Winstub S'Rosestiebel, 3, rue de la Gare, 67700 Saverne
☎ 03 88 91 10 19
chez.jean@wanadoo.fr

Hotel le Boeuf Noir, 22, Grande Rue, 67700 Saverne

Kleiber, 37, Grande Rue, 67700 St Jean Saverne (N of Saverne)
☎ 03 88 91 11 82
info@kleiber-fr.com

STAGE 3 SAVERNE TO NIEDERBRONN-LES-BAINS

Campsites
Dossenheim-sur-Zinsel
Camping Plage Loisirs ★★
Open 1 April–30 September

Oberbronn
Municipal Eichelgarten ★★ (between Zinswiller and Oberbronn)

Niederbronn-les-Bains
Camping Heidenkopf ★★ (3.5km NW of Niederbronn-les-Bains; take route de Bitche to outskirts then R uphill)

Hotels
Ingwiller
Aux Comtes de Hanau, 139 rue Général de Gaulle, 67340 Ingwiller
☎ 03 88 89 42 27
aux.comtes.de.hanau@wanadoo.fr

Niederbronn-les-Bains
Muller
16 Ave de la Libération, 67110 Niederbronn-les-Bains
☎ 03 88 63 38 38
hotel.muller@wanadoo.fr

Le Bristol, 4 place de l'Hôtel de Ville, 67110 Niederbronn-les-Bains
☎ 03 88 09 61 44
hotel.lebristol@wanadoo.fr

STAGE 4 NIEDERBRONN-LES-BAINS TO HAGUENAU

Campsites
Haguenau
Camping Municipal ★★

Strasbourg
Camping La Montagne Verte ★★★★

Hotels
Niedersteinbach
Cheval Blanc, 11 rue Principale, 67510 Niedersteinbach

☎ 03 88 09 55 31
contact@hotel-cheval-blanc.fr

Strasbourg
Vendome, 9 Place de la Gare, 67000 Strasbourg
☎ 03 88 32 45 23
hotel.vendome1@wanadoo.fr

For further information on accommodation, see Appendix B

ROUTE 4

AN ALPINE EXPERIENCE: GENEVA TO GRENOBLE

ROUTE SUMMARY

From	To	Km	Terrain
Geneva	St Jean-de-Sixt	53	Undulating, then very hilly
St Jean-de-Sixt	Albertville	51	Very hilly
Albertville	St Jean-de-Maurienne	73	Mountainous
St Jean-de-Maurienne	Le Bourg d'Oisans	68	Mountainous
Le Bourg d'Oisans	Alpe d'Huez and back	14	Mountainous
Le Bourg d'Oisans	Grenoble	49	Long descent, then one hill

Stage 1 Geneva to St Jean-de-Sixt

Distance	53km/33 miles (23km/14 miles from Bonneville)
Terrain	Undulating, then very hilly
Climb	600m

Note Few shops between La Roche-sur-Foron and St Jean-de-Sixt.

How to get to Geneva
Reaching Geneva by train from Paris There are regular TGV trains from Paris Gare de Lyon to Geneva (most are

direct) and journey time is only 3½–4hr. You can then get a train from Genève Gare des Eaux Vives station to Bonneville if you do not want to start the tour from Geneva.

Reaching Geneva/Bonneville from Geneva airport If you decide to start this tour from Bonneville (or from Geneva centre) but have flown to Geneva airport, train tickets can be purchased at the ticket office just before 'Baggages' at the airport. Take bikes in the lift beyond the nearby escalator down to the train platforms underground. You have to make a short train journey to Genève CFF station (passport control here) followed by a 2km bike ride or taxi transfer across the Pont du Mont Blanc with the lake on your L to the Gare des Eaux Vives, which is situated L off the busy Route de Chêne.

You may need to book a space for your bicycle on the train to/from Genève CFF (Gare de Cornarvin) station from the airport, otherwise a surcharge of CHF10 (Swiss currency) may be payable; ask when you buy your ticket. The bike compartment is usually in the end carriage. Journey time is 6min and costs CHF5. From the Gare des Eaux Vives to Bonneville journey time is 1hr, TER service (bikes go free but space is limited).

Starting this tour from Geneva airport Bicycle bags can be left at 'Baggages' (open 7am–7.30pm) situated on your R after the revolving doors. Cost at time of going to press was CHF7 deposit per item, then CHF7 a day until your return. (**Tip** If you have two or more bags, roll them all up inside one to save money.) There are several shops beyond the 'Baggages', and a Migros supermarket at the far end open 8am–8pm, seven days a week, which also sells detailed maps of Geneva (recommended).

The route
From Geneva airport follow signs to Geneva Centre past the lake L (Pont du Mont Blanc), then continue SE through the city centre following signs to Malagnou (suburb) to Place Guyenot. Continue SE along Route de

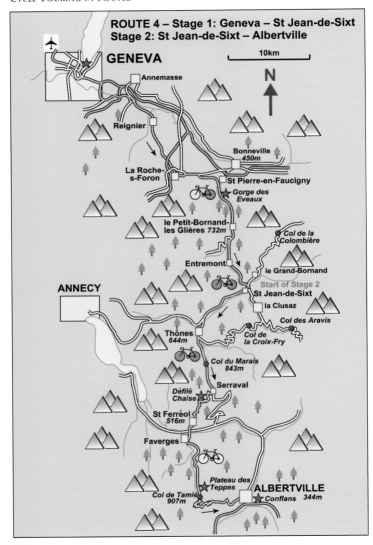

ROUTE 4 – Stage 1: Geneva – St Jean-de-Sixt
Stage 2: St Jean-de-Sixt – Albertville

10km

N

GENEVA

Annemasse

Reignier

Bonneville
450m

La Roche-
s-Foron

St Pierre-en-Faucigny

*Gorge des
Eveaux*

le Petit-Bornand-
les Glières *732m*

Col de la
Colombière

Entremont

le Grand-Bornand

ANNECY

Start of Stage 2

St Jean-de-Sixt

la Clusaz

Col des Aravis

Thônes
644m

*Col de
la Croix-Fry*

*Col du Marais
843m*

*Défilé
Chaise*

Serraval

St Ferréol
516m

Faverges

*Plateau des
Teppes*

ALBERTVILLE

*Col de Tamié
907m*

Conflans 344m

Malagnou for 2.5km to a turning R (chemin Naville) before reaching the Pont du Vallon bridge over the Seymaz. Turn L at the end along Route de Florissant and over the Arve river (Pont de Sierne) to Veyrier and the old border control. Turn L after this onto the N206, and follow signs to Annemasse (bridge over Autoroute) and turn R signposted Monetier-Mornex (D906A) up to a chapel L and château R. Descend to a junction and go L to Reignier (D2). Bear R past church to the centre of **Reignier** (*two supermarkets*) then continue on the recently resurfaced D2 to **La Roche-sur-Foron** (cycle lane for most of the way). Bear L in town centre (*Autres Directions*) then N203 towards Bonneville.

Descend to Vozerier and take first R by a wooden bridge, then first L (Route de Saint Pierre). Go straight (E) at next junction, then R after 200m, 'Route de la Restat'. Turn L at junction (Rue Saint Maurice). At the rdbt bear R (D6) for La Clusaz and R at T-junction for **le Petit-Bornand** (D12). A scenic gradual climb up the **Gorge des Eveaux** with its sheer limestone walls and deep gorge on your R opens out with views of the Rochers de Leschaux which can be seen from as far away as La Roche-sur-Foron,

Le Grand-Bornand from above St Jean-de-Sixt

shaped like a shark's fin. This gradual climb ends at Termine. There are two campsites at Saxias/le Petit-Bornand soon after (732m). A descent to Glières and **Entremont** is followed by three short tunnels as the road snakes through Les Etroits, the narrow limestone cleft created by the Borne river (865m). A short, punchy climb then leads up to the D4 junction. Turn R here for **St Jean-de-Sixt** (L for le Grand-Bornand) and R again (steep road) before reaching the village if you intend camping at one of two campsites on the ridge overlooking St Jean-de-Sixt. Excellent view of le Grand-Bornand in the valley to the NE from this ridge.

Stage 2 St Jean-de-Sixt to Albertville

Distance	51km/32 miles
Terrain	Very hilly
Climb	700m
Map	See Stage 1

The route

From **St Jean-de-Sixt** take the D909 to Thônes, a 7.5km descent. Look out for the sharp filter L for **Thônes** as the D909 flattens out, and from the centre of this picturesque little town follow signs to Faverges. A pleasant, gradual climb to the **Col du Marais** (D12) at 843m (*bar/restaurant on R after col and campsite 0.5km on L*) is followed by a descent to **Serraval** (*alimentation*). A short ascent to 759m follows, before a long descent again following the verdant **Chaise gorge** with wonderful views of the surrounding hills and crags. The D12 descends to **St Ferréol**, situated in a wide, open valley basin that forms a small part of the Bauges National Park.

The Plateau des Teppes near the Col de Tamié

Take the new road over the N506 through an industrial estate into **Faverges** and follow signs for the Col de Tamié. This climb is quite steep in places and offers little shelter from the sun until you reach the junction for Seythenex after 4km. Here the D12 follows a babbling stream through woodlands, the climb much less acute and becomes very pleasant as it crosses the grassy **Plateau des Teppes** before reaching the **Col de Tamié** at 907m and entering the *département de la Savoie*. At the junction after the col, go R (D201c) for Albertville, a long pleasurable descent with lots of hairpin bends to Plancherine and Gemilly before reaching the D990 in the valley. Go L here for **Albertville**, a busy town in the Isère Valley that hosted the 1992 Winter Olympics.

Conflans, a medieval village perched on the hill overlooking Albertville, can be reached from the Pont des Adoubes in the centre of Albertville. Follow the Montée Adolphe Hugues road up to a parking area and past the cemetery to the Chemin des Capucins that leads up to this interesting village.

There is an excellent cycle shop for repairs and so on, Cycles Pecchio, just 200m S of the Halle Olympique in Albertville (open Tues–Sat, 9am–12pm and 2–7pm).

119

Stage 3 Albertville to St Jean-de-Maurienne

Distance	73km/45.5 miles
Terrain	Mountainous
Climb	1750m

The route

Note Buy food and plenty of water in Albertville before setting off. Few shops/bars between Albertville and La Chambre.

Take the D909 to **La Bâthie** with its old castle ruins L just beyond the EDF plant. A path, 'Montée du Château', leads up to it. After crossing the railway line continue straight, signposted Lagnon, then R (D66A) at the rdbt by a railway tunnel for **Rognaix**, crossing over the busy N90. Stay on this road (D66) to a junction (*L for Feissons – no shops*) where you will see the first sign for the Col de la Madeleine straight ahead of you and Pussy/Bonneval.

Climb to the Col de la Madeleine Without doubt this *hors categorie* climb is one of the toughest in the Alps, and is often included in the Tour de France. The southern slopes of the Madeleine certainly do not inspire one to make the long ascent from La Chambre, north of St Jean-de-Maurienne, geared as they are now for the winter ski season. In stark contrast the unspoilt northern side, with its smattering of picturesque Alpine villages in which time seems to have stood still, provides a much greater sense of isolation and a feeling of being at one with nature.

Note A very early start is required if you are intent on completing the climb in one day.

The climb starts from the Isère Valley near the village of **Feissons-sur-Isère** (410m) and is 26km long, culminating at an altitude of 2000m. There are several long, steep sections reaching a gradient of 11%, and only one short respite halfway up where the road descends slightly for less than 1km. If you are intending to stay in hotels or B&Bs note that there is a distinct lack of either between Albertville and La Chambre. If you are staying at campsites and carrying extra weight in your panniers (tent,

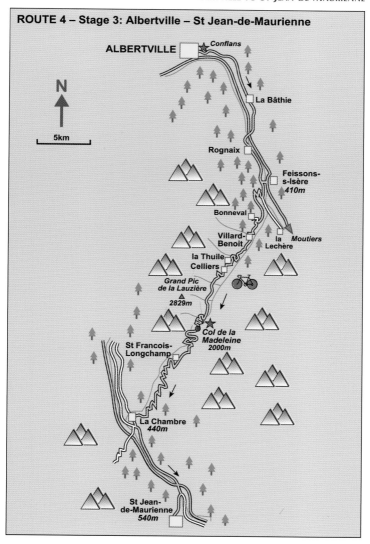

ROUTE 4 – Stage 3: Albertville – St Jean-de-Maurienne

ALBERTVILLE *Conflans*

N

5km

La Bâthie

Rognaix

Feissons-s-Isère
410m

Bonneval

Moutiers

Villard-Benoit

la Lechère

la Thuile
Celliers

Grand Pic de la Lauzière
▲
2829m

St Francois-Longchamp

Col de la Madeleine
2000m

La Chambre
440m

St Jean-de-Maurienne
540m

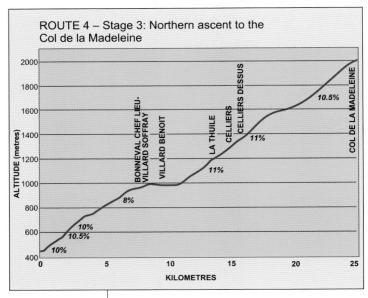

ROUTE 4 – Stage 3: Northern ascent to the Col de la Madeleine

cooking gear and so on) be prepared for a night in the mountains if the weather turns nasty or if, for some reason, things do not go according to plan.

The Madeleine climb starts on the R and is immediately hard, a steep hairpin ascent (10–10.5%) for 1km in woods that provide plenty of shade, but can be very humid in summer. As the woods thin out so the climb becomes kinder, soon arriving at the turning R for Bonneval (D213B). Stay on the D213, signposted Celliers (7km) and Col de la Madeleine (18km.). After 0.5km you reach the village of Bonneval chef lieu – Villard Soffray overlooking the Eau Rousse Valley (*information bureau doubling as an alimentation selling local produce, water and bread, open daily in summer 9am–12.30pm, 3–7pm; public toilets next door*).

The road flattens and descends slightly before climbing steeply once more to **La Thuile** (max 11%). Continue on up to the picturesque village of **Celliers** (*flattish grassy area with picnic tables beyond*) then on to Celliers Dessus (*Auberge du Glacier – menu journalier 12 euros, sandwiches 4 euros*). The road twists and turns quite steeply now (11%) before levelling out a little, passing two waterfalls R before the final push up to the col which can now be seen (max 10.5%). Half a dozen traverses of the mountainside and you're at the **Col de la Madeleine**! The 2000m sign on your L tells you so. Enjoy a bite to eat in La Banquise 2000 (*restaurant/brasserie/pizzeria where bottled water and beer can be purchased; open every day June–early October, depending on snow conditions at start and end of summer, tel: 04 79 59 10 60; also another restaurant, Les Mazots*). On a clear day you can see the Mont Blanc Massif to the NE and the Aiguilles d'Arve and Meije to the S.

The descent is long, seemingly never-ending past the ski village of **St Francois-Longchamp** and on down to **St Martin sur la Chambre** in the Arc Valley. There are two campsites at St Martin sur la Chambre, the first on your R as you reach the village ('Le Petit Nice') and then further down on your L, 'Camping Le Bois Joli', some 400m before reaching La Chambre. If you are pretty whacked by this point and planning on camping I would recommend grabbing a pitch at one of these two campsites, especially at the height of summer.

Lance Armstrong (in yellow) on the Col de la Madeleine, Tour de France 2004

Turn L in **La Chambre** past the church and information office, following signs for St Jean-de-Maurienne and getting onto the RN6 which is mostly flat. Turn off R just opposite a ruined tower on a rocky outcrop following signs to St Jean-de-Maurienne and Col de la Croix de Fer (D906) over the River Arc. Follow the road up into **St Jean-de-Maurienne**; the Romanesque cathedral here has some beautifully carved stalls and a 15th-century ciborium of alabaster inside.

Stage 4 St Jean-de-Maurienne to Le Bourg d'Oisans

Distance	68km/42.5 miles
Terrain	Mountainous
Climb	1620m

Note Buy food and plenty of water in St Jean-de-Maurienne. Few shops/bars between St Jean-de-Maurienne and Allemont.

The route

From the centre of town head SE past the cathedral and L'Hôtel de Ville, then signs for Vallée de l'Arvan, turning R up the D926. The D926 climbs steeply from St Jean-de-Maurienne past a restored, square, ancient watchtower, but thereafter flattens with lovely views up the valley. A steepish section (7–8.5%) leads to a junction where the D78c veers off R to St Pancrace and the sign for the Croix de Fer tells you there are 26km to the col! Turn L at the next junction for Montrond, St Jean d'Arves (14km) and St Sorlin d'Arves (18km.). A 1km descent past a derelict house (1892 inscribed on central roof beam) on your L and pleasant woodland soon after is followed by a grand view of Gevoudaz in the valley below after passing through Le Cret.

The D926 then climbs again, traversing the wooded slopes before a series of steep hairpins (mostly 8.5–9%)

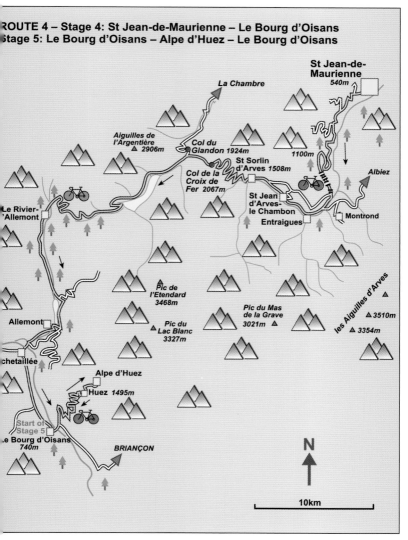

ROUTE 4 – Stage 4: St Jean-de-Maurienne – Le Bourg d'Oisans
Stage 5: Le Bourg d'Oisans – Alpe d'Huez – Le Bourg d'Oisans

La Chambre

St Jean-de-Maurienne
540m

Aiguilles de
l'Argentière
△ 2906m

Col du
Glandon 1924m

St Sorlin
d'Arves 1508m

1100m

Col de la
Croix de
Fer 2067m

Albiez

St Jean
d'Arves-
le Chambon

Le Rivier-
d'Allemont

Entraigues

Montrond

Pic de
l'Etendard
3468m

Pic du Mas
de la Grave
3021m △

les Aiguilles d'Arves

△ 3510m

Pic du
Lac Blanc
3327m

△ 3354m

Allemont

Alpe d'Huez

chetaillée

Huez 1495m

Start of
Stage 5

Le Bourg d'Oisans
740m

BRIANÇON

N

10km

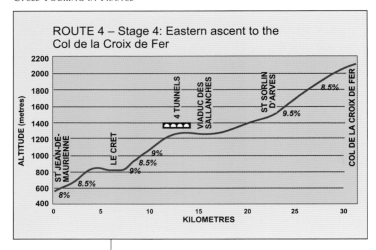

ROUTE 4 – Stage 4: Eastern ascent to the Col de la Croix de Fer

to Charvin, a viewpoint (approx 1100m) with St Jean de Maurienne to the N and the rocky pinnacles known as Aiguilles d' Arves to the SE. Four tunnels follow at 1250m. (Bike lights recommended, especially for the third tunnel which is about 300m long.) Immediately upon exiting this tunnel look up at the gully R which has two very strange rocky monoliths at the top near the ridge. After the fourth and shortest tunnel you reach a junction where both roads are signposted for St Jean d'Arves. The Col de Croix de Fer is now only 15km away. Stay on the D926 (L), a short descent to the Viaduc des Sallanches, with glimpses of Montrond and the Aiguilles d'Arves and a small dam by the junction for the Col du Mollard (D80). Stay on the D926 to **St Jean d'Arves-le Chambon** which is a gradual, easy ascent. This village has an *alimentation*. The climb to **St Sorlin d'Arves**, a ski resort in winter, is again gradual and easy (*mini-super-market, open every day, bars and restaurants open in summer*). A steep climb out of St Sorlin d'Arves is followed by the final push to the col past a disused camp-site, a series of long traverses of a grassy scree slope that offers no shade. The views are superb as you climb higher. The final traverse is flanked by loose rock walls and as you turn the corner you reach the **Col de la Croix de Fer** (2067m). There are great views of the craggy Aiguilles de l'Argentière before you, the Col du Glandon below them. It is worth cycling along the track L opposite the Chalet du Col de la Croix de Fer bar/restaurant for 100m for a wonderful view of the Aiguilles d'Arves to the SE. Cycle on down (potholes!) to a junction where there is another bar and bear R here, a very short ascent (D927) up to the **Col du Glandon** (1924m) from where you can again see Mont Blanc on a clear day.

Return to the D926 signposted Allemont and descend to a reservoir (slight ascent as you cycle round it). There are some very steep hairpin bends on the descent from the Grand Maison dam as you drop down into the wooded Defilé de Maupas, after which there is a punchy 50m climb to a flattish section to **Le Rivier-d'Allemont**. A very long, steep descent follows all the way down to just before the Vaujany turning. The scenery opens out now across the Verney reservoir. Take the D526 across the Barage du Verney signposted **Allemont**, and descend to the RN91 at **Rochetaillée**. Turn L here and follow the RN91 to **Le Bourg d'Oisans** (7km) which has an interesting geology museum, the Musée des Mineraux et de la Faune des Alpes.

The final push to the Col de la Croix de Fer

Stage 5 Le Bourg d'Oisans to Alpe d'Huez and back

Distance	13.8km/8.5 miles (not including descent back to Le Bourg d'Oisans)
Terrain	Mountainous
Climb	1130m
Map	See Stage 4

The most famous climb in the Tour de France! First included in 1952 and won by the legendary Fausto Coppi, l'Alpe d'Huez has played a decisive part in many Tours since. Incorporating 21 marked hairpin bends over 13.8km, with a height gain of 1130m and an average gradient of 7.9%, Coppi took just 45min 22 sec to complete the climb… after a 252km ride from Lausanne! Marco Pantani, another great Italian rider, scaled it in 37min 35sec in 1997, the 'official' record to date.

Note Buy food and water in Le Bourg d'Oisans before setting off.

The route

From Le Bourg d'Oisans take the N91 E towards Briançon, then the D211 L signposted La Garde 3.5km/ Alpe d'Huez 13km. The real climbing does not start until about 0.3km from this turning when you reach the bridge over the Sarennes and the campsites beside it. The numbered bends give you an idea of your progress, and it is not surprising how quickly you gain height as the first few kilometres are pretty steep (10–10.5%), easing off somewhat after bend 17. Look out for the names of triumphant Tour de France riders on plaques on the numbered bends (bend 20 – Joop Zoetemelk and Iban Mayo, for example). The gradient averages about 8% after the village of La Garde and steepens after bend 10, only to then relent again. Climbing higher now – with even less shade offered than on the lower slopes – you do at least get some cracking views from the roadside looking down to the Romanche Valley. Bend 6 belongs

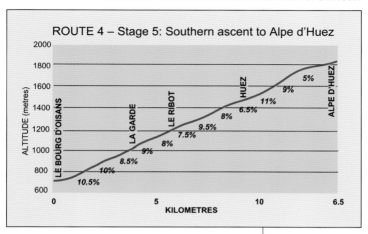

to Gianni Bugno, first to the top in the 1990 and 1991 Tours. The last few bends open out with excellent views across the valley as you climb into Alpe d'Huez, leaving just 2km to reach the open area where the Tour always finishes near the ski station.

See Stage 4 for accommodation.

Stage 6 Le Bourg d'Oisans to Grenoble

Distance	49km/30.5 miles
Terrain	Long descent, then one hill
Climb	150m

The route
From **Le Bourg d'Oisans** return to **Rochetaillée** (RN91), after which there is a wonderful 25km descent down the Gorges de la Romanche to **le Péage-de-Vizille**. Turn next

R (D101) for the **Château de Vizille** which was built between 1600 and 1619 by François de Bonne, Duc de Lesdiguières. The Château and Museum of the French Revolution are certainly worth a visit (*open every day except Tues; free admission April–September 10am–6pm; closed 1 May. Free admission to extensive park April, May, September 9am–7pm; June, July, August 9am–8pm*). From the Place du Château cycle up Rue de Gaulle and uphill (D5) towards **Brié**, involving a steepish

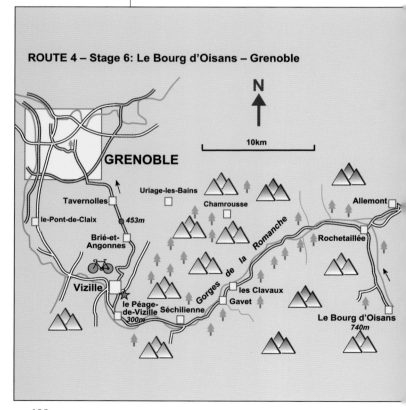

ROUTE 4 – Stage 6: Le Bourg d'Oisans – Grenoble

N

10km

GRENOBLE

Tavernolles

Uriage-les-Bains

Chamrousse

Allemont

le-Pont-de-Claix

453m

Brié-et-
Angonnes

Rochetaillée

Vizille

les Clavaux

Gorges de la Romanche

le Péage-
de-Vizille
300m

Séchilienne

Gavet

Le Bourg d'Oisans
740m

The Château de Vizille

1km section followed by views of the vast wooded hills below Chamrousse R. A pleasant descent follows to the Grenoble suburb of Eybens; after approx 1.5km follow the cycle path signs L in parkland for *centre ville/gare* that leads you to the centre of **Grenoble** and its SNCF train station, crossing tramlines en route.

Grenoble, the birthplace of Stendhal in 1783, has an historic centre and interesting old quarter, St Laurent, on the north bank of the Isère. Dating back to Roman times, Grenoble has been the capital of the Dauphiné region since the 12th century, and hosted the 1968 Winter Olympics. There is a great view of the city from the Fort de la Bastille, reached in a cable car that starts from the Quai Stéphanie Jay on the south bank. This viewpoint can also be reached on foot via a steep footpath.

Descent to Grenoble

How to get back to Geneva

If you want to return to the start of the route take a regional train via Chambery to Culoz (N of the Lac du Bourget) and change here for Geneva. There is a good train service from Grenoble to Paris Gare de Lyon, sometimes involving a change at Chambery or Lyon Part Dieu which would involve a combination of TER then TGV (3½–4hr). There is also an occasional direct train (TGV), which takes 3hr.

SELECTED ACCOMMODATION
ROUTE 4

**STAGE 1 GENEVA TO
ST JEAN-DE-SIXT**

Campsites
Bonneville
Municipal du Bois des Tours, route des Bairiers
☎ 04 50 97 04 31

Le Petit-Bornand-les-Glières
Municipal Les Marronniers (N, 1.5km)
☎ 04 50 03 54 74
Open June–mid-September

Le Grand-Bornand
L'Escale
☎ 04 50 02 20 69
Open June–September

Le Clos du Pin
☎ 04 50 02 27 61
Open mid-June–mid-September

St Jean-de-Sixt
Le Cret
☎ 04 50 35 80 54
Open mid-June–mid-September

la Clusaz (3km S of St Jean-de-Sixt)
Le Plan du Fernuy (1.5km E of la Clusaz)

☎ 04 50 02 44 75
Open mid-June–mid-September

B&Bs
Le Grand-Bornand (NE of St Jean-de-Sixt)
De Lajarte
La Ferme de Vanille, 74450 Le Grand-Bornand
☎ 04 50 09 08 32
delajarte@wanadoo.fr
www.lafermedevanille.com

St Jean-de-Sixt
Missillier
La Passerelle, 74450 St Jean-de-Sixt
☎ 04 50 02 24 33
info@gites-chaletlapasserelle.com
www.gites-chaletlapasserelle.com

Hotels
Bonneville
Hotel d'Arve, Rue du Pont, 74130 Bonneville

Le Grand-Bornand
Les Glaieuls, 74450 Le Grand-Bornand
☎ 04 50 02 20 23
info@hotel-lesglaieuls.com

La Croix Saint Maurice, Place de l'Eglise, 74450 Le Grand-Bornand
☎ 04 50 02 20 05
info@hotel-lacroixstmaurice.com

St Jean-de-Sixt

Beau-Site, 74450 St Jean-de-Sixt
☎ 04 50 02 24 04
hotelbeausite@hotmail.com

Les Villards sur Thones (4km SW of St Jean-de-Sixt)
Le Viking, 74230 Les Villards sur Thones
☎ 04 50 02 11 78
hotelviking@wanadoo.fr

STAGE 2 ST JEAN-DE-SIXT TO ALBERTVILLE

Campsites
Thônes
Camping Le Tréjeux
Open June–September

St Ferréol
Camping Municipal (E of village by a stream)
Open mid-June–mid-September

Albertville
Camping Les Adoubes, Centre Ville (La Maladière, D909 just outside Albertville en route to La Bâthie)

La Bâthie (8km beyond Albertville on D909)
Le Tarin ★★
☎ 04 79 89 60 54
Open all year, small site

B&Bs
Thônes
Taleb
Glapigny/La Closette, Châlet Les Lupins, 74230 Thônes
☎ 04 50 63 19 96
leslupins@aol.com
www.pagesperso.aol.fr/leslupins

Hotels/Auberges
Faverges
Du Parc – Manoir du Baron Blanc, 74210 Faverges
☎ 04 50 44 50 25
info@lhotelduparc.com

Albertville
Albert 1er Hotel Restaurant, 38–40, Av Victor Hugo, 73200 Albertville
☎ 04 79 37 77 33
contact@albert1er.fr

Auberge de Costaroche, 1 chemin Pierre du Roy, 73200 Albertville
☎ 04 79 32 02 02

Hotel de Savoie, 355 Ave JB Mathias, Albertville
☎ 04 79 37 90 73

Le Passé Simple, 21 Ave Jean Jaurès, Albertville
☎ 04 79 37 42 21
hoteldesavoie1@aol.com

STAGE 3 ALBERTVILLE TO ST JEAN-DE-MAURIENNE

Campsites
La Bâthie (8km beyond Albertville on D909)
Le Tarin ★★
☎ 04 79 89 60 54
Open all year, small site

St Martin sur la Chambre
Le Petit Nice ★★
☎ 04 79 56 37 12
westphal@net-up.com
www.outcamp.fr/petitnice
Open all year

Le Bois Joli ★★
☎ 04 50 45 48 30
camping-le-bois-joli@net-up.com
Open early April–mid-October

St Jean-de-Maurienne
Camping des Grands Cols ★★★
Ave du Mont Cenis, 73300 St Jean-de-Maurienne
☎ 04 79 64 28 02
camping@saintjeandemaurienne.fr
Open mid-May–late September

Hotels/Auberges
La Bâthie
Chalet du Grand Mont, 73540 La Bâthie
☎ 04 79 31 01 87

Bonneval chef lieu – Villard Soffray
Auberge de la Valle de L'Eau Rousse, Bonneval chef lieu, 73260 Bonneval Tarentaise
☎ 04 79 22 59 15

Celliers
Auberge La Ferme du Rocher, Celliers Dessus, 73260 Celliers
☎ 04 79 24 05 82

St Francois Longchamp
Les Airelles, 73130 St Francois Longchamp
☎ 04 79 59 10 63
hotel@lesairelles.net

La Chambre
L'Eterlou, 405 Grande Rue, 73130 La Chambre
☎ 04 79 56 20 39
eterlou73@ifrance.com

Ste Marie-de-Cuines (3km S of La Chambre)
Le Grand Chatelard, chef lieu
☎ 04 79 59 49 75
acbridon@aol.com

St Avre (near St Martin sur la Chambre)
Le Vergier Fleuri, 371 rue du Rivet
☎ 04 79 56 21 70

St Jean-de-Maurienne
Hotel de l'Europe, Ave du Mont-Cenis, 73300 St Jean-de-Maurienne
☎ 04 79 64 06 33
heurope@icor.fr

Hotel du Nord, place du Champs de Foire, St Jean-de-Maurienne
☎ 04 79 64 02 08
www.hoteldunord.net

STAGE 4 ST JEAN-DE-MAURIENNE TO LE BOURG D'OISANS

Campsites
Allemont
Municipal le Plan
☎ 04 76 80 76 88
Open all year

Le Grand Calme
☎ 04 76 80 70 03
Open all year

Rochetaillée
Belledonne ★★★★
☎ 04 76 80 07 18
Open June–early September

Le Château
☎ 04 76 80 21 23
Open June–mid-September

Le Bourg d'Oisans
A la rencontre du Soleil ★★★
☎ 04 76 79 12 22
Open late May–mid-September

La Cascade ★★★★
☎ 04 76 80 02 42

Camping La Piscine ★★
☎ 04 76 80 02 41]
Open June–September

Le Colporteur
☎ 04 76 79 11 44
Open June–September

Caravaneige le Venis ★★★
☎ 04 76 80 02 68
Open early June–mid-September

B&Bs
Le Bourg d'Oisans
Durdan
Les Petites Sources, Le Vert, 38520 Le Bourg d'Oisans
☎ 04 76 80 13 92
durdan@club-internet.fr

Hotels
St Sorlin d'Arves
Beausoleil, 73530 St Sorlin d'Arves
☎ 04 79 59 71 42
info@hotel-beausoleil.com
Open only 1 July–31 August

Le Bourg d'Oisans
Le Terminus Rest, Moulin des Truites Bleues, Ave de la Gare,
38520 Le Bourg d'Oisans
☎ 04 76 80 00 26
Open only 20 May–25 September

Hotel Beau Rivage, rue des Marquis de l'Oisans, 38520 Le Bourg d'Oisans
☎ 04 76 80 03 19

STAGE 6 LE BOURG D'OISANS TO GRENOBLE

Campsites
Rochtaillée
Belledonne
☎ 04 76 80 07 18
Open June–early September

Le Châyeau
☎ 04 76 80 21 23
Open June–mid-September

Vizille
Municipal du Bois de Cornage (N of Vizille in outskirts/suburbs)
☎ 04 76 68 12 39
Open May to mid-October

B&Bs
Séchilienne (Gorges de la Romanche) Chemin
Cotte Fournier, Au Bout du Chemin, 38220 Séchilienne
☎ 04 76 72 15 06
cheminj@wanadoo.fr

Hotels
Grenoble
Institut Hotel, 10, rue Barbillon, 38000 Grenoble
☎ 04 76 46 36 44
contact@institut-hotel.fr

Alizé, 1 place de la Gare, 38000 Grenoble
☎ 04 76 43 12 91

Hotel d'Angleterre, 5 place Victor Hugo, 38000 Grenoble
☎ 04 76 87 37 21
www.hotel-angleterre.fr

For further information on accommodation, see Appendix B

ROUTE 5

THE LAND OF LAVENDER: PROVENCE

ROUTE SUMMARY

From	To	Km	Terrain
Arles	Cavaillon	46	Undulating, hilly, then flat
Cavaillon	Caromb	50	Hilly, then undulating
Caromb	Buis-les-Baronnies	34	Mostly hilly
Buis-les-Baronnies	Sault	37	Hilly
Sault	Mt Ventoux and back	52	Mountainous
Sault	L'Isle-sur-la-Sorgue	64	Gorge descent, then flattish

Stage 1 Arles to Cavaillon

Distance	46km/29 miles
Terrain	Undulating, hilly, then flat
Climb	230m

How to get to Arles
From Marseille–Provence airport You have two options: cycle to Rognac and catch a train from there, or take the shuttle bus to Marseille Gare St Charles and take a train.

- From Arrivals follow *Toutes Directions* past a petrol station for 0.5km, then follow the sign for Rognac/Berre (D20), taking care crossing over to it from the main stretch of road. Follow signs to Vitrolles (L). Continue straight at rdbt (third exit) for Rognac and Berre on the D20. Continue to Rognac on the D20 and find the train station on your R. Take a train from here to Arles, which may involve changing trains at Miramas. Most local trains will take bicycles at the discretion of the conductor.

- The shuttle bus service from Marseille–Provence airport to Marseille's Gare St Charles leaves every 20min from 6.10am until the last evening flight arrival. A one-way ticket costs 8.50 euros.

From Marseilles Gare St Charles From here take a train to Arles (express trains going on to Avignon and Lyon) or to Miramas (local service) where you can catch another train to Arles.

From Montpellier airport (Aéroport Montpellier Mediterranée) Shuttle bus service from airport (outside gate A) to coach station in Montpellier city centre from 8.35am–10.40pm Mon–Fri, 9.20am–10.40pm Sat and Sun (shuttle departs approx every 1¼hr). Single ticket costs 5 euros. Train service from Montpellier St Roch station in city centre to Arles direct (IC or Corail service) takes 1hr. Otherwise change at Avignon for Arles (TER then IC/TER service) which takes 2½hr from Montpellier.

From Nîmes-Arles-Camargue airport (near Garons) Shuttle bus service from Terminal to Nîmes *centre ville*. Single ticket costs 4.30 euros. Train service from Nîmes station to Avignon and Arles (trains arriving from Montpellier previously mentioned). Journey takes 1¾hr to Arles via Avignon, or 30min direct to Arles.

From Avignon Train service to Arles (TER or IC/TER) direct, or change at Tarascon (TER) for Arles. Shuttle bus service to Arles from Avignon (Gare routière) four times daily, stopping at Avignon TGV station en route (more frequent bus service from here).

If arriving from Paris on the TGV you need to get off at Avignon TGV station and either take the shuttle bus (*navette*) to Arles, or cycle or get a taxi to Avignon Centre railway station. Avignon TGV station is situated in the S suburbs of Avignon, 3km from Avignon Centre station.

See also Getting There in the Introduction for TGV transfer from Paris CDG.

Note Easyjet also fly to Nice from Belfast, Bristol, Liverpool, London Gatwick, London Luton, London Stansted and Newcastle.

From Avignon airport By taxi (Taxis Avignonnais) a 10min journey into Avignon centre, otherwise an 8km cycle ride NW along the N7 into Avignon. From Avignon to Arles as described above. ◀

Arles boasts the impressive Arena (*Les Arènes*) situated not far from the railway station. It is one of the best-preserved Roman monuments to be found in the south of France, and dates back to the 2nd century. The Arles Festival is staged at the nearby Roman theatre (dating from the reign of Augustus – 27BC–AD14) in July. The Venus d'Arles, now in the Louvre in Paris, was discovered here. Also worth a visit is the Eglise St Trophime in Place de la République, which has a striking 12th-century portal with an array of statues of apostles and saints depicting Christ's childhood, the Last Judgement and Apocalpyse. Van Gogh lived in Arles for just over a year (1888–89), during which time he painted more than 200 portraits and landscapes on canvas.

The route

From Arles train station take the road N from the rdbt that has a fountain at its centre, under the railway line towards Les Baux, and take first R at the rdbt that follows after 1km for Fontvieille and Les Baux (D17). Go straight at the next rdbt after which a pleasant, gentle ascent leads to the **Abbaye de Montmajour** situated on top of a hill overlooking an expanse of flat fields. Founded in the 10th century, the Romanesque abbey church (12th century) has interesting cloisters. The fortified watch-

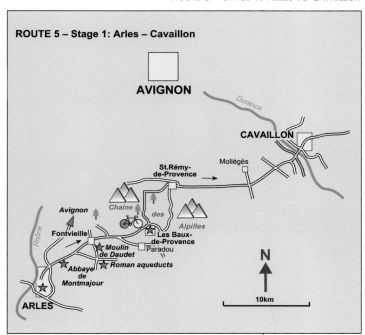

tower grants great views of the surrounding countryside if you don't mind the climb. Open daily 9am–7pm, April–September and every day except Tues 10am–1pm, 2–5pm, October–March.

From the Abbaye de Montmajour continue E on the D17 past the Eglise Sainte Croix R to the large village of **Fontvieille** ('Old Spring'). Close by is situated the wind-mill where the famous writer Alphonse Daudet (1840–97) lived for a time seeking solitude and inspiration from the surrounding countryside. From the centre of Fontvieille turn R uphill to the **Moulin de Daudet** (D33) which you can reach via a parking area and path L near the top of the hill. There is a lovely view from the wind-mill and a tiny museum here can be visited daily 9am–7pm, April–September and 10am–12pm, 2–5pm,

141

Abbaye de Montmajour	October–March. Note the plaque with Daudet's quotation: *Tout ce beau paysage provençal ne vit que par la lumière.*

If you decide to stop for the night in Fontvieille, take an early evening ride up to the moulin when the hordes of tourists have gone. Continue uphill on the D33 before a pleasant descent to a junction where you turn L; the road cuts through some ruined Roman aqueducts after 0.2km. From here return W along the D82 (do not turn R back up the hill at the junction) and stay on the D82 as it winds its way around the hill to the D17 again and from here back to Fontvieille.

From Fontvieille, continue E on the D17 which has a wide cycle strip for 3km (gradual ascent) to a junction where you turn L for Les Baux (D78). This scenic road cuts between olive fields overlooked by limestone crags and climbs gradually before a moderately steep section up to the village of **Les Baux-de-Provence**. Over a million tourists visit this famous fortified citadel yearly, the ruined Citadelle de la Ville Mort (Dead City) granting superb views of the legendary Val d'Enfer below. The living village beneath it is worth exploring with its charming alleyways and steep narrow streets lined with quaint Renaissance houses. Half a dozen museums can be found here too, as well as the charming Chapelle des Pénitents Blancs in Place de l'Eglise.

From Les Baux return down the hill you have just climbed (two hairpins) and turn R for Maillane (D27). This scenic, snaking road cuts straight through limestone

Moulin de Daudet, Fontvieille

outcrops to the **Cathédrale des Images**, a huge gallery hewn into the rock face R, once quarried for the bauxite discovered here in 1821 and now site of spectacular audio-visual shows. From here continue up to the col at 223m and turn R for some superb views of Les Baux, Provence to the SE, and some remarkable rocky crags that have been sculpted by the strong winds high up on the hill. Returning to the col there is a pleasant descent N down through pine and birch woodland for 4.5km to the Tour de Cardinal.

Turn R at the first crossroads along the Vieux Chemin d'Arles, a flat, quiet country road (good road surface) that leads directly into the typically Provençal town of **St Rémy-de-Provence** with its boulevards lined with *platanes* (plane trees), so common in this part of France.

Plane trees, which the Crusaders discovered on their trips to the East, provide plenty of shade during the hot summer months and do not lose their leaves despite the strong Mistral wind hereabouts. It is reported that Napoleon specifically ordered that these trees should be planted along the main roads so that, once mature, they would provide ample shade for his weary troops on the march.

Follow signs for Cavaillon (D99A), going through the town to join up with the D99 outside St Rémy-de-Provence. This road is often busy, but is flat and fast, mostly well surfaced, and lined with plane trees for 4km offering shade from the sun and protection from strong winds. After 3km there are views R of the craggy Chaîne des Alpilles, and your first view of Mont Ventoux in the distance to the N. It might appear that the summit slopes of Mont Ventoux are covered in snow in summer, but this illusion is due to the barren landscape of shattered, white rock; nothing can grow there due to the tremendously strong winds that batter the mountain. The D99, still quite well shaded as far as Plan d'Orgon, crosses over the Autoroute du Soleil. Follow signs to **Cavaillon** *centre ville* (third exit at rdbt), then stay on the main road into town and turn R to Apt/Pertuis to the SNCF station.

Distance	50km/31 miles
Terrain	Hilly, then undulating
Climb	600m

The route

From the SNCF railway station in Cavaillon follow signs to Apt/Gordes, then keep straight at traffic lights for Apt/Robion (D2). Pass through Les Taillardes and Robion (D2) before forking R (Chemin du Carraire) for **Maubec**.

The road leading up to Maubec offers good views of the village L. There is a Municipal campsite straight ahead just after the bend L up into **Maubec**. Maubec is one of several picturesque hill villages hereabouts; Oppede-le-Vieux, 3km E, is also certainly worth a visit. From the old village of Maubec on the ridge drop down to the Grand Rue (*Mairie and information office R and alimentation L*) and turn L at the mini rdbt that follows (D29), then second R into Route de Coustellet. Go straight at the next junction with the D3 to reach the D2 again. Bear R here for Coustellet and Gordes. Go straight at the main crossroads in **Coustellet** and past the Musée de la Lavande on your R (*free admission*/www.museede-lalavande.com). The road begins to climb after passing the junction for Les Imberts and is moderately steep to the turning L for the Village des Bories and the mini rdbt where you go L for Gordes/Abbaye de Sénanque (D15).

The **Village des Bories** is an enclosed village of strangely shaped drystone huts called *bories* that were common during the Roman occupation of Gaul. Despite its primitive appearance, however, this village was inhabited only from the 16th–20th centuries. It is open to the public daily throughout the year. A few hairpin bends follow after which there is a stunning view of **Gordes** from an open belvedere (caution – no safety rails).

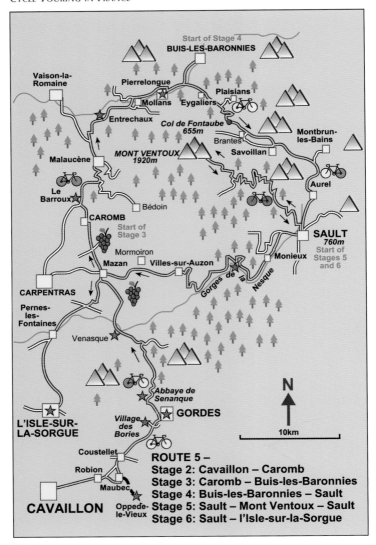

BUIS-LES-BARONNIES

Start of Stage 4

Vaison-la-Romaine

Pierrelongue

Plaisians

Mollans

Eygaliers

Entrechaux

Col de Fontaube 655m

Brantes

Montbrun-les-Bains

MONT VENTOUX 1920m

Savoillan

Malaucène

Aurel

Le Barroux

Bédoin

CAROMB

Start of Stage 3

Mormoiron

Mazan

Villes-sur-Auzon

SAULT 760m Start of Stages 5 and 6

Monieux

Gorges de la Nesque

CARPENTRAS

Pernes-les-Fontaines

Venasque

Abbaye de Senanque

N

Village des Bories

★ **GORDES**

10km

L'ISLE-SUR-LA-SORGUE

Coustellet

Robion

Maubec

CAVAILLON

Oppede-le-Vieux

ROUTE 5 –
Stage 2: Cavaillon – Caromb
Stage 3: Caromb – Buis-les-Baronnies
Stage 4: Buis-les-Baronnies – Sault
Stage 5: Sault – Mont Ventoux – Sault
Stage 6: Sault – l'Isle-sur-la-Sorgue

Gordes

Gordes is one of the most picturesque hill villages in Provence. It is particularly stunning as the rays of the setting sun turn the stone houses golden-ochre. Despite suffering serious damage in World War II, the village came to life again thanks to the artist/designer Victor Vasarely and other contemporaries such as Chagall. Vasarely restored the 16th-century château at the very top of the village to house his work in a museum, opened in 1970. Many of the houses perched on the steep slopes beneath this castle date back to the 16th century.

From Gordes, return down the D15 to the junction R (D177) for the Abbaye de Sénanque/Venasque. A punchy climb leads up to the Côte de Sénanque with a good view L of a desolate limestone canyon below. Descending from the Côte de Sénanque there is a view over the cliff to the **Abbaye de Sénanque** after 100m. Continue downhill to the turning L which leads you past lavender fields to the abbey, one of the finest Cistercian monasteries in France. This delightful building, half-hidden in the hollow of a wooded valley, was founded in 1148 and has sheltered Cistercian monks ever since. Its church (1160) does not face east simply because the valley is too narrow! Open 10am–12pm and 2–6 pm, Mon–Sat March–October, 2–6pm Sun.

Return to the D177 and turn L to undertake a series of fairly steep hairpins for 3km up to a crossroads at 575m. Go straight here for Venasque, an enjoyable 5km descent where low-growing oak trees cover the hillsides either side of the road, followed by a steep section (take care when the surface is wet) down into a limestone gorge.

At the T-junction that follows turn L (D4) towards Venasque passing vineyards and cherry orchards. Turn L soon after for the lovely village of **Venasque** – if you don't mind a detour – otherwise continue on down the D4 and turn R after 1.5km (D77) for Malemort-du-Comtat past more vineyards and cherry orchards. A short rise is rewarded on a clear day with a view of Mont Ventoux straight ahead of you. Turn R for Malemort at the next junction, then immediately L for Mazan (D158) before reaching the village of Malemort. Then turn L again (D77) for Mazan and look out for a turning L after 0.5km, the D163 (sign hard to read). Passing by vineyards the D163 leads you to **Mazan**. Go through this large bustling village and take a turning R for Caromb (D70) past more vineyards. Continue straight at the next crossroads for **Caromb** (*mini-supermarket in the centre*).

Limestone gorge near Venasque

Distance	34km/21 miles
Terrain	Mostly hilly
Climb	300m
Map	See Stage 2

The route

Follow the D13 N to the D938, turning R here (Malaucène) and cycling through a short tunnel before reaching a turning L that leads up to the village of Le Barroux (D78). **Le Barroux** is worth visiting with its medieval château, Notre-Dame la Brune chapel and historic fountains. Return to the D938 and continue the ascent up past the junction R for Bédoin after which the D938 soon descends all the way into **Malaucène** (*mini-supermarket opposite Le Blé en Herbe Hotel in town centre*). It is worth visiting the labyrinth of twisting streets and narrow alleyways in the old part of town.

Returning to the D938 head N towards Vaison-la-Romaine, a gradual 2km descent past vineyards to the junction R for Entrechaux/Buis-les-Baronnies. Take this road (D13) which soon offers views across vineyards L of

Entrechaux

149

Pierrelongue

the hill village of Le Crestet before reaching the similarly attractive village of **Entrechaux** with its ruined fortifications perched high on the hilltop. Continue along the D13 towards Mollans and Buis-les-Baronnies, a short ascent to the Pas du Voltiguer (328m) offering views N of the Baronnies hills. A pleasant, long descent follows down the recently resurfaced road to the large village of Mollans-sur-Ouvèze, passing now into the *département* of Drome and leaving Vaucluse. Turn R at the T-junction for **Pierrelongue** (D5), the road surface again extremely good and a wide cycle strip for good measure. Pierrelongue, a sleepy village (*no shops*) with an extraordinary church built on a rocky outcrop, can be seen from the D5 across olive fields.

After Pierrelongue there is a short climb to the Col St Michel after which you pass a small lake R with a view of the Rochers St Julien straight ahead. This rocky mountain resembles a shark's fin and is a popular destination for rock climbers, there being many interesting routes up the S face. This towers above the small town of **Buis-les-Baronnies** (*good selection of accommodation plus shops, mini-supermarkets and restaurants; bicycle shop: Serge Coutton, 4 Grand Rue, tel: 04 75 28 08 01, 9am–12pm/3–7pm*).

Stage 4 Buis-les-Baronnies to Sault

Distance	37km/23 miles
Terrain	Hilly, remote and rugged
Climb	580m
Map	See Stage 2

The route

From Buis-les-Baronnies return down the D5 towards Pierrelongue to the junction at Cost, and turn L here over the River Ouvèze. This is the scenic D72 that climbs gradually to the old village of **Eygaliers** overlooking the babbling Derbous stream. The road has also been recently resurfaced. The valley opens out now as the D72 climbs through craggy, forested country, a beautifully tranquil part of this southerly *département* of the

Note Buy food and water in Buis-les-Baronnies before setting off.

Mont Ventoux from the Col de Fontaube

Col de Fontaube
alt. 655 m

Rhône–Alpes region which sees little traffic. Most people travelling by car hereabouts prefer the D40 which follows the Toulourenc river on the other side of the Montagne de Bluye to the S; the two roads eventually meet up near Savoillan, 20km E of Mollans-sur-Ouvèze.

The D72 steepens slightly after passing the junction L for Plaisians, a series of hairpin bends leading up to the **Col de Fontaube** with the occasional pine and oak tree offering shade on a hot, sunny day. There are good views down valley. The final kilometre to the col at 655m is easy, with good views of the massive N face of Mont Ventoux. The road follows a ridge now. At the junction R for Brantes, a classic hill village, continue straight for the Col des Aires (640m), a subsidiary col in effect, on the D41 towards Sault. A long, refreshing descent to the village of **Savoillan** follows (*picnic area beyond the car park behind the church*). ◄

From Savoillan take the D72 E to Reilhanette, after which there is a view of Montbrun-les-Bains L beyond farmland. Take R turn (D542) towards Sault, a pleasant ascent through upper pastures, cycling back into the Provence-Alpes-Côte d'Azur region where the road number changes to D942 (back in the *département* of Vaucluse). The road climbs gradually through oak woodland after which the countryside opens up again before reaching the hill village of **Aurel**. From here the road descends slightly over 5km to **Sault** (*information office, restaurants and shops plus Ecomarché supermarket –not open Sundays – and Albion Cycles 1.5km up the D950 towards St Trinit, NE of Sault*). The local, very large campsite is situated in woods on the R approx 1km after the supermarket.

If you want to explore **Brantes**, turn R before the Col des Aires and continue on down to the Vallée de Toulourenc and follow the D40 L for Savoillan.

Distance	52km/32.5 miles
Terrain	Mountainous
Climb	1232m
Map	See Stage 2

The route

From Sault (760m) return to the D942 towards Aurel and take the turning L signposted 'Mont Ventoux' (D164) downhill to farmland at 680m. The route then climbs gradually past lavender fields, yellow/black marker poles lining the road to gauge the depth of snow in winter. At 870m you enter pine forest. At Gollet de Puy (1000m) there is a sheltered picnic area L and a tiny chapel on the hillside R. The countryside opens up a little as you pass through oak woods into the Forêt Domaniale du Ventouret, again predominantly oak and pine offering abundant shade in the early morning. The climb steepens hereabouts but is still not hard, and is then followed by a very slight descent down one side of a wooded valley

Note Buy food and water in Sault before setting off. **Start very early in summer (no later than 7am)** to take advantage of the shade offered by trees hugging the D164 up the first 20km to le Chalet-Reynard (1419m).

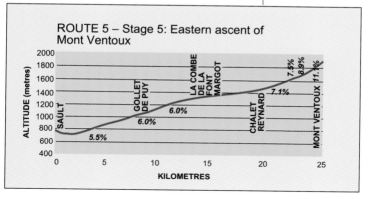

153

The summit of Mont Ventoux is within sight!

and an easy ascent of the other side to a viewpoint at 1280m, La Combe de la Font Margot. Here there are wonderful views of the Plateau d'Albion, Sault in the middle distance, and the Grand Luberon mountains on the horizon.

The D164 continues through woods, climbing gradually to le Chalet-Reynard (*snack bar/restaurant*) at 1419m. This is where the hard part of the Ventoux climb begins. Six kilometres of steep, long, snaking road with no trees to offer shade on a hot, sunny day, just barren slopes covered in shattered white rock where the wind can blow you off your bicycle. I was fortunate enough to cycle up Mont Ventoux when there was minimal wind and completed the whole climb in 4hr from the campsite near Sault. Whatever the weather forecast, be sure to take a windproof jacket and, if you don't mind the extra weight, a pair of thermal gloves might come in handy!

Mostly 7% in gradient to and beyond the Fontaine de la Grave (1500m) the road then steepens to 7.5% at 1602m where there is a distinct lack of vegetation. Still hovering around the 7–7.5% to 1740m, the gradient increases to 8.9% at 1750m.

Here you will see the memorial to Tom Simpson on the R, a British rider who sadly died during the ascent of Mont Ventoux in the 1967 Tour de France. Many who tackle Mont Ventoux on a bicycle leave a piece of personal cycling accessory at the memorial as a mark of respect, be it a water bottle or cycling mitt, inner tube or bicycle pump. A small plaque on the memorial reads 'There is no mountain too high... Your daughters: Jane and Joanne, July 13th 1997'.

At 1839m the gradient reaches 11.1% for the final kilometre to the Bar Restaurant Vendran below the observatory on the summit (1912m). On a clear day it's worth climbing the steps above the souvenir shop to the actual summit to savour spectacular views all around, especially the Alps in the distance to the NE.

See Stage 4 for accommodation in Sault.

Stage 6 Sault to L'Isle-sur-la-Sorgue

Distance	64km/40 miles (77km/48 miles to Avignon)
Terrain	Short climb, long gorge descent, then flattish arable land and vineyards
Climb	140m
Map	See Stage 2

The route

From the centre of Sault take the D942 signposted Carpentras/Gorges de la Nesque downhill (R after 200m). Take the L turn after la Loge for Gorges de la Nesque, a pleasant descent past lavender fields, and fields full of poppies early summer, passing a violet-coloured cart on your R before reaching the village of **Monieux** (640m).

Note Buy food and water in Sault for the ride down the Gorges de la Nesque to Villes-sur-Auzon.

155

Monieux

A gentle ascent for 2.5km to 740m leads up to a wonderful viewpoint of the **Gorges de la Nesque** below, followed by an outstanding view from the belvedere 200m further on. This is considered the second-most breathtaking gorge in Provence after the Gorges du Verdon (which few gorges could compete with world-wide!). Four road tunnels through the rock follow, each only about 25m long, and a scenic gradual descent of 20km down the N side of the gorge to **Villes-sur-Auzon**.

Note If you plan to take a train from Avignon back to your original starting point/airport turn R at the first rdbt on the D938, following the D28 all the way into Avignon (22km).

Stay on the D942 towards Mormoiron/Carpentras following the Auzon stream through vineyard country-side to **Mazan**, the start and end of your circular tour of Mont Ventoux. Upon entering Mazan turn L by a monument fountain surrounded by three trees for **Pernes-les-Fontaines**/St Didier, going straight at the rdbt that follows (D1) to Pernes. The road into Pernes is very bumpy indeed at the time of writing. Turn L at the T-junction over the Nesque (here just a whispering stream!) on the D938 for **L'Isle-sur-la-Sorgue** (11km) on a good road surface. ◂

L'Isle-sur-la-Sorgue, quite literally 'the Island on the Sorgue' since it branches across five courses of the river, is a popular tourist destination situated close to the well-known Fontaine-de-Vaucluse, and famous for its antiques market on Sundays.

How to get back to the start
Trains run from here to Avignon Centre station (TER service/25min) for onward journey to Nîmes, Montpellier or Avignon airports or Avignon TGV station, or Cavaillon/Miramas and change at Miramas for Rognac (towards Marseille) if you are returning to Marseille–Provence airport.

Gorges de la Nesque

SELECTED ACCOMMODATION
ROUTE 5

STAGE 1 ARLES TO CAVAILLON

Campsites
Vitrolles (4km N of Marseille-Provence airport at l'Agneau)
Camping Le Castor, Plage de l'Agneau, 18127 Vitrolles
☎ 04 42 89 30 74
Open all year, limited space for tents

Arles
Camping du Gardian, Raphèle-les-Arles (6km SE of Arles), 13637 Arles
☎ 04 90 98 46 51
corinneprotche@wanadoo.fr

Fontvielle
Camping Les Pins ★★★, Rue Michelet, 13990 Fontvielle
☎ 04 90 54 78 69
www.fontvieille-provence.com
Open Easter–mid-October

St Rémy-de-Provence
Camping Monplaisir, 13538 St Rémy-de-Provence
☎ 04 90 92 22 70
www.camping-monplaisir.fr

Camping Pegomas, 13538 St Rémy-de-Provence
☎ 04 90 92 01 21

contact@campingpegomas.com.
www.campingpegomas.com.

B&Bs
Le Paradou
Joly
L'Espélido, route des Tours de Castillon, 13520 Le Paradou
☎ 04 90 54 38 55
lespelido@wanadoo.fr

St Rémy-de-Provence
Dieuleveult/Xiberras
Le Mas de Manon, Chemin des Lônes, 13210 St Rémy-de-Provence
☎ 04 32 60 09 86
masdemanon@libertysurf.fr
www.alpilles.com/mas_manon.htm

Feige
Mas de Clair de Lune, BP 90, 13533 St Rémy-de-Provence
☎ 04 90 92 02 63

Plan d'Orgon
Rodet
447 route des Ecoles, Mas de la Miougrano, 13750 Plan d'Orgon
☎ 04 90 73 20 01
lamiougrano@net-up.com
www.lamiougrano.fr.st

Orgon (SE of Plan d'Orgon)
Guenot/Lorieux
Route de Cavaillon, Domaine de St
Veran, 13360 Orgon
☎ 04 90 73 32 86
d1jour@wanadoo.fr
www.avignon-et-
provence.com/bb/saint-veran

Cavaillon
Maurel
Le Mas du Platane, 22 quai des Trente
Mouttes, 84300 Cavaillon
☎ 04 90 78 29 99
noel.maurel@wanadoo.fr
www.lemasduplatane.free.fr

Lepaul
Mas du Souléou, 5 chemin St. Pierre
des Essieux, 84300 Cavaillon
☎ 04 90 71 43 22
nadine.lepaul@club-internet.fr
www.souleou.com
See also Robion (E of Cavaillon) in
Stage 2.

Hotels
Arles
Amphitheatre, 5–7 Rue Diderot
☎ 04 90 96 10 30
contact@hotelamphitheatre.fr
www.hotelamphitheatre.fr

Calendral, 5 Rue Porte de Laure
☎ 04 90 96 11 89
contact@lecalendal.com
www.lecalendal.com

Cavaillon
Toppin, 70 Cours Gambetta, 84300

Cavaillon
☎ 04 90 71 30 42
resa@hotel-toppin.com

STAGE 2
CAVAILLION TO CAROMB

Campsites
Maubec
Camping les Royères du Prieuré ★★,
84660 Maubec
☎ 04 90 76 50 34
www.campingmaubec-luberon.com
Open April–mid-October

Malemort-du-Comtat
Camping Font Neuve, 84570
Malemort-du-Comtat
☎ 04 90 69 90 00
camping.font-neuve@libertysurf.fr

Mazan
Le Ventoux (3km N of Mazan/D70)
☎ 04 90 69 70 94

Caromb
Camping Le Bouquier, route de
Malaucène, 84330 Caromb (1km N of
Caromb via D13)
☎ 04 90 62 30 13
lebouquier@wanadoo.fr

B&Bs
Robion
Charvet
Domaine Canfier, 84440 Robion
☎ 04 90 76 51 54
info@domainedecanfier.fr
www.domainedecanfier.com

159

Amiguet/Bourquin
Le Domaine d'Anthyllis, Le Plan de
Robion, 84440 Robion
☎ 04 32 52 91 30
domaine@anthyllis.com
www.anthyllis.com

Pomarede
Mas la Pomarede, Chemin de la
Fourmillère, 84440 Robion
☎ 04 90 38 16 58
www.maslapomarede.com

Gordes
Cortasse
La Badelle, 84220 Gordes
☎ 04 90 72 33 19
badelle@club-internet.fr
www.la-badelle.com

Doat
Les Coucourdons,
Près de St Pantaleon, 84220 Gordes
☎ 04 90 72 43 90
mas-des-oliviers@club-internet.fr

Peyron
Les Martins, 84220 Gordes
☎ 04 90 72 24 15

Camus
Mas de la Beaume, 84220 Gordes
☎ 04 90 72 02 96
la.beaume@wanadoo.fr
www.labeaume.com

Modène (E of Caromb)
Monti
Villa Noria, 84330 Modène
☎ 04 90 62 50 66
post@villa-noria.com
www.villa-noria.com

St Pierre-de-Vassols (E of Caromb)
Andre/Poncet
La Barjaquière, 84330 St Pierre-de-
Vassols
☎ 04 90 62 48 00
welcome@barjaquiere.com
www.barjaquiere.com

Hotels
Venasque
Hotel-Restaurant La Garrigue
☎ 04 90 66 03 40

Malemort-du-Comtat
Auberge les Engarouines
☎ 04 90 69 92 25

Mazan
Hotel le Secret des Malauques
☎ 04 90 69 63 63

Crillon-le-Brave (NE of Caromb)
Hostellerie de Crillon le Brave ★★★
☎ 04 90 65 61 61

Caromb
Hotel-Restaurant La Mirande ★★,
Place de l'Eglise, 84330 Caromb
☎ 04 90 62 40 31
infos@mirandecaromb.com
www.mirandecaromb.com

STAGE 3 CAROMB TO BUIS-LES-BARONNIES

Campsites
Entrechaux
Camping Les 3 Rivières
(after Entrechaux, L turn)

Pierrelongue
Les Castors, 26170 Pierrelongue
☎ 04 75 28 74 67
castorscamp@aol.com
Open April–October

Cost (D72 to Eygaliers)
Camping Le Moulin de Cost
☎ 04 75 28 09 82
Swimming pool and *table d'hôtes*

Buis-les-Baronnies
Three campsites: cross River Ouvèze in town centre and turn L to reach Camping Municipal and Camping de Sejour immediately after the CM; if these are full, return to the river and follow the road along N side to Camping Les Ephélides (1km), 26170 Buis-les-Baronnies, ☎ 04 75 28 10 15, open 15 May–1 September.

Camping La Fontaine d'Annibal ★★★, 26170 Buis-les-Baronnies (NE of Buis-les-Baronnies on the road to Séderon)
☎ 04 75 28 03 12
fontaine.annibal@free.fr

B&Bs
Le Barroux
Pillet

L'Aube Safran, Chemin du Patifiage, 84330 Le Barroux
☎ 04 90 62 66 91
contact@aube-safran.com
www.aube-safran.com

Malaucène
Dallaporta-Bonnel
Le Château Crémessières, 84340 Malaucène
☎ 04 90 65 11 13
e.dalla@provenceservices.com

Entrechaux
Subiat
L'Esclériade, route de St. Marcellin, Les Esclériades, 84340 Entrechaux
☎ 04 90 46 01 32
lescleriade@wanadoo.fr
www.escleriade.com

Mollans-sur-Ouvèze
Grenon
Les Fouzarailles, route de Veaux, Vallée du Toulourenc (D40A towards Veaux), 26170 Mollans-sur-Ouvèze
☎ 04 75 28 79 05

Cost (D72 to Eygaliers)
Lou Donjon
☎ 04 75 28 03 96
Open all year

Buis-les-Baronnies
L'Ancienne Cure, 2 rue du Paroir, 26170 Buis-les-Baronnies
☎ 04 75 28 22 08
contact@ancienne-cure.com
www.ancienne-cure.com

Hotels
Mollans-sur-Ouvèze
Hotel-Restaurant Le Saint Marc, 26170 Mollans-sur-Ouvèze
☎ 04 75 28 70 01
le-saint-marc@club-internet.fr
www.saintmarc.com

Buis-les-Baronnies
Les Arcades Le Lion D'Or, Place du Marché, 26170 Buis-les-Baronnies
☎ 04 75 28 11 31
info@hotelarcades.fr
www.hotelarcades.fr

Hotel-Restaurant Sous l'Olivier, 26170 Buis-les-Baronnies
☎ 04 75 28 01 04
www.guideweb.com/prov/hotel/sousolivier

STAGE 4 BUIS-LES-BARONNIES TO SAULT

Campsites
Cost (D72 to Eygaliers)
Camping Le Moulin de Cost
☎ 04 75 28 09 82
Swimming pool and *table d'hôtes*

Montbrun-les-Bains
Municipal Le Pré des Arbres ★★
☎ 04 75 28 85 41
Open 1 April–31 October

Sault
Camping Le Defends★★, route de Saint-Trinit, 84390 Sault
☎ 04 90 64 07 18
2km NE of Sault on the D950.

Open 16 April–30 September

B&Bs
Cost (D72 to Eygaliers)
Lou Donjon
☎ 04 75 28 03 96
Open all year

Eygaliers
Paesan
Le Petit Collet
☎ 04 75 28 16 32
Situated 0.2km after Eygaliers.
le-petit-collet@wanadoo.fr

Plaisians
Théodore
Le Clos des Molières, Domaine de la Bergerie, Plaisians
☎ 04 75 28 23 23
www.plaisians.com

Col de Fontaube (1km W of col)
Le Crouton Fontaube
☎ 04 75 28 13 45

Aurel
Pierre de Lune
☎ 04 90 64 13 58

La Bastie
☎ 04 90 64 08 58

Le Richarnau
☎ 04 90 64 03 62

Sault
Jamet
Les Bourguets, 84390 Sault
☎ 04 90 64 11 90

Bonnard
Piedmoure, route de St Christol,
Piedmoure, 84390 Sault
☎ 04 90 64 09 22
piedmoure@aol.com

Le Grand Jas, route de St Christol,
Sault
☎ 04 90 75 08 96

Chez Nous, route de la Lavande, Sault
☎ 04 90 64 09 72

Hotels
Aurel
Relais du Mont Ventoux, Aurel
☎ 04 90 64 00 62

Sault
Hostellerie du Val de Sault, route de
St Trinit, Sault
☎ 04 90 64 01 41

Hotel d'Albion, Ave de l'Oratoire, Sault
☎ 04 90 64 06 22

Le Louvre, Place du Marché, Sault
☎ 04 90 64 08 88

Le Signoret, Ave de la Résistance, Sault
☎ 04 90 64 11 44

STAGE 6 SAULT TO L'ISLE-SUR-LA-SORGUE

Campsites
Villes-sur-Auzon
Camping Les Verguettes, Route de
Carpentras, Villes-sur-Auzon

info@provencecamping.com
www.provence-camping.com

L'Isle-sur-la-Sorgue
Camping 'La Sorguette', route d'Apt,
RN 100, 84800 L'Isle-sur-la-Sorgue
☎ 04 90 38 05 71
sorguette@wanadoo.fr
www.camping-sorguette.com

B&Bs
Monieux
Giardini
Ferme Le Viguier, 84390 Monieux
☎ 04 90 64 04 83
le.viguier@wanadoo.fr

Le Moulin, 84390 Monieux
☎ 04 90 64 04 64

Mormoiron
Escoffier
Lou Mas de Carboussan, 500 chemin
de Carboussan, 84570 Mormoiron
☎ 04 90 61 93 02
loumasdecarboussan@tiscali.fr
www.loumasdecarboussan.chez.tiscal.fr

Pernes-les-Fontaines
Maintenant
Domaine de Nesquière, 5419 route
d'Althen, 84210 Pernes-les-Fontaines
☎ 04 90 62 00 16

Desbordes
Le Mas Pichony, 1454 route de St Didier
(D 28), 84210 Pernes-les-Fontaines
☎ 04 90 61 56 11
mas-pichony@wanadoo.fr
www.maspichony.com

Forte
Moulin de la Baume, 182 route d'Avignon, 84210 Pernes-les-Fontaines
☎ 04 90 66 58 36
www.moulindelabeaume.com

Veleron
Hickl
Villa Veleron, rue Roquette, Villa Veleron, 84740 Veleron
☎ 04 90 20 12 31
www.villaveleron.com

L'Isle-sur-la-Sorgue
Sundheimer
Domaine de la Fontaine, 920 chemin du Bosquet, 84800 L'Isle-sur-la-Sorgue
☎ 04 90 38 01 44
www.domainedelafontaine.com

Soubrat
La Coudoulière, 1854 route de Carpentras, 84800 L'Isle-sur-la-Sorgue
☎ 04 90 38 16 35
masdelacoudouliere@wanadoo.fr

Konings
Mas les Fontanelles, 114 route de Lagnes, 84800 L'Isle-sur-la-Sorgue
☎ 04 90 20 72 59
lesfontanelles@wanadoo.fr
www.lesfontanelles.com

Hotels
L'Isle-sur-la-Sorgue
Mas de Cure Bourse, route de Caumont, 84800 L'Isle-sur-la-Sorgue
☎ 04 90 38 16 58

Hotel Cantosorgue, route de Carprentas, 84800 L'Isle-sur-la-Sorgue
☎ 04 90 20 81 81

Hotel Le Pescador, Le Partage des Eaux, 84800 L'Isle-sur-la-Sorgue
☎ 04 90 38 09 69

Hotel Les Nevons, chemin des Nevons, 84800 L'Isle-sur-la-Sorgue
☎ 04 90 20 72 00

For further information on accommodation, see Appendix B

ROUTE 6

MEADOWS AND MOUNTAINS: PYRÉNÉES

ROUTE SUMMARY

From	To	Km	Terrain
Foix	St Girons	54	Fairly hilly; wide valleys
St Girons	St Bertrand-de-Comminges	56	Hilly; river plain, meadows, woods
St Bertrand-de-Comminges	Arreau	41	Undulating, then hilly; farmland, then forested valley
Arreau	Bagnères-de-Bigorre	38	Mountainous, then long descent
Bagnères-de-Bigorre	Argelès-Gazost	49	Fairly hilly, then flat cyclepath and one short climb in wide valley
Argelès-Gazost	Col d'Aubisque and back, then Lourdes	75	Mountainous, then flat cyclepath in wide valley

Stage 1 Foix to St Girons

Distance	54km/34 miles
Terrain	Fairly hilly; wide valleys
Climb	400m

Note Buy food and water in Foix before setting off. Few shops en route.

How to get to Foix

Paris to Toulouse by train Direct service from Paris Montparnasse (TGV) which takes 5hr, or a combination of TGV and Corail trains via Bordeaux (6hr). It is also possible to leave from Paris d'Austerlitz for Toulouse on Corail Lunéa trains, which take 7–8hr. Visit **www.voyages-sncf.com** for timetable information.

Flying to Toulouse From the UK, Easyjet fly from London Gatwick to Toulouse and Flybe fly from Bristol and Birmingham. Domestic flights from Paris with Air France.

A shuttle bus service connects Toulouse airport with the central SNCF train station Matabiau. These buses have large baggage holds for bikes, and one leaves the airport every 20min from 7.35–12.15am (from 9.15am on Sun and Bank Holidays) and leaves from Matabiau train station every 20min from 5am–8.20pm (until 7.40pm on Sat). Tickets cost 4 euros single trip/6 euros return (☎ 05 34 60 64 00; visit **www.navettevia-toulouse.com** for more information). The Vélo Station at Matabiau hires out bicycles if required. It is situated close to the bay where the airport shuttle bus arrives.

Then take a train from Toulouse Matabiau railway station to Foix (1¼hr).

Foix is a charming town on the Ariège river with some houses in the centre dating back to the 14th century. Dominating the town are the imposing château ruins with three splendid, different shaped towers. There are wonderful views of the valley and surrounding mountains from the square, central tower. Open daily, 9.30am–6.30pm July and August, 9.45am–12pm and 2–5.30pm May, June, September. Open 10.30am–12pm and 2–5.30pm October–April.

The route

From Foix station go R onto the RN20 and take the first bridge over the river. Follow signs through cobbled streets to the abbey, and take road L of this (D1) over bridge over a small gorge towards Vernajoul. The D1

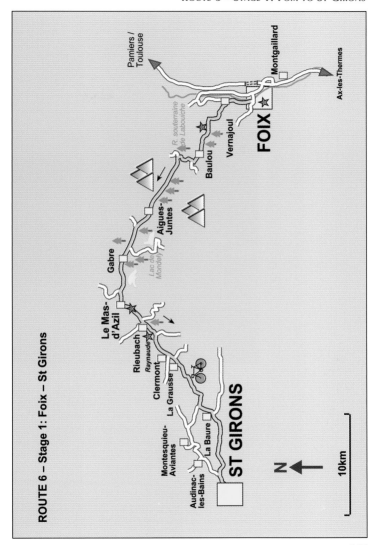

*The Grotte du Mas
d'Azil*

follows the Ariège river on R side, with limestone crags to its L. It's a slow, easy climb to **Vernajoul**. Stay on the D1, a gentle, scenic road amidst oak woods and green fields to the fascinating **Labouiche** underground river. After this the valley opens out at Clarac. Shortly after **Baulou** turn R at T-junction signposted Loubens and Vallée de la Lèze. At the bottom of a 1km descent through woods turn L (D1A) signposted **Aigues Juntes**, Gabre, Grotte du Mas d'Azil.

A very long, gradual descent follows down a wide valley with a long limestone escarpment R and undulating wooded hills L. A short ascent to **Gabre** is followed

by another long descent in woods to a junction. Go L
(D119) signposted **Mas d'Azil** to the village and its
immense cave. The D119 and Arize river run through
this famous cave, which is 0.5km long and 70m high in
places (bike lights recommended). Deep inside there is a
museum of sorts, several chambers displaying prehistoric
artefacts including mammoth bones. Continue along the
D119 to the village of Rieubach. Soon after, look out for
an interesting church and several small chapels behind it
on the hill at **Raynaude** on your R.

The D119 flattens out here for 4km to **Clermont**
(*shop open Sun for water and provisions – Alimentation
– Bar – Tabac Bruel*). A steady climb follows through
woods offering plenty of shade, reaching 479m where
there is a signpost for Montesquieu straight ahead
(D119). Take this road if camping at **Audinac-les-Bains**,
keeping straight on at the first junction and L at the next
on the D18. Otherwise, stay on the main road,
descending to the D117 to **La Baure** and R for **St Girons**.

Raynaude

Stage 2 St Girons to St Bertrand-de-Comminges

Distance	56km/35 miles
Terrain	Hilly; river plain, meadows, woods
Climb	360m

The route

From St Girons centre follow signs to **St Lizier** (D3), a very pretty village with goldfish swimming in the fountain in the Place de l'Eglise.

St Lizier

Dating back to Roman times, the village of **St Lizier** has not one, but two cathedrals. The 12th-century Cathédrale St Lizier has Romanesque frescoes and an interesting cloister. The village is worth exploring on foot as there are good views of the Pyrenean peaks from the upper part where the other cathedral, the Cathédrale de la Sède, is located.

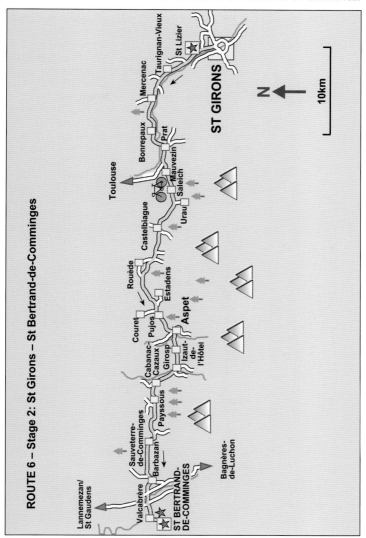

ROUTE 6 – Stage 2: St Girons – St Bertrand-de-Comminges

Return to the D3 and continue N alongside the River Salat to **Taurignan-Vieux**. Soon after this village go L to Taurignan-Castet; there's a good view of the River Salat from the bridge at Taurignan-Castet. At the next rdbt go straight, D34 to **Mercenac**. A brief climb to this village is followed by a descent to a large plain and two weirs at Prat-Bonrepaux. Take the D234 here for **Prat**. Turn R on to the D117 and follow this busy road for 1km to a cream-coloured church R. Opposite this take the D133 to **Mauvezin-de-Prat** (campsite before the village). A tough little climb is soon rewarded by a descent to **Saleich**.

Continue straight to a junction (Christ on a cross) staying on the D60 R to Castelbiague. At the crossroads in **Castelbiague** go L and immediately R to Aspet, staying on the D60. Mostly flat, this road cuts through a tranquil landscape of meadows and munching cows beyond which are undulating wooded hills very similar to Umbria and Tuscany in Italy. There is a campsite down R turn for Couret before descent to Aspet and another campsite in **Aspet**. Cross the River Ger, continue uphill through woods on the D34 to **Girosp** where the scenery opens out with a leisurely descent to Izaut de l'Hotel. An interesting guidebook to this part of the Ariège, *Le canton de Aspet* by Jacques Ducos, is on sale in the village mini-market. The River Job runs alongside the west wall of the village church!

About 1km after **Cabanac-Cazaux** go L at a T-junction for Barbazan. At Brucan take R turning D9 signposted Labarthe-Rivière and Valentine uphill, then D26 to **Barbazan**. Pine trees alongside the road herald the arrival of the Hautes-Pyrénées and your departure from the Ariège. The château at Barbazan L just before a steep descent into the village is being restored. At the bottom of the hill turn R, D26 to St Bertrand-de-Comminges, crossing the D33 in the valley. Follow signs to St Bertrand-de-Comminges across the bridge over the River Garonne, then turn first R.

In Valcabrère take the L turning signposted **Basilique St Just**, a cycle path which is one of the *parcours cyclable*

*Basilique St Just and
St Bertrand-de-
Comminges*

de la Garonne. The Basilique St Just is an impressive
11th-century Romanesque basilica, once the Cathedral
of Comminges. Follow another cycle path W signposted
'St Bertrand-de-Comminges' past Es Pibous campsite
from here. Turn R when the cycle path ends, then L up
the steep road into the centre of **St Bertrand-de-
Comminges**, a charming hill village dominated by the
grand 12th-century Cathédrale Ste Marie that can be seen
from miles around. Inside the cathedral are 66 beautifully
carved Renaissance choir stalls and a magnificent 16th-
century organ in the short nave. Good food is available
at 'La Bergerie' opposite the cathedral.

Stage 3 St Bertrand-de-Comminges to Arreau

Distance	41km/25.5 miles
Terrain	Undulating, then hilly; farmland, then forested valley
Climb	325m

The route

Having explored St Bertrand-de-Comminges, return to the valley and take the L turn D26A towards **Tibiran-Jaunac**. Mostly ups and downs to **Aventignan** through farmland and past the turning to the **Grottes de Gargas** (famous for their unusual prehistoric handprints) the D26 flattens out to Nestiers with views S of the Hautes-Pyrénées. Turn L at a T-junction for **Nestier**, then R to **Anères** and bear R here over a river and a stream with an interesting 20ft-high rock monolith beside it (R of the road) with a Madonna statue on top. At rdbt go L towards Tuzaguet and stay on this road up a long gradual climb, after which there are more views S of the mountains.

At **La Barthe-de-Neste** take the third exit at rdbt signposted Hèches – D929 – which is mostly flat or downhill all the way to **Hèches**. ◄

If you are planning on staying at the campsite 2km beyond the village of Hèches, buy food and water in Hèches before you get there (*alimentation, tabac and boulangerie*). The D929 now becomes a gradual climb all the way to the charming, small town of **Arreau** (703m). You see the turn-off for the start of the Col d'Aspin on your R just before you get to Arreau.

During July and August this road can be busy as it leads to Spain through the Bielsa tunnel.

Arreau stands at the junction of the Rivers Louron and Aure, and has some interesting old buildings, many half-timbered, as well as excellent food shops and restaurants to prepare you for the climb to the Col d'Aspin!

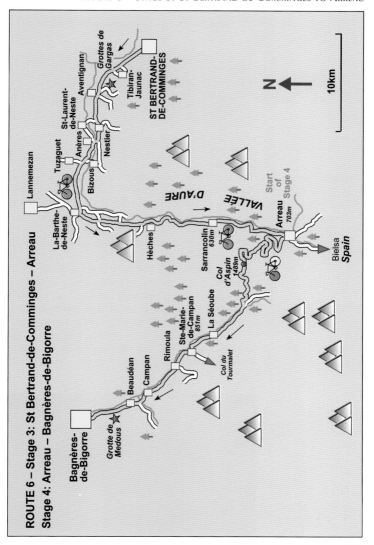

ROUTE 6 – Stage 3: St Bertrand-de-Comminges – Arreau
Stage 4: Arreau – Bagnères-de-Bigorre

Stage 4 Arreau to Bagnères-de-Bigorre

Distance	38km/24 miles
Terrain	Mountainous, then long descent
Climb	796m
Map	See Stage 3

The route

Note Buy food and plenty of water in Arreau for the climb to the Col d'Aspin and descent to Campan.

The climb to the **Col d'Aspin** starts off easily enough at 3% for the first 3km, which is kind on the legs – and there's plenty of shade. However, it then increases to 8% near the turning L to Aspin-Aure and the scenery opens up after the first major hairpin bend. It then becomes 5–6% for 2km and 7% at 950m with good views of the Vallée d'Aure and the occasional tree offering shade. At 1080m it turns into 9.5% – a long stretch with little or no shade – but the views of the towering l'Arbizon (2831m) L more than make up for it, especially as it relents a little thereafter to 7.5% and you can see the Col d'Aspin up on the ridge ahead. There are also great views of Pic Schrader, Pic des Gourgs Blanc and Pic Perdiguère in the distance, straddling the border between France and Spain. The final 3km stretch to the col (1489m) is mostly 8%.

On the climb to the Col d'Aspin

The 13km descent through pine forests passes quite quickly, a series of tight hairpin bends before it opens out at Payolle and the road straightens. There is camping just beyond the village of **La Séoube** R, L'Orée des Monts, a useful base if you fancy tackling the climb to the **Col du Tourmalet** (2115m), an extremely serious undertaking starting at **Ste Marie-de-Campan**. The campsite is open all year, but only has 66 pitches, so book in advance to secure a pitch during July and August. There is also a small campsite 1km S of Ste Marie-de-Campan, Camping Les Rives de l'Adour, and camping in St Roch and Campan.

The **Col du Tourmalet** is usually open by early June, but late snowfalls can mean that the road beyond the ski village of La Mongie may only be clear in high summer. Phone the *office de tourisme* in Campan (☎ 05 62 91 70 36) for the latest on the road conditions between Ste Marie-de-Campan and the Col du Tourmalet. There is also an information board in Ste Marie-de-Campan which states whether the Col du Tourmalet is *ouvert* or *fermé*.

The D935 road from Ste Marie-de-Campan (851m) to Bagnères-de-Bigorre is a long, gradual descent of 11km.

Bagnères-de-Bigorre is a bustling little town. The grounds of the Mairie are very pretty with benches positioned around the trunk of a giant sequoia that was planted in 1860 and measures approx 36m high and nearly 10m in circumference. The Mairie is also home to a colourful peacock often seen strutting proudly round the grounds!

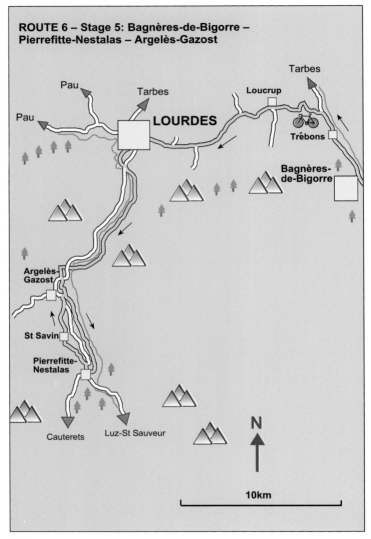

ROUTE 6 – Stage 5: Bagnères-de-Bigorre –
Pierrefitte-Nestalas – Argelès-Gazost

Distance	49km/30.5 miles
Terrain	Fairly hilly, then flat cycle path and one short climb in wide valley
Climb	200m

The route

From Bagnères-de-Bigorre take the flat road for Tarbes, and after the village of **Trébons** turn L for Lourdes, a steep, punchy climb to **Loucrup** followed by a shaded, steep descent to farmland and thereafter mostly flat all the way to **Lourdes**.

If you can put up with the masses visiting **Lourdes** and the town's concentration of tourist shops selling kitsch religious artefacts, the Basilique du Rosaire et de l'Immaculée Conception and the underground Basilique St Pie X are worth visiting (**Note** you cannot wheel your bicycles past the entrance gates). More than 7 million people come to Lourdes each year, the majority Catholic pilgrims who come to visit the Grotte de Massabielle where the young Bernadette Soubirous had a vision of the Virgin Mary in 1858. The spring water from this grotto is believed to have healing powers.

There is a cycle path from Lourdes all the way to Pierrefitte-Nestalas. Follow signs for Argelès-Gazost from the centre of Lourdes, passing a pretty park and then the impressive Hôtel de Ville/Mairie (dark red building) L cycling along Ave Francis Lagardere. After approx 0.5km, just beyond the turning R for the Tribunale d'Instance, look out for the overhead cables where the old railway line used to be. This has now been converted into an excellent cycle path 'La Voie Verte des Gaves'. Every 0.5km or so between Lourdes and Pierrefitte-Nestalas there are 7ft-high green information boards giving

Cycle path from Lourdes to Pierrefitte-Nestalas

information about the nearby villages, churches or towers in several languages. There is an interesting church at Boo-Silhen L after which you cross the Gave de Pau via an iron bridge. The cycle path then goes under the N21 and soon after passes two campsites L, Les Trois Vallées being the second, larger site. There are usually pitches available at the far end. These campsites in the valley below Argelès-Gazost make a good base if you are planning to cycle up the Val d'Azun to the Col d'Aubisque the following day, and there is also a big Champion supermarket opposite the entrance to Les Trois Vallées.

Continue along the cycle path from **Argelès-Gazost** to the disused railway station of **Pierrefitte-Nestalas**. The information board here describes how the 'Chemin de Fer Lourdes–Nestalas', opened in the summer of 1871, used to follow the Gave de Pau upstream for 17km from Lourdes. The first steam trains, up to six a day, covered the distance in 45min, less than 30kmph. From 1898 onwards passengers could get off at Pierrefitte-Nestalas and continue to Cauterets (or Luz St-Sauveur from 1901) by taking the 'P.C.L', the little train of the Pierrefitte–Cauterets–Luz electric railway company. The cycle path finishes just beyond the station.

Continue on round to the other side of the station through a car parking area and go past the Grand Hotel de France in Avenue General Leclerc. Follow this road to the Mairie with its picturesque fountains. If you wish to cycle to Cauterets or Gavarnie, turn L here and follow signs to one or the other after 100m. Otherwise turn R and after a 300m descent turn L after a Christ on the cross on your L, signposted D13 St Savin.

The D13 is a gradual ascent through lovely woodland, a monument L after 1km in memory of the poet Despourrin (1698–1749), erected in 1867 by the Société Academique des Hautes-Pyrénées. Soon after this there is an excellent view of St Savin village and the valley below, and also the aquamarine waters of the Gave de Pau. Just beyond this viewpoint take the steep track L to the quaint Chapelle de Piétat, well worth a visit (unfortunately usually closed) and an excellent shady place for a picnic lunch with far-reaching views of the valley. Continue to **St Savin**, a very picturesque village, and just after passing the church bear L for Argelès-Gazost, descending to the main road below the *centre ville.*

Take the valley road towards Lourdes at the rdbt after this descent from St Savin to return to the cycle path. The path passes the entrance to Les Trois Vallées campsite (if you are camping); if not turn sharp L at the rdbt before this campsite and the Champion supermarket up the shaded D101 to the village of **Argelès-Gazost**.

Chapelle de Piétat near St Savin

181

Stage 6 Argelès-Gazost to the Col d'Aubisque and back, then Lourdes

Distance	75km/47 miles
Terrain	Mountainous, then flat cycle path in wide valley
Climb	1500m

The rdbt near the Champion supermarket and Les Trois Vallées campsite is, in effect, the start of the climb to the Col du Soulor (1474m) and the Col d'Aubisque beyond (1709m). This is a beautiful climb, steep at the start then very gradual up the Val d'Azun to Arrens, followed by the final assault up to the Col de Soulor high above the valley. Stunning views and picturesque villages make this an ideal outing on a clear day.

Note Buy food and plenty of water in advance for this climb. Few shops en route.

The route

From the rdbt near the Champion supermarket take the steep, shaded D101 road opposite to Argelès-Gazost *centre ville*. Turn R before the main square and church, signposted Col d'Aubisque/Val d'Azun. The climb to **Arras-en-Lavedan** is unforgiving, but hang on in there because it will soon relent with wonderful views of the Vallée d'Estaing and the village of Sireix L with Grande Fache in the distance. There are three campsites at Arras-en-Lavedan, open in summer. Soon after the Pic de Gabizos appears ahead, a majestic peak that dominates the scenery right up to the Col de Soulor. It is worth stopping off at **Aucun** to explore this quaint, unspoilt village.

The village of **Arrens** just after Aucun has a mini-supermarket, pharmacy and *boulangerie* together with Camping La Heche, open all year. There is also camping at Marsous: Le Gerrit and Le Moulian. The climb proper to the **Col du Soulor** starts from Arrens at 7.5% and is mostly 7.5–8%, an ascent of 559m from the village and 7km of twists and turns up the slopes to the shoulder of

ROUTE 6 – Stage 6: Argelès-Gazost – Col d'Aubisque – Argelès-Gazost – Lourdes

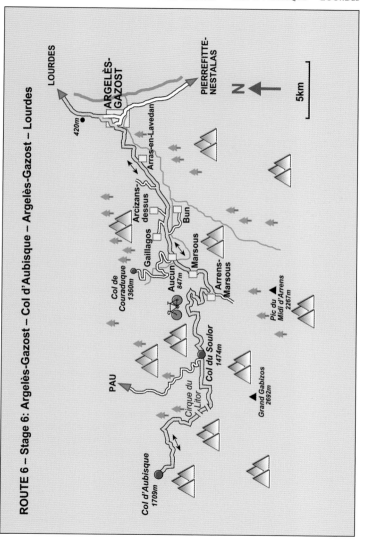

183

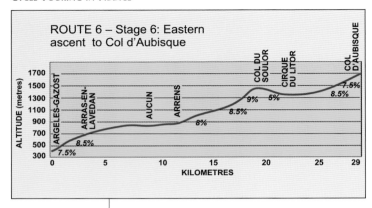

the Pic de Gabizos. There is a café here beside the descending D126 to Arbeost and Ferrières.

If the road to the Col d'Aubisque is open (usually clear of snow by early June) hardened cyclists will be tempted to continue on to this higher col. This involves a 100m descent and traverse of a steep, rocky, concave slope with tunnels, the **Cirque du Litor** (pay particular attention when wet and windy and/or foggy), before a 350m climb. Be prepared, however, for that 100m ascent back up to the Soulor upon your return!

Return to Argelès-Gazost, then continue on down to the cycle path in the valley to return to Lourdes.

How to get back to Toulouse
There is a good train service from Lourdes to Toulouse Matabiau, or to Pau, west of Lourdes, from where Ryanair also operates flights to London Stansted.

Col du Soulor

SELECTED ACCOMMODATION
ROUTE 6

STAGE 1 FOIX TO ST GIRONS

Campsites
Foix
Camping Le Lac de Labarre ★★★ (on
L on N20 N of the station)
☎ 05 61 65 11 58
Open May–October

Mas d'Azil
Camping Municipal ★★

Audinac-les-Bains
Camping Audinac ★★★
Open May–September

St Girons
Camping Parc de Palètes ★★★

B&Bs
Rimont (4km E of la Baure)
Vansteenkiste
Terrac, 09420 Rimont
☎ 05 61 96 39 60

Hotels
Foix
Du Lac, Route de Toulouse (Labarre,
N off D331), 09000 Foix
☎ 05 61 65 17 17
hotel.du.lac.foix@free.fr

Lons, 6 place G. Dutilh, 09000 Foix
☎ 05 34 09 28 00
hotel-lons-foix@wanadoo.fr

St Girons
La Clairière, Ave de la Résistance,
09200 St Girons
☎ 05 61 66 66 66
contact@domainedebeauregard.com

La Flamme Rouge, 15–19 Ave
Galliéni, 09200 St Girons
☎ 05 61 66 12 77
laflammerouge@wanadoo.fr

Le Valier, 29, Ave d'Aulot, 09200 St Girons
☎ 05 61 66 22 25
contact@hotel-levalier.com
Open May–October

Hostellerie La Rotonde, 28 Ave de la
Résistance, 09200 St Girons
☎ 05 34 14 01 40
la.rotonde.09@wanadoo.fr

STAGE 2 ST GIRONS TO ST
BERTRAND-DE-COMMINGES

Campsites
Mauzevin de Prat
Camping l'Estelas ★

Aspet
Camping Municipal Ger ★

St Bertrand-de-Comminges (in the valley, E of St Bertrand-de-Comminges)
Camping Es Pibous ★★
Open 1 March–31 October

B&Bs
Labroquère
Sipieter
Chateau de Vidaussan, 31510 Labroquère
☎ 05 61 95 05 68
christiane.sipieter@wanadoo.fr

Hotels
Barbazan
Hostellerie de l'Aristou, Route de Sauveterre de Comminges, 31510 Barbazan
☎ 05 61 88 30 67

St Bertrand-de-Comminges
L'Oppidum, Rue de la Poste, 31510 St Bertrand-de-Comminges
☎ 05 61 88 33 50
oppidum@wanadoo.fr

STAGE 3 ST BERTRAND-DE-COMMINGES TO ARREAU

Campsites
Tibiran-Jaunac
Camping Le Rural ★

Montrejeau
Camping Midi-Pyrénées ★★
Camping ESSI Les Hortensias ★

St Laurent-de-Neste
Camping La Neste ★★

Hèches
Camping La Bourie ★★

Arreau
Camping Municipal ★
☎ 05 62 98 65 56
Closed October

Camping Le Refuge★★
☎ 05 62 98 63 34
N of Arreau, open all year

B&Bs
St Laurent-de-Neste
Garcia
4 rue de l'Ancienne Poste, La Souleillane, 65150 St Laurent-de-Neste
☎ 05 62 39 76 01
www.souleillane.com

Hotels
Arreau
Hotel de l'Arbizon
☎ 05 62 98 64 35

Hotel d'Angleterre
☎ 05 62 98 69 66
Closed May and October

STAGE 4 ARREAU TO BAGNÈRES-DE-BIGORRE

Campsites
La Séoube
L'Orée des Monts ★★★
☎ 05 62 91 83 98
www.camping.oree-des-monts.com
Open all year

Ste Marie-de-Campan
Camping Les Frênes ★★
☎ 05 62 91 81 97
Open all year

Camping Les Rives de l'Adour ★★
(1km S of Ste Marie-de-Campan, D918)
☎ 05 62 91 83 08
Open all year

Campan St Roch
Camping Le Saint-Roch ★★
Open 15 June–1 September

Campan
Camping Le Layris ★★
Open 1 November–1 June, 15 June–1 October

Bagnères-de-Bigorre
Camping Le Monlôo ★★★
www.lemonloo.com

Camping Les Fruitiers ★★
Le Bigourdan ★★★
Bellevue des Palomières ★★★

B&Bs
La Séoube
Huteau
La Laurence, La Séoube, 65710 Campan
☎ 05 62 91 84 02
lalaurence@wanadoo.fr
www.gites-france-65.com/lalaurence

Ste Marie-de-Campan
Contard
Chez Bernatou, Chemin de Trassouet, 65710 Ste Marie-de-Campan
☎ 05 62 91 88 41

Campan
Duffau
Lahore, chemin d'Angoué, 65710 Campan
☎ 05 62 91 77 95
lahore@wanadoo.fr

Bagnères-de-Bigorre
Magnien
La Caminade, 65130 Bourg-de-Bigorre
☎ 05 62 39 08 63

Hotels/Auberges
Payolle
L'Arcochi, Payolle, 65710 Campan
☎ 05 62 91 89 01
Open 1 May–30 September

Ste Marie-de-Campan
Auberge des Pyrenees, Route de La Mongie, Ste Marie-de-Campan, 65710 Campan
☎ 05 62 91 82 46
Open all year

Chalet Hotel, Ste Marie-de-Campan, 65710 Campan
☎ 05 62 91 86 64
Open 10 May–30 October

Campan
Hotel Beauséjour
☎ 05 62 91 75 30

Bagnères-de-Bigorre
Les Fleurs d'Ajoncs, 3 place du Forail, 65200 Bagnères-de-Bigorre
☎ 05 62 95 27 29
les.fleurs.dajonc@wanadoo.fr
www.les-fleurs-dajonc.com

Le Florian, 24 Allee des Coustous, 65200 Bagnères-de-Bigorre
☎ 05 62 91 17 21

Le Frascati et du Parc, Boulevard de l'Epéron, 65200 Bagnères-de-Bigorre
☎ 05 62 95 21 14

STAGE 5 BAGNÈRES-DE-BIGORRE TO ARGÈLES-GAZOST

Campsites
Lourdes
Camping Le Sarsan ★★★
Camping Plein Soleil ★★★
Camping Relais Océan Pyrénées ★★★

Boo Silhen
Camping Le Deth Potz ★★
☎ 05 62 90 37 23
www.deth-poth.fr
100 pitches

Pierrefitte-Nestalas
Camping Larbey ★★★
Route de Cauterets
☎ 05 62 92 70 28

Argèles-Gazost (campsites in the valley)
Camping La Bergerie ★★
☎ 05 62 97 59 99
50 pitches

Camping Les Trois Vallées ★★★
☎ 05 62 90 35 47
400 pitches
3-VALLEES@wanadoo.fr
www.les-campings.les-3-vallees.fr

Camping du Lavedan ★★★
44 route des Vallées
☎ 05 62 97 18 84
www.lavedan.com

B&Bs
Montgaillard
Cazaux
67 le Cap de la Vielle, 65200 Montgaillard
☎ 05 62 91 54 29

Orincles
Grimbert
Passage du Moulin, 65380 Orincles
☎ 05 62 45 40 65
moulindo@free.fr

Boo-Silhen
Brouillet
Les Aillans, 65400 Boo-Silhen
☎ 05 62 97 59 22
franc.brouillet@wanadoo.fr
www.brouilletfranck.com

Pierrefitte-Nestalas
Dubarry
21 rue Parmentier, 65260 Pierrefitte-Nestalas
☎ 05 62 92 74 77

Hotels
Lourdes
Just cycle in and take your pick – hundreds of hotels!

Argelès-Gazost
Le Soleil Levant, 17 Ave des Pyrenees
☎ 05 62 97 08 68

Victoria, 25 rue de l'Yser
☎ 05 62 97 08 34

Au Primerose, Ave de l'Yser
☎ 05 62 97 06 72
primerose@wanadoo.fr

Les Fleurs, Place de la Mairie
☎ 05 62 97 00 24

Le Puits Fleuri, 18 Ave de la Marne
☎ 05 62 97 01 08

Le Relais, 25 rue maréchal Foch
☎ 05 62 97 01 27

STAGE 6 ARGELÈS-GAZOST TO THE COL D'AUBISQUE AND BACK, THEN LOURDES

Campsites
Arras-en-Lavedan
Camping l'idéal ★★
☎ 05 62 97 03 13
60 pitches

Camping Le Picorlet ★★

Camping Relais de l'Aubisque ★★

Arcizans Dessus
Camping l'Edelweis ★★
☎ 05 62 97 09 45
jean-michel.miqueu@wanadoo.fr
38 pitches

Aucun/Arrens Marsous
Camping La Heche ★★
Camping Le Gerrit ★★
Camping Le Moulian ★★

Hotels
Aucun
Le Picors
☎ 05 62 97 40 90
www.hotel-picors.com
hotelpicors@aol.com
See Stage 5 for accommodation in Argelès-Gazost and Lourdes.

For further information on accommodation, see Appendix B

RIVERS AND CASTLES: DORDOGNE AND LOT

ROUTE SUMMARY

From	To	Km	Terrain
Brive-la-Gaillarde	St Céré	61	Hilly, then river valleys
St Céré	Figeac	40	Very hilly; woods
Figeac	Cahors	90	River valleys
Cahors	Monpazier	69	River valley, then hilly
Monpazier	La Roque-Gageac	46	High plateau, river valley
La Roque-Gageac	Souillac	38	River valley

Stage 1 Brive-la-Gaillarde to St Céré

Distance	61km/38 miles
Terrain	Hilly, then river valleys
Climb	450m

How to get to Brive-la-Gaillarde
By train From Paris Austerlitz via Limoges Benedictin (4hr).

By air You can fly from the UK to Limoges or Bergerac with Ryanair from London Stansted or East Midlands (Nottingham) airports, or with Flybe from Southampton.

Flybe also fly from Bristol to Bordeaux and Bergerac, and from Birmingham to Bergerac.

If flying to Limoges the train journey takes just 1hr. If flying to Bergerac, it would be easier to start this circular tour from Siorac-en-Périgord (see Stage 5), which can be reached by train from Bergerac railway station in 1hr. Otherwise, a much longer train journey via Libourne. Taxi service from Limoges airport to Limoges takes 10min.

Gaillarde translates as 'bold', and **Brive-la-Gaillarde** acquired its full name because of the courage shown by its inhabitants defending the town against the English throughout the Hundred Years' War. The suburbs are bland, but the old town still boasts some charming turreted buildings of beige sandstone. One in particular, the 'Tour', can be found in the narrow Rue des Echévins just south of the 12th-century church of St Martin.

The route

From Brive-la-Gaillarde SNCF station follow Avenue Jean Jaurés to Rue Célestin Lafeuille and continue along this E for 300m before turning L up Rue de Noailles to Boulevard Brune. Go R here (E) until you reach the turning R (D38) towards Meyssac. The D38 goes over the railway line and climbs out of Brive-la-Gaillarde in woodland for 8km to a crossroads where the countryside opens up. The D38 here climbs L towards Meyssac. Instead, continue straight on the D8 to Jugéals-Nazareth (2.5km), with a scenic viewpoint L just before reaching the village. The Mairie in Jugéals-Nazareth has a few vaulted chambers underground, used to house lepers about the time of the First Crusade.

Continue S on the D8 past the privately owned Château de la Peyrousse L to the village of **Turenne**. Once the seat of the very powerful Viscounts of Turenne – who ruled over more than 1000 villages in the 15th century and minted their own coins until the 18th century – this charming village is dominated by the ruined hilltop château with its two fine towers, the Tour

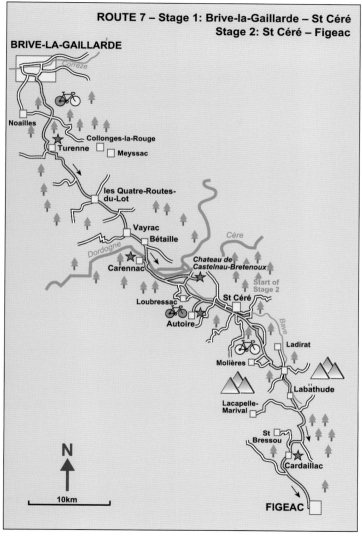

ROUTE 7 – Stage 1: Brive-la-Gaillarde – St Céré
Stage 2: St Céré – Figeac

BRIVE-LA-GAILLARDE

Corrèze

Noailles

Turenne · Collonges-la-Rouge · Meyssac

les Quatre-Routes-du-Lot

Vayrac · Bétaille

Cère

Dordogne

Carennac · Château de Castelnau-Bretenoux

Start of Stage 2

Loubressac · St Céré

Autoire

Bave

Ladirat

Molières

Labathude

Lacapelle-Marival

St Bressou

Cardaillac

N

10km

FIGEAC

de l'Horloge and the Tour du César. The Clock (*horloge*) Tower is now privately owned, but you can still climb to the top of the 12th-century Caesar's Tower for a superb view over the surrounding hilly countryside. Open daily 10am–7pm July and August, 10am–12pm and 2–6pm April–June, September and October. The Tour du César can be reached via Rue de l'Eglise and up the steep hill between the Chapelle des Capucins and the Maison Tournadour.

The D8 descends SE to the Gare de Turenne and across the railway line. This road now becomes the D820 as you cycle into the *département* of Lot and leave Corrèze behind. Road, rail and *rau* (a common word for stream) travel alongside each other to **les Quatre-Routes-du-Lot** (the Four Roads of Lot) where, naturally, you will find a crossroads.

Continue straight on here to Condat and St Michel de Bannières before a gradual descend to **Vayrac** with the Puy d'Assolud due W. Turn L (E) along the D803, which runs from Souillac to Bretenoux, for 3km to **Bétaille**. Just before leaving this village turn R (D20), crossing the railway line. This straight road takes you past a *parc aquatique* R and to a bridge over the River Dordogne. Turn R at the junction to visit the village of **Carennac**.

Carennac is one of the prettiest villages along the Dordogne, its typically medieval Quercynois houses with their brown-tiled turreted roofs and towers all huddled together within the original ramparts. Its fortified gate still exists, but most who visit Carennac come to see the charmingly peculiar **Tower of Télémarque**, where it is said that Fénelon wrote his masterpiece *Les Aventures de Télémarque* in the late 17th century.

Return to the junction with the D20 and continue straight on (D30) along the pretty south bank of the Dordogne. Pass the village of Gintrac on the steep hillside R to a crossroads (approx 5km from Carennac); turn L here (D43) over the Bave river, passing the chapel of Pauliac and bearing L at the next junction to the village of

Prudhomat. Behind it towers the impressive **Château de Castelnau-Bretenoux** which can be reached by staying on the D43 that climbs from the valley. This magnificent, triangular-shaped castle is one of the finest examples of French medieval military architecture with its red stone ramparts, haughty towers and huge square keep. You can, apparently, make out the towers of Turenne from its ramparts on a clear day.

The Tower of Télémarque (right), Carennac

Return to Prudhomat and turn L (SW) along the D14 and across the Bave river via the Pont de Maday. Turn L here to rejoin the D30 and follow this SE for 3.5km to the turning R for **Autoire** (D38). This is an interesting detour, a 3km climb up a picturesque valley to one of France's prettiest and best-preserved villages, again typical of the Quercy region with its brown-tiled turreted manor houses and dovecots (*pigeonniers*) built of an ochre-coloured limestone that collectively resemble a cluster of miniature châteaux. ►

Return to the D30 and turn R along the Bave Valley to another enchanting castle, the Chateau de Montal. A medieval exterior of steep *lauze* roofs (see Route 8, Stage 2) and austere round towers, complete with loopholes through which arrows may have been fired, contrasts radically with the inner courtyard that takes on the

Autoire can also be admired from the Cirque d'Autoire, 1.5km further on, by continuing up the D38 to a car park where a path leads to a bridge over the Autoire river and up to a great viewpoint.

195

Autoire

character and charm of the Renaissance period. The turning R to the château comes soon after the crossroads where the D807 climbs R to St Jean-Lespinasse. Continue E along the Bave Valley road (now the D673) to the medieval town of **St Céré**, dominated by the ruined Château de St Laurent-les-Tours.

Stage 2 St Céré to Figeac

Distance	40km/25 miles
Terrain	Very hilly; woods
Climb	525m
Map	See Stage 1

The route

Note Buy food and water in St Céré before setting off.

From the centre of St Céré take the D940 towards Figeac over the Bave river and turn L along the D48 towards Leyme. After 0.5km leave this road for the D19 which follows the south bank of the Bave before crossing the

Rau de Mellac. Keep R at the junction as the D19 climbs through a wooded ravine alongside the Mellac stream. Immediately you sense a distinct change in the landscape from that of Stage 1. This NE corner of Lot divides the limestone causses of Gramat and Martel from the Mont du Cantal. This is the Ségala – undulating terrain with deep, wooded valleys where hillside village (*villages perchés*) houses have steep-pitched slate roofs sourced from the nearby volcanic region of the Auvergne.

Continue at a junction up the D19 to a crossroads at 357m and straight on here, downhill to the Vialgues stream. Cross this and the D19 climbs again to Plagnes, sandwiched between three hills, before reaching the village of Terrou where you encounter the Bave again, here a babbling stream. Cross the Bave and follow it up the narrow valley via the D19 for 7km, passing **Labathude** to a junction with the D653 that marks the top of the climb at Rouqueyrou (600m). Turn L here along the ridge, then immediately R onto the D19 again, as far as a crossroads where you stay on the D19 for Cardaillac (do not take the D89 L which climbs the hill). Turn R (D18) at another crossroads after 4km through woods, the road twisting and turning to the hillside village of **Cardaillac**.

Two very diverse towers – once part of a 12th-century fort – dominate the skyline in **Cardaillac**. The Tour de Saignes is square with a flat roof terrace, while the 'Baron's Tower' – probably named after Hugues de Cardaillac who was the local baron in the mid-14th century – is cylindrical with a pitched roof. The latter, like so many in Lot, contains a dovecot from which doves' droppings were collected for use as manure.

From Cardaillac all roads S lead to the Drauzon Valley and Figeac. From the church by the stream you can either take the D15 or D115 to the N140 and turn L for Figeac, or from the village you can continue on the D18 (SW) which skirts a hill, then descend to Fourmagnac and the N140 and L for **Figeac**.

Figeac, situated on the River Célé, is a medieval town where past and present mingle happily. The old town is worth visiting with its narrow streets lined with half-timbered and beige sandstone houses, each street also bearing its alternative Occitan name. A scenic route around the old quarter starts from the Tourist Information Centre in Place Vival.

Stage 3 Figeac to Cahors

Distance	90km/56 miles
Terrain	River valleys
Climb	200m

Stage 3 is different again, involving cycling beside two of the most beautiful, meandering rivers in SW France, the Célé and the Lot. There is only one short climb to St Cirq-Lapopie, otherwise this stage, although long, is pretty much flat. It could be split into two days if you want to spend more time exploring.

The route
Leave Figeac on the D802 (W) for Cahors, which follows the N side of the Célé river. After passing the 15th-century château of Ceint d'Eau (4km), the road goes under a railway line. Soon after this, take the D41 L just before the main road passes under the railway line again. The D41 follows the Célé faithfully for the next 47km as it snakes its way across the Parc Naturel Régional des Causses du Quercy, babbling below high limestone cliffs and past narrow fields of maize, tobacco and walnut trees. Popular with canoeists, this is a wonderful valley for cyclists as well, especially out of season.

ROUTE 7 – Stage 3: Figeac – Cahors

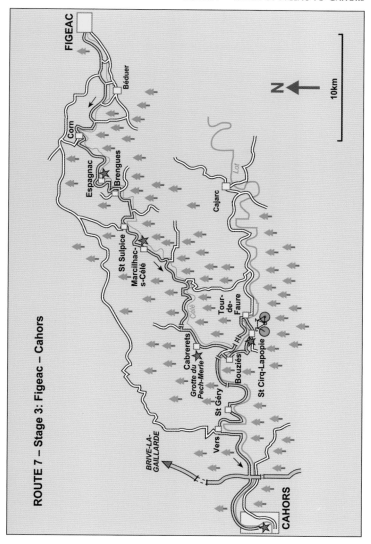

FIGEAC

Béduer

Corn

Espagnac

Brengues

St Sulpice

Marcilhac-s-Célé

Cajarc

Lot

Célé

Cabrerets

Tour-de-Faure

Grotte du Pech-Merle

Bouziés

St Géry

St Cirq-Lapopie

BRIVE-LA-GAILLARDE

Vers

CAHORS

N↑

10km

199

The valley narrows at Boussac after 5km and the Célé performs the first of a score of tortuous turns before **Corn**, whose ruined castle tower dominates this quaint village. Continue downstream past the cliffs at St Eulalie, where prehistoric cave engravings were discovered, to an old stone bridge L that leads to the beautiful village of **Espagnac**. Here you will find the priory of Val-Paradis, which has a lovely half-timbered belfry tower with octagonal lantern.

Return to the D41 and continue along it to **Brengues** (9km from Corn) which, like so many of the villages in the Célé Valley, is perched beneath vertical cliffs dotted with fortified caves known as the *châteaux des anglais*. The names comes from marauding English soldiers who made their presence felt here during and after the Hundred Years' War. About 5km further on is **St Sulpice** whose castle is owned by the Hébrards, once a very powerful family who ruled the entire Célé Valley. After this comes the picturesque village of **Marcilhac-sur-Célé**, overlooked by an amphitheatre of huge limestone cliffs, its old houses huddled about the ruins of an 11th-century Benedictine abbey that flourished until the Hundred Years' War. Sauliac-sur-Célé, 6.5km downstream, is yet another old village clinging to a precipitous cliff with fortified caves. The Vallée du Célé narrows considerably here, and is densely wooded for 6km to a road tunnel that cuts through the cliff, 3km before Cabrerets.

Shielded by poplar trees, the village of **Cabrerets** is overlooked by two castles, the ruined Château du Diable (Devil's Castle) dating back to 1259, and the Château de Gontaut–Biron (14th century). Cabrerets is perhaps better known for the **Grotte du Pech-Merle** nearby.

In 1922 two local teenage boys stumbled upon a concealed fissure in the rocky limestone plateau which they duly reported to Abbé Lemozi, the priest in Cabrerets. A keen prehistorian, Lemozi climbed through the crack into a vast cave system that contains remarkable prehistoric wall paintings and engravings, possibly 30,000 years old. Guided tours daily from 9.30am–12pm and 1.30–5pm, April–October.

The D41 and the Célé river snake their way S down a narrow canyon for 4km that finally spills out into the broad Vallée du Lot. Turn L here (D662) along the N bank of the Lot over the Quercy railway line and through two tunnels (the first is longer than the second) for 4km to **Tour-de-Faure**.

St Cirq-Lapopie

Turn R before the village, crossing the railway line and the Lot to climb the steep hill to the spectacular village of **St Cirq-Lapopie**. Perched precariously on the edge of a vertical cliff overlooking the Lot, St Cirq-Lapopie has a late 15th-century church with a cylindrical turret flanking its main belfry tower. Steep, narrow streets lined with 14th- and 15th-century half-timbered houses help to enhance one of the most beautiful villages in France.

Go through St Cirq-Lapopie and turn R (D40) at a fork; follow this road which skirts the steep wooded hillside to a belvedere that looks down on the Lot before a descent to **Bouziés**. Cross the suspension bridge over the Lot here to rejoin the D662, above which there is another *château des anglais* cave. This stretch along the Lot is called the *Défilé des Anglais* (Pass of the English). Turn L towards Cahors, the road passing through two short tunnels before going under the railway line and around the bend to **St Géry**. Another 5km further on comes **Vers** where there are remains of a Gallo-Roman aqueduct. The D662 joins up with the D653 here. Go L at the junction past N.D. de Velles. The Lot valley opens up near Savanac, after which the D653 goes under the Viaduc du Lot and passes through Laroque-des-Arcs, past its château and on to **Cahors**.

Cahors is built on a tongue of land created by the looping Lot. The Pont Valentré, which spans the Lot on the western side of the great meander, is a superb example of medieval architecture. It has three enormous square towers with turrets, the middle one known as the Tour du Diable. The Cathédrale St Etienne in the old part of the town dates back to the late 11th century and has a splendid Romanesque portal.

Distance	69km/43 miles
Terrain	River valley, then hilly through woods and arable land
Climb	525m

The route

From the Cahors side of the famous Pont Valentré, go N along Avenue P. Semard which becomes Rue Lattre de Tassigny, running alongside the railway line for 1km. At the rdbt take the second exit (D8), crossing the Lot via the Pont des Remparts. Turn R at the junction on the W bank and follow the D8 to a rdbt. Go straight here, under the N20 and bear L to another rdbt where you take the third exit (D8) to Pradines. The D8 then curls SW, following the course of the Lot to **Douelle**. This stretch of the valley – flatter and more fertile – is home to the vineyards of Cahors. A number of local châteaux are open to the public for wine tasting.

The D8 cuts W for 5km to Caunezit. Take the second exit at the rdbt that follows, and turn immediately R for Luzech which, like Cahors, is located inside a loop of the snaking river Lot. **Luzech** is sandwiched between two hills, one overlooking the southern end of the loop – La Pistoule – and another, L'Impernal, to the N. Inhabited since prehistoric times because of its strategic position, L'Impernal was also chosen as the site for a Gallo-Roman oppidum where excavations started in 1873. Having crossed the Lot to visit the old town of Luzech, follow the road S that goes round La Pistoule to the N.D. de l'Ile, a tiny chapel set in a picturesque position amidst vines and walnut trees near the river.

Continue on round the hill to the W side of Luzech and follow the D9 along the N bank of the Lot past the very pretty church of Camy to the *bastide* village of

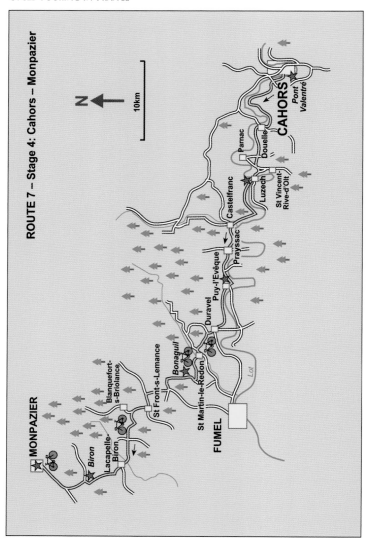

ROUTE 7 – Stage 4: Cahors – Monpazier

Castelfranc (8km). Here the Masse and Vert rivers converge and join into the Lot, and the D9 meets the D811. Go L along this to sprawling **Prayssac** and continue W for 4.5km on the D811 to the much prettier **Puy-l'Evêque**. Cross the bridge over the Lot to appreciate the best view of this small town with its array of old golden-stone houses descending from the cliff right down to the riverbank. From the Esplanade de la Truffière, next to the big square 13th-century keep that dominates the town, there is another good view, this time looking across the wide valley covered with vineyards and fields. Continue along the D811 for 6km to Duravel beneath wooded hills to the N. Cycle up through these on the D58 towards Montcabrier turning L shortly at a junction, a narrow road that climbs the hill to 200m. (bear R at the next junction) before a descent to Caze Marnac in the Thèze Valley. Turn L here (D673) towards Fumel, then R after 0.5km into the village of **St Martin-le-Redon**.

Cross the Thèze stream and turn R, then a sharp L and keep L at the next junction, a steep climb of 100m in height before a descent W to a picturesque narrow valley and a T-junction. Turn R here along the D158 towards the majestic castle of **Bonaguil** that dominates

Cycling towards the castle of Bonaguil

the valley, a huge fairytale fortress dating back to the
15th century. Bonaguil has 13 towers and turrets and is
considered a masterpiece of medieval military architecture. Open daily from 10am–5.30pm July and August,
10am–12pm and 2–5pm June, 10.30am–12pm and
2.30–5pm February–May, September–November.

From Bonaguil take the road N into the *département*
of Dordogne up a wooded valley for 2.5km, turning L
after a brief climb at a junction (220m), then R at a crossroads (D440) which descends through Lastreilles and
across the Lémance to a T-junction in the valley. Turn L
(SW) along the D710 to a crossroads (**St Front-sur-
Lémance**). Turn R here along the Bromance Valley
(D426) for 2km, after which the road crosses the
Bromance stream L, shortly before reaching the village of
Blanquefort and climbing up through a lovely wooded
ravine to a crossroads by the cemetery of la Sauvetat.

Go straight here down through woods to **Lacapelle-
Biron**. With the village church L take the D255 (W) out
of Lacapelle-Biron, turning immediately R for Biron on
the D150. This becomes the D53 as you cross into
another commune, with the **Château de Biron** dominating the surrounding countryside N. Dating from the
11th century, the building developed into the substantial
castle seen today thanks to the Gontaut-Biron family; 24
generations of the family owned the Renaissance-style
château from the 12th to early 20th centuries. From Biron
continue N on the D53 down to the D2 in the Dropt
Valley and turn R here. One final climb leads up into the
best-known *bastide* town of all, marvellous **Monpazier**.

Monpazier is perhaps the very best example of a *bastide* town in France and
is one of many in the *départments* of Lot and Dordogne. Deriving from the
Occitan *bastido*, these towns first appeared in the early 13th century.
Monpazier was founded by the English king Edward I in 1284. Unlike towns
and villages that grew up around churches or castles, bastides developed
round market places. Monpazier's central square, the charming Place des
Cornières, is surrounded by medieval houses with magnificent arches.

Distance	46km/29 miles
Terrain	High plateau, arable land, then river valley
Climb	30m

The route

From Monpazier take the D53 which cuts NE across high countryside for 17km to **Belvès**. There is little to see en route to Belvès, making the sudden view of it perched on a limestone promontory all the more enchanting. Resist the temptation to move straight on to the Dordogne Valley and take time to explore the old part of this town. Then descend the D53 on the other side of Belvès to the D710 and head L (N), now down the Nauze Valley by the railway line to the Dordogne river. The D710 passes under the Bergerac–Sarlat railway line to a major rdbt in **Siorac-en-Périgord**.

Go straight here over the Dordogne river and bear R at the next rdbt (D703 E) for **St Cyprien**. Surrounded by steep wooded hills, St Cyprien's focal point is its huge 12th-century church, around which huddle the old village houses. Join the D703 S of St Cypien and go L here (SE) towards Beynac. The valley is broad, flat and fertile; a wide variety of crops – strawberries to tobacco to cereals – are cultivated here on account of the good soil and kind climate. St Vincent-de-Cosse, a small, charming village 8km E of St Cyprien, lies off the beaten track and deserves a visit. Look out for the turning L to it 2km before Beynac. The Château les Milandes on the S bank of the Dordogne opposite was built in 1489 by François de Caumont and was the home of the great American caberet entertainer Josephine Baker and her adopted children during the 20th century.

ROUTE 7 – Stage 5: Monpazier – la Roque-Gageac
Stage 6: La Roque-Gageac – Souillac

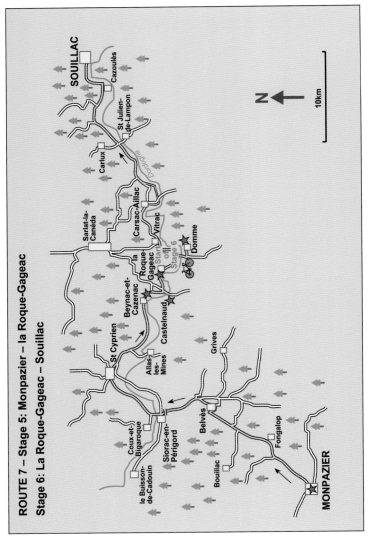

The next village along the N bank of the Dordogne is **Beynac-et-Cazenac** (Cazenac is a smaller village in the hills nearby), dominated by its spectacular château perched high on the cliff edge above. From the terrace of this 12th-century castle there is a fantastic view S of three other grand châteaux along the Dordogne: Marquessac, Fayrac and Castelnaud.

Continue E along the D703 under the railway line and turn R at the junction for La Roque-Gageac. At le Luc (1.5km) take the D57 R which crosses the valley and the Dordogne river before an ascent to Castelnaud and the impressive ruins of its 12th-century castle, from which there are outstanding views of the Dordogne and Léon valleys. There is also an excellent museum of medieval warfare. Return to the D703 and continue E to one of the most picturesque villages along the Dordogne, if not in the whole of France – **La Roque-Gageac**. A row of quaint, old houses lines the road overlooking the river. Behind them, others with turrets or steeply pitched roofs crowd the steep slope beneath a vertical cliff. The Manoir de Tarde, with its distinctive pepperpot tower, overlooks the eastern end of the village.

Stage 6 La Roque-Gageac to Souillac

Distance	38km/24 miles
Terrain	River valley
Climb	250m
Map	See Stage 5

The route

Continue along the D703 for 3km to another bridge over the Dordogne to Cénac. Take the road from Cénac (D50) that climbs L beneath the cliffs of a promontory and around an old fortress site to the Port del Bos, the western gateway to the well-preserved, sandstone *bastide* town of **Domme**. The Belvédère de la Barre on the northern edge of the town grants a wonderful view of the Dordogne stretching from Beynac in the W all the way to the Cingle de Montfort upriver. Return to the D703 and continue E for 3 km to **Vitrac**, after which the road veers NE between two hills to Montfort and the river again. Here you will find the privately owned Château de Montfort standing on a rocky promontory overlooking the Cingle de Montfort, a perfect loop on the meandering Dordogne.

On to **Carsac-Aillac** which has a very pretty little 12th-century church housing some interesting carvings as well as more modern work by the Russian artist Leon Zack. In Carsac-Aillac you can leave the road for a cycle path (disused railway line from Sarlat/good tarmac surface) that follows the D704 S around a hill, passing through a cutting with ferns and then shaded by trees to a junction where the cycle path veers S, crossing the Dordogne. Instead, keep to the shaded cycle path L (E) that passes a walnut tree orchard and offers views of Groléjac on the S side of the river. Cross over the D704; the cycle path goes over a road and after 1.5km runs parallel with the D703 to Aillac with views of the Château de Vayrignac on the south bank of the Dordogne. Rejoin the D703 hereabouts, turning R at the junction soon after for Calviac-en-Périgord and then Rouffilac, whose château is situated in oak woods on the steep hillside L overlooking the bridge to **St Julien-de Lampon**. Here the valley really begins to widen. Continue along the D703, soon leaving the *département* of Dordogne and returning to that of Lot, a gentle ride of 7km into the town of **Souillac**.

How to get back to Brive-la-Gaillarde
From here by train (direct) to Brive-la-Gaillarde (30min).

SELECTED ACCOMMODATION
ROUTE 7

**STAGE 1 BRIVE-LA-GAILLARDE
TO ST CÉRÉ**

Campsites
Brive-la-Gaillarde
Camping Municipal La Ferme des Iles
★★★

les Quatres-Routes-du-Lot
Camping Municipal Le Vignon ★★

Vayrac
Camping Les Granges ★★★
Camping Municipal La Palenquière ★★
Camping Municipal La Peupleraie ★

Carennac
Camping l'Eau Vive ★★

Loubressac
Camping La Garrigue ★★★

St Céré
Camping Le Soulhol ★★★

B&Bs
Turenne
Soustre
Au Bontemps, 19500 Turenne
☎ 05 55 85 97 72

Sourzat
Le Clos Marnis, Le Bourg, 19500
Turenne
☎ 05 55 22 05 28
keny.sourzat@wanadoo.fr

Couvrat-Desvergnes
La Croix de Belonie, 19500 Turenne
☎ 05 55 85 97 07
bruno.couvrat-desvergnes@wanadoo.fr

les Quatres-Routes-du-Lot
Eymat
St Julien, 46110 les Quatres-Routes-
du-Lot
☎ 05 65 32 11 82
www.cafecouette-st-julien.com

Autoire
Graves
La Rivière, 46400 Autoire
☎ 05 65 38 18 01

Hotels
Brive-la-Gaillarde
Le Chapon Fin, Place de Lattre de
Tassigny, 19100 Brive-la-Gaillarde
☎ 05 55 74 23 40
lechaponfinbrive@wanadoo.fr

Le Chene Vert, 24 Boulevard Jules
Ferry, 19100 Brive-la-Gaillarde
☎ 05 55 24 10 07

Le Montauban, 6 Ave Edouard
Herriot, 19100 Brive-la-Gaillarde
☎ 05 55 24 00 38
lemontauban@free.fr

Carennac

Hostellerie Fenelon, 46110 Carennac
☎ 05 65 10 96 46
contact@hotel-fenelon.com

Autoire

Auberge de la Fontaine, 46400
Autoire
☎ 05 65 10 85 40
auberge.de.la.fontaine@wanadoo.fr

St Céré

Le Victor Hugo, 7, Ave des Maquis.
46400 St Céré
☎ 05 65 38 16 15
vichugostcere@wanadoo.fr

STAGE 2 ST CÉRÉ TO FIGEAC

Campsites
Figeac
Camping Les Rives du Célé ★★★
(1.5km E, N140)
☎ 05 65 34 59 00
Open April–September

B&Bs
Fons
Spindler-Glass
La Piale, 46100 Fons
☎ 05 65 40 19 52

Lissac-et-Mouret (NW of Figeac)
Gay
L'Oasienne Clavies, 46100 Lissac-et-
Mouret
☎ 05 65 34 40 98
loasienne@hotmail.com

Hotels
Figeac
Hostellerie de l'Europe, 51 Allée
Victor Hugo. 46100 Figeac
☎ 05 65 34 10 16
sa.delsahut@wanadoo.fr

STAGE 3 FIGEAC TO CAHORS

Campsites
St Sulpice
Camping Municipal ★★

Marcilhac-sur-Célé
Camping Municipal ★★

Cabrerets
Camping Si Cantal ★★

Cahors
Camping Rivière de Cabessut ★★★
☎ 05 65 30 06 30
Open April–October

Camping Municipal Saint-Georges
★★

B&Bs
Marcilhac-sur-Célé
Menassol
Les Tilleuls, 46160 Marcilhac-sur-Célé
☎ 05 65 40 62 68
michellemenassol@wanadoo.fr
www.les-tilleuls.fr.st

Cabrerets
Bessac
Place de la Mairie, 46330 Cabrerets
☎ 05 65 31 27 04

Tour-de-Faure
Druot
Combe de Redoles, 46330 Tour-de-Faure
☎ 05 65 31 21 58
druot@club-internet.fr
www.redoles.com

St Géry
Ladoux
Domaine du Porche, 46330 St Géry
☎ 05 65 31 45 94

Mauduit
Le Mas de la Pommeraie, Les Masseries, 46330 St Géry
☎ 05 65 31 99 43

Vers
Crepin
Le Bois Noir, 46090 Vers
☎ 05 65 31 44 50
www.closdesdryades.com

Hotels
Vers
Les Chalets, 46090 Vers
☎ 05 65 31 40 83
les.chalets.vers@wanadoo.fr

Cahors
Chartreuse, Rue Saint-Georges, 46000 Cahors
☎ 05 65 35 17 37
la-chartreuse@wanadoo.fr

STAGE 4 CAHORS TO MONPAZIER

Campsites
Luzech
Camping Municipal de l'Alcade ★★

Prayssac
Camping de la Source ★★

Duravel
Camping Club de Vacances Duravel ★★★★

Sauveterre-la-Lémance
Moulin du Périé ★★★★ (3 km E)
☎ 05 53 40 67 26
Open April–September

Monpazier
Camping Le Veronne ★★ (3km NW, Marsalès)
☎ 05 53 22 65 23
Open mid-June–mid-September

213

Moulin de David ★★★★ (3km SW, D2)
☎ 05 53 22 65 25
Open mid-May–mid-September
www.moulin-de-david.com

B&Bs
Pradines
Faille
Valrose, Le Poujal, 46090 Pradines
☎ 05 65 22 18 52
claude.faille@libertysurf.fr

Luzech
Martinot
Le Peyrou, 46140 Luzech
☎ 05 65 30 51 98
m.martinot@wanadoo.fr

Prayssac
Becht
Les Cambous, Chateau Onésime, 46220 Prayssac
☎ 05 65 36 54 57
www.chateau-onesime.com

Sauveterre-la-Lémance
Lemoine
La Carelle, 47500 Sauveterre-la-Lémance
☎ 05 53 01 63 04

Hotels
Pradines
Le Clos Grand,Lieu-dit Labéraudie, 46090 Pradines
☎ 05 65 35 04 39

Puy l'Eveque
La Truffiere, 46700 Puy l'Eveque

☎ 05 65 2134 54
hotellatruffiere@aol.com

Henry, 46700 Puy l'Eveque
☎ 05 65 21 32 24

Monpazier
Hotel-Restaurant Edward 1er, 5 rue Saint-Pierre, 24540 Monpazier
☎ 05 53 22 44 00
info@hoteledward1er.com
http://www.hoteledward1er.com
www.hoteledward1er.com

De Londres, place du Foirail Nord, 24540 Monpazier
☎ 05 53 22 60 64

STAGE 5 MONPAZIER TO LA ROQUE-GAGEAC

Campsites
Belves
Camping Le Moulin de la Pique ★★★★
Camping Les Nauves ★★

St Cyprien
Camping Municipal Le Garrit ★★★

Beynac
Camping Le Capeyrou ★★

La Roque-Gageac
Camping Beau Rivage ★★★
Camping Le Lauzier ★★
Camping La Butte ★★
Camping Verte Rive ★

B&Bs
Siorac-en-Perigord
Santerre
Les Deux Tours, chemin de Barthalem, 24170 Siorac-en-Perigord
☎ 05 53 29 33 64
info@lesdeuxtours.fr

Hotels
St Cyprien
La Terrasse, Place Jean Ladignac, 24220 St Cyprien
☎ 05 53 29 21 69
hotel-laterrasse@wanadoo.fr

Beynac-Cazenac
Hostellerie Maleville, 24220 Beynac-Cazenac
☎ 05 53 29 50 06
hostellerie.maleville@wanadoo.fr

La Roque-Gageac
Le Perigord, 24250 La Roque-Gageac
☎ 05 53 28 36 55
hotel-le-perigord@wanadoo.fr

Belle Etoile, rue Principale, 24250 La Roque-Gageac
☎ 05 53 29 51 44
hotel.belle-etoile@wanadoo.fr

STAGE 6 LA ROQUE-GAGEAC TO SOUILLAC

Campsites
Domme
Camping La Rivière ★★
Camping Le Bosquet ★★
Camping Le Perpetuum ★★

Camping Le Bras ★
Camping Moulin de Caudon ★

Carlux
Camping Les Ombrages de la Dordogne ★★

Souillac
Camping La Paille Basse ★★★★
Camping Municipal ★★★

Brive-la-Gaillarde
Camping Municipal La Ferme des îles ★★★

B&Bs
Carlux
Pigeon
La Vigerie, 24370 Carlux
☎ 05 53 28 65 94
la.vigerie@wanadoo.fr

Hotels
Souillac
Belle Vue, 68, Ave Jean Jaurès, 46200 Souillac
☎ 05 65 32 78 23
hotelbellevue.souillac@wanadoo.fr

Les Ambassadeurs, 12, Ave du Général de Gaulle, 46200 Souillac
☎ 05 65 32 78 36
contact@ambassadeurs-hotel.com

La Vielle Auberge, 1, rue de la Recège, 46200 Souillac
☎ 05 65 32 79 43
r.veril@la-vieille-auberge.com
For accommodation in Brive-la-Gaillarde see Stage 1.

ROUTE 8

RUGGED AND REMOTE:
AUVERGNE AND LANGUEDOC

ROUTE SUMMARY

From	To	Km	Terrain
Meymac	Riom-ès-Montagnes	73	Undulating or hilly
Riom-ès-Montagnes	St Flour	65	Mostly hilly, high rolling country
St Flour	Marvejols	70	Undulating or fairly hilly
Marvejols	Florac	63	Hilly, mostly flat in a gorge
Florac	Alès	83	Very hilly, a long descent, then undulating

Stage 1 Meymac to Riom-ès-Montagnes

Distance	73km/45.5 miles
Terrain	Undulating or hilly
Climb	780m

How to get to Meymac
By rail From Paris Austerlitz railway station to Limoges Benedictins station which takes approx 3hr (fast train service). Change here for Meymac (TER service) which takes 1½hr. You can also leave from Paris Gare de Lyon station for Clermont-Ferrand (3½–4hr/Corail) and change

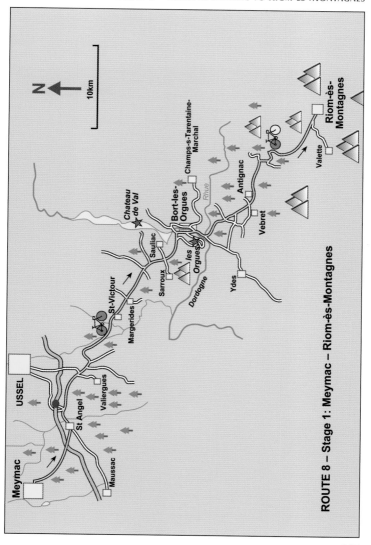

ROUTE 8 – Stage 1: Meymac – Riom-ès-Montagnes

here for Meymac (TER service) which takes 2hr 20min. By air Ryanair operate flights from London Stansted and East Midlands (Nottingham) airports to Limoges airport and also from Nîmes airport (not far from Alès) back to Stansted and East Midlands. Taxi service from Limoges airport to Limoges takes 10min.

Meymac is situated on the edge of the high Plateau des Millevaches, mostly a mixture of forest, peat bog and heathland. The old town is full of character with grey, granite houses, steeply pitched roofs and pepperpot turrets, and an old clock tower beyond which there is a lovely little square with a fountain.

The route

From Meymac train station go L towards **Meymac** (the road passes under the railway line) and turn L at the junction, D979 (R for Meymac) towards St Angel/Ussel. The D979 climbs to a viewpoint R at 738m looking across the Luzège countryside, followed by a descent, passing over the A89 Autoroute and into **St Angel**.

Follow the N89 E out of St Angel towards Ussel, and after a 2km ascent turn R at the crossroads (straight on for the Autoroute), once more on the D979 through woods

Château de Val and the Dordogne

Steep climb near la Troubade

to Lestrade and then on to la Serre. Stay on the D979 at the junction (R for Neuvic/D982) after which there is a lovely descent to the Diège river (552m) and the village of la Vialatte. Having crossed the Rau d'Ozange soon after there is a climb to **St Victour**. Continue straight, past the turning R for Margerides to Nuzéjoux.

Just after the D27 junction L for Thalamy, take the D82 L for la Troubade, bearing R at each junction. From the top of the hill here there is a good view of the fairy-tale 15th-century **Château de Val** and the Dordogne river. If you don't mind the steep climb back, continue NE down through beautiful woods to the river for closer inspection. Return to the D979 and continue SE for 2km to la Chassang and then the Belvédère des Aubazines a couple of kilometres further on.

This is a popular viewpoint with a picnic area overlooking the huge Bort dam and the Dordogne, more of a reservoir here than a river. A road runs across the top of the dam that is almost 400m long. It is the first of five major barrages along the Dordogne as it worms its way across Auvergne and Périgord to Bergerac and beyond.

The D979 takes you into **Bort-les-Orgues**. A short, interesting detour can be made up the D127 R before the cemetery to **les Orgues**, huge blocks of 100m-high basalt rock that look like a series of giant organ pipes. Steps lead up to their base in Chantery, approximately 2km from Bort. Returning to Bort-les-Orgues and the D979 turn R passing the cemetery and then over the Dordogne (returned to river status here).

Go R now along the busy D922 for 1km before turning L (D45) immediately after crossing the Rhue river. You are now about to leave the *département* of Corrèze and cycle into Cantal. The D45 becomes the D3, which passes through woodland and is followed by a railway crossing. Continue straight at the crossroads with the D22, then L at the T-junction, following the D3 into the Parc Naturel Régional des Volcans d'Auvergne. The D3 passes **Antignac** which boasts a 12th-century church, St Pierre aux Liens, and Salsignac which has the 15th-century gothic chapel of St Ferréol, as it travels E alongside the Sumène stream. Stay on the D3 as it climbs steeply from a crossroads with the D205 up onto the St Angeau plateau and **Riom-ès-Montagnes**.

Riom-ès-Montagnes (Riom of the Mountains) is the last sizeable settlement before cycling up into the beautiful volcanic mountains of Cantal. A rural trading post throughout the centuries, Riom-ès-Montagnes is well known throughout the Auvergne for its cattle and cheese fairs, and also for producing an alcoholic aperitif, made from the roots of gentian plants that grow high up in the Parc Naturel Régional des Volcans d'Auvergne.

Stage 2 Riom-ès-Montagnes to St Flour

Distance	65km/40.5 miles
Terrain	Mostly hilly, high rolling country
Climb	800m

The route

From Riom-ès-Montagnes continue SE on the D3 which climbs gradually to the junction with the D49 (3km). If you don't mind the detour climb, then take the narrow D49 R to visit the lovely village of **Apchon** with its ancient drinking fountain in the square, and appreciate the panoramic views from its ruined castle (10min walk from the village). There is a good view of the Cheylade valley to the S with Puy Mary in the distance, while all around stretch undulating green slopes dotted with red Salers cattle. From Apchon you can rejoin the D3 by taking the D49 S out of the village and turning immediately L downhill (steep) to the Petite Rhue stream and L again. The ruins of Apchon castle can also be admired from below on the D3, which curls around its northern flank.

Note Buy food and water in Riom-ès-Montagnes before setting off.

The ruins of Apchon castle from the D3

221

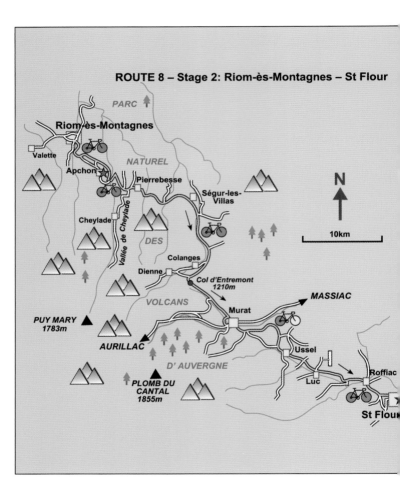

ROUTE 8 – Stage 2: Riom-ès-Montagnes – St Flour

PARC

Riom-ès-Montagnes

Valette

NATUREL

Apchon

Pierrebesse

Ségur-les-Villas

Cheylade

Vallée de Cheylade

DES

N

10km

Colanges

Dienne

Col d'Entremont
1210m

VOLCANS

PUY MARY
1783m

Murat

MASSIAC

AURILLAC

Ussel

D' AUVERGNE

Luc

Roffiac

PLOMB DU
CANTAL
1855m

St Flour

The D3 climbs to the Plateau du Limon, a vast, open landscape of soft, rolling, grassy pastures 1000m above sea level with only the odd farmhouse or shepherd's hut – simply breathtaking. There is, however, little shade up here, so pick up plenty of water in Riom-ès-Montagnes before setting off as the only village of any note on the 30km stretch between Apchon and Murat in the Vallée de l'Alagnon is **Ségur-lès-Villas** (1013m) above the Santoire stream. The D3 follows this stream, a popular destination for anglers in search of mountain trout, up to the **Col d'Entremont** (1210m), a scenic, gradual 9km climb, followed by a pleasant 7km descent to the busy little town of **Murat**.

Many of the old houses in the centre of **Murat** are roofed with *lauzes*, semi-circular, thickly cut wedges of dark stone which overlap each other and resemble the scales of a fish. Roofs tiled with *lauzes* are often seen in Cantal. A giant 19th-century statue of the Virgin Mary stands on a hill overlooking Murat, very much in keeping with the more famous one in Le Puy.

From the station in Murat head E on the N122, taking the turning R over the railway line and Alagnon river for St Flour (D926). A long, gradual climb follows to Meymargues, where a large sign states that you are leaving the Parc Naturel Régional des Volcans d'Auvergne. Soon there are views W of the Plomb du Cantal (1855m) as the D926 passes through **Ussel** and reaches a plateau near **Luc** (993m), just N of which is the Aérodrome de St Flour-Coltines. From the next village, Mons, the D926 descends a wooded slope to **Roffiac**, which has an attractive Romanesque church and characteristic *château-fort* tower. Crossing the Ander, the road now climbs for 1km to a major junction with the D921. Bear L here for St Flour, continuing straight at the rdbt that follows and along Avenue du Lioran before turning L up Rue Marcelin Boudet to a rdbt. Keep straight on here (Rue de Collège and Rue du Breuil) before turning R to reach the Cathédrale Saint-Pierre.

St Flour has an upper and lower town. The old, upper town stands on the edge of a basalt plateau huddled about its cathedral and watches over the lower town in the Ander Valley. From the valley you can make out the dark square towers of the Cathédrale St Pierre, built of local stone, poking above the wall of old houses high up the hill. Inside this cathedral is a life-size Christ made of dark wood dating back to at least the 15th century. Known as the Bon Dieu Noir of St Flour, it is the only black Christ figure in France.

Stage 3 St Flour to Marvejols

Distance	70km/44 miles
Terrain	Undulating or fairly hilly
Climb	600m

The route

Note Few shops en route.

A steep, narrow road to the rear of the cathedral leads down to Avenue de Verdun. Go L (E) here to cross the l'Ander once more. Go R at the rdbt and along Avenue de la République/D909 for about 3km, the first kilometre of which is sandwiched between the railway line and the river. Just before reaching the A75 Autoroute continue on the D909, which swings SE towards the Viaduc de Garabit. Cross the Rau de Vabres stream, make a gradual climb to a roundabout (880m), then continue straight on for 2km to la Gazelle and past the turning R for Anglards-de-St Flour. A descent with hairpin turns to the Gorges de la Truyère and the historic railway bridge, the **Viaduc de Garabit**.

The D909 crosses the Truyère and then proceeds to climb the hill beneath the bridge before reaching Lair and la Bessaire (888m), thereafter passing under the A75. A gradual ascent past a turning R for the Château de

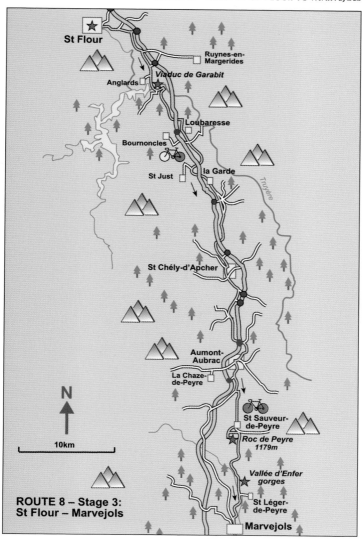

ROUTE 8 – Stage 3:
St Flour – Marvejols

Viaduc de Garabit Before the Barages de Grandval was built across the Truyère some 20km due south of St Flour, this incredible railway viaduct towered more than 100m above the river. It is 0.5km long and was built over two years (1882–4) by Gustav Eiffel, who later went on to build the Eiffel Tower in Paris.

Pompignac and a turning L for the village of Loubaresse, the D909 flattens out somewhat as you leave Cantal for Lozère, the least populated *départment* in the whole of France. You also leave the Auvergne and enter the region of Languedoc-Roussillon, Lozère being its most northerly *départment*. The D909 now becomes the N9 of old, and passes under the A75 a couple more times before another climb to **la Garde** (1042m) and the high point of 1132m in woods alongside the A75. Although the road gets unfortunately close to the autoroute in stretches, it's certainly quieter than it was just over a decade ago when the autoroute did not exist and the D909 was a very busy Route Nationale. A long descent leads to **St Chély-d'Apcher**. There's not much to see here, but it's a useful place to stock up on water/provisions or spend the night if necessary.

Continue S, keeping to the N9 at a fork (R) after 1km heading for **Aumont-Aubrac** through which a famous pilgrim route, the Way of St James, passes.

Starting in Le Puy the pilgrim route travels 100km via the GR65 path over the Montagne de la Margeride to Aumont-Aubrac before continuing SW across the remote, high Aubrac countryside to Conques. The final destination of this mammoth pilgrimage is Santiago de Compostela in Spain.

Ride through Aumont-Aubrac, still on the N9, thereafter passing timber mills and a campsite on your R before taking a turning L to la Chazotte and continuing on to the sprawling village of **St Sauveur-de-Peyre**. Take the D73 SW out of the village to a junction with the D3 and cross over S to a road that leads up to the **Roc de**

Peyre. This rocky monolith with a large white cross on its summit grants superb views of Lozère and its never-ending sea of rugged hills, wild and remote.

Return to the junction and take the D3 E where it joins up with the D303, and turn R (S) for le Grach soon after. After le Grach the road descends steeply and crosses the Chapchinies stream and then a railway line before joining the D2. Go R here, after which the countryside opens up with a view of the Viaduc d'Enfer railway bridge and the wild, rugged **Vallée d'Enfer**, a gorge through which the narrow D2 threads its way down the E side. Spectacular scenery, but don't take your eyes off the twisting road as the drop on your R is a long one! Like most old roads that journey through gorges in mountainous areas, the D2 also succumbs to the occasional rockfall – another good reason to take the 5km descent slowly as you don't know what may be strewn across the road round the next bend. Having passed the turning L for the village of **St Léger-de-Peyre** halfway down the Vallée d'Enfer the D2 eventually joins up with the N9. Go L here (S) to the medieval town of **Marvejols**, which has high fortified gates on three sides. From the N you pass through the impressive Porte de Soubeyran, which has a decidedly unflattering statue of Henri IV in front of it.

Stage 4 Marvejols to Florac

Distance	63km/39.5 miles
Terrain	Hilly, then mostly flat in a gorge
Climb	525m

The route

Note Buy plenty of water for the climb from Chanac.

Leaving Marvejols through the S gate, ignore the N9 turning R for Chirac at the junction that follows and take the N108 across the Colange river (Pont Pessil). Follow this SE for 2.5km to the turning R for Palhers. Cross the Jordane river. A steep climb through the village of **Palhers** follows, then keep uphill via the D31, eventually to be rewarded by a wonderful view ahead of the wooded Causse du Villard proudly overlooking the Lot river valley. A scenic descent to Chabannes and the N88 follows, where you turn L for 3.5km to the Pont Vieux R. Cross the Lot here for **Chanac**.

Chanac from the climb to Champerboux

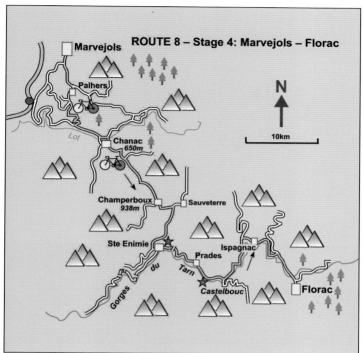

Chanac is a thriving and pleasant place, a perfect base for exploring the Lot and the awe-inspiring Gorges du Tarn to the S, so understandably popular with holidaymakers. Take the D31 (SE) uphill for St Enimie, a series of twists and turns offering good views of Chanac and the Lot Valley as you climb to a junction at 830m. Woodland peters out, marking the onset of the rugged, barren plateau of the Causse de Sauveterre; not a place to be at high noon on a hot July or August day. Continue straight at the junction, (D44), leaving the D31 which veers off L. A gradual ascent to Champerboux follows. Continue straight on through this village to a junction after 2km and turn R here (D986) for St Enimie. Stay on the D986 at le Bac, after which the road skirts the steep hillside and is a very gradual descent offering spectacular views of the immense Gorges du Tarn. A sharp L turn below a rock wall after 3km or so takes you down to **St Enimie** in the gorge.

The **Gorges du Tarn** rates as one of the most beautiful canyons in Europe. It is a spectacular corridor that cuts through the limestone plateaux of the Causses de Sauveterre and Méjean, in places 500m deep and 1500m wide. Unlike many gorges which can only be viewed from above, this canyon can also be appreciated from deep inside, as the D907bis road follows the river Tarn faithfully for nearly 60km from le Rozier to Ispagnac. The south-facing slopes are mostly barren, whilst the north-facing slopes are wooded in places and home to cliff-nesting birds such as swifts and rock thrushes as well as birds of prey including kites, eagles and even giant griffon vultures.

Castelbouc

Head E along the D907bis, a fairly flat road that looks down on the Tarn river R for the next 16km. This is a truly scenic stretch, especially outside July and August when there are fewer tourists. It passes though the lovely villages of **Prades** and Blajoux with wonderful views of **Castelbouc** and its houses perched precariously on the rocky southern bank of the Tarn. Ispagnac, 9km from Blajoux, is another historic village as well as being the last one in the gorge at its eastern end. About 4km after Ispagnac the D907bis joins up with the N106. Turn R here, a 5km ride to **Florac**.

Florac, a busy little town, is overlooked by the craggy Rochers de Rochefort. The headquarters of the Parc National des Cévennes are located in the restored castle here. The Parc National des Cévennes covers an area of some 3000sq km of rugged, quasi-mountainous country, rich in both flora and fauna. There are wonderful views of it from the Corniche des Cévennes, a long, high ridge you will cycle up to on Stage 5.

Stage 5 Florac to Alès

Distance	83km/52 miles
Terrain	Very hilly, a long descent, then undulating
Climb	625m

The route

From the centre of Florac take the D907 S with the Tarnon river on your L for 5km to le Mazel. Bear L here over the river, after which the road (D983) starts to climb quite steeply to **St Laurent-de-Trèves** (875m), well known for the 190-million-year-old dinosaur footprints

Note Buy food and water in Florac before setting off.

that were discovered here on a rocky platform near the village. Onwards and upwards to the Col de Rey at 992m where the D983 descends L to Barre-des-Cévennes. Instead, continue on up to the **Col des Faisses** (1026m) on the D9 and enjoy the effortless ride along the **Corniche des Cévennes** ridge, which grants magnificent views of the Parc National des Cévennes.

Parc National des Cévennes

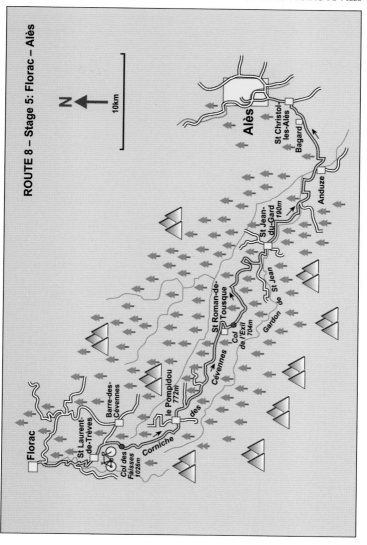

ROUTE 8 – Stage 5: Florac – Alès

N

10km

Florac

St Laurent-de-Trèves

Col des Faïsses 1026m

Barre-des-Cévennes

le Pompidou 772m

Corniche des Cévennes

St Roman-de-Tousque

Col de l'Exil 704m

Gardon de St Jean

St Jean-du-Gard 190m

Anduze

Bagard

St Christol-les-Alès

Alès

233

The road then wriggles its way down to the village of **le Pompidou** (772m) before a gradual climb of some 50m, then a wonderful 20km descent to the Gardon Valley, which includes the **Col de l'Exil** (704m) and Col de St Pierre (597m). The latter marks the boundary between Lozère and Gard as well as being a point where the GR70, better known as the Robert Louis Stevenson Trail, passes. The author crossed the Cévennes with a donkey in 1878, and an account of his journey was published in 1879. Upon reaching the Gardon de St Jean (hot brake pads?) turn L along the D907 to **St Jean-du-Gard**, a very pleasant place. Continue SE for 7km on the D907, which follows the Gardon de St Jean river to a junction. Go L here then take the second exit at the rdbt for Anduze, still the D907. The road passes under the Cévennes steam railway line and once more sticks close to the river, skirting the north side of a wooded hill before turning S and going under the railway line again. Cross the river in **Anduze** and follow the D910A (climb from the river) to **St Christol-les-Alès** (9km) before turning L (second exit at rdbt – Rond Point du 8 Mai 1945) onto the N110. Take the second exit (N) at the next rdbt after 3km (Avenue d'Anduze) for Alès *centre ville,* crossing the Gardon d'Alès river to reach the train station.

How to get back to Clermont-Ferrand/Nîmes

You can get a direct train from Alès N to Clermont-Ferrand (TER or other service) which takes 4hr, and from here to Paris Gare de Lyon (4hr) or a train S to Nîmes (40min/TER service) for Nîmes airport or Montpellier airport further SW. There are also rail connections from Nîmes to Avignon Centre station (and then from Avignon TGV station to Paris by TGV) and from Avignon Centre station to Marseille. See Route 5 Introduction for some information on airports hereabouts. Avignon TGV station is situated in the S suburbs of Avignon, 3km from Avignon Centre station.

SELECTED ACCOMMODATION
ROUTE 8

**STAGE 1 MEYMAC TO
RIOM-ÈS-MONTAGNES**

Campsites
Meymac
Camping La Garenne ★★★ (NE on D30)
☎ 05 55 95 22 80
Open mid-May–mid-October

Ussel
Camping Municipal du Centre
Touristique de Ponty ★★★

Bort-les-Orgues
Camping Les Aubazines ★★★
Camping Municipal Beausoleil ★★
Camping Municipal Le Toulourou ★

Vebret
Camping Municipal ★

Riom-ès-Montagnes
Camping Municipal le Sédour ★★
(E on D678)
☎ 04 71 78 05 71
Open May–September

B&Bs
Sarroux
Vennat
Puy de Bort, 19110 Sarroux
☎ 05 55 96 05 10

Bort-les-Orgues
Bourdoux
51 Boulevard de la Nation, Place de
l'Eglise, 19110 Bort-les-Orgues
☎ 05 55 96 00 58

Vebret
Galvaing
Verchalles, 15240 Vebret
☎ 04 71 40 21 58
guy.galvaing@wanadoo.fr

Hotels
Meymac
Le Limousin, 76 Ave Limousine,
19250 Meymac
☎ 05 55 46 12 11

Bort-les-Orgues
Central Hotel, 65 Ave de la Gare,
19110 Bort-les-Orgues
☎ 05 55 96 81 05
sarl.jokotel.central.hotel@libertysurf.fr

Riom-ès-Montagnes
Le Panoramic, Les Mazets. Route de
Murat, 15400 Riom-ès-Montagnes
☎ 04 71 78 06 41
lagriffoul@wanadoo.fr

Le Saint-Georges, 5 rue du Capitaine Chevalier, 15400 Riom-ès-Montagnes
☎ 04 71 78 00 15
hotel.saint-georges@wanadoo.fr

STAGE 2 RIOM-ÈS-MONTAGNES TO ST FLOUR

Campsites
Apchon
Camping Municipal ★★

Cheylade
Camping Municipal de la Biaugue ★

Murat
Camping Municipal de Stalapos ★★

St Flour
Camping Municipal les Orgues ★★
19 Ave Dr Mallet (Ville-haut)
☎ 04 71 60 44 01
Open mid-May–mid-September

Camping International La Roche Murat ★★ (4.5 km NE towards junction 28 of A75)
☎ 04 71 60 43 63
Open April–October

B&Bs
La Chappelle-d'Alagnon (E of Murat)
Medard
Gaspard, 15300 La Chappelle-d'Alagnon
☎ 04 71 20 01 91
denis.medard@wanadoo.fr

Roffiac
Brouard
Le Bourg, 15100 Roffiac
☎ 04 71 60 11 33

Hotels
Segur-les-Villas
De La Santoire, 15300 Segur-les-Villas
☎ 04 71 20 70 68

Murat
Les Messageries, 18, Ave du Docteur Louis Mallet, 15300 Murat
☎ 04 71 20 04 04
info@hotel-les-messageries.com

St Flour (lower town)
Auberge de la Providence, 1 rue du Château d'Alleuze, 15100 St Flour
☎ 04 71 60 12 05
info@auberge-providence.com

Le Saint Jacques, 8 place de la Liberté, 15100 St Flour
☎ 04 71 60 09 20
www.hotelsaintjacques.com

St Flour (upper town)
Grand Hotel de l'Europe, 12–13, Cours Spy des Ternes, 15100 St Flour
☎ 04 71 60 03 64
info@saint-flour-europe.com

STAGE 3 ST FLOUR TO MARVEJOLS

Campsites
St Chély-d'Apcher
Camping Municipal ★★

Marvejols
Camping Municipal Europe ★★★ (1.5km E)
☎ 04 66 32 03 69
Open June–September

Hotels
St Chély-d'Apcher
Les Portes d'Apcher, Ave de Saint-Flour. 48200 St Chély-d'Apcher
☎ 04 66 31 00 46

Aumont-Aubrac
Chez Camillou, 10 route du Languedoc, 48130 Aumont-Aubrac
☎ 04 66 42 80 22
camillou@club-internet.fr

Marvejols
De la Gare et Des Rochers, Place de la Gare, 48100 Marvejols
☎ 04 66 32 10 58
hotel.rocher@worldonline.fr

STAGE 4 MARVEJOLS TO FLORAC

Campsites
Chanac
Camping Municipal La Vignogne ★★

Ste Enimie
Camping Le Couderc ★★★
Camping Les Fayards ★★★
Camping de Mr Solanet ★★
Camping du Centre de Plein Air ★★
Camping Le Castel Bouc ★★

Ispagnac
Camping Municipal ★★★
Camping de l'Aiguebelle ★★
Camping Le Vieux Moulin ★★
Camping Les Cerisiers ★★

Florac
Camping Municipal Le Pont du Tarn ★★ (2km N)
☎ 04 66 45 18 26
Open April–mid-October
Camping Le Velay ★

B&Bs
Chanac
Pradeilles
48230 Chanac
☎ 04 66 48 21 91

Quezac
Mejean
La Maison de Marius, 8 rue du Pontet, 48320 Quezac
☎ 04 66 44 25 05
www.chez.com/maisondemarius

Hotels
Chanac
Des Voyageurs, 48230 Chanac
☎ 04 66 48 20 16
lesvoyageurschanac@wanadoo.fr

Florac
Le Rochefort (2 Km N on N106),
48400 Florac
☎ 04 66 45 02 57
ledolmen.lerochefort@wanadoo.fr

Des Gorges du Tarn, 48, rue du
Pêcher, 48400 Florac
☎ 04 66 45 00 63
gorges-du-tarn.adonis@wanadoo.fr

STAGE 5 FLORAC TO ALÈS

Campsites
Le Pompidou
Camping Municipal Bel Air ★★

St Jean-du-Gard
Camping La Cam ★★★
Camping La Forêt ★★★
Camping Les Sources ★★★

Anduze
Camping Le Malhiver ★★★★
Camping Cevennes Provence ★★★
Camping l'Arche ★★★
Camping Le Pradal ★★★
Camping Les Fauvettes ★★★
Camping Castel Rose ★★

Alès
Camping Municipal des Châtaigniers ★
☎ 04 66 52 53 57
Open June–mid-September

La Croix Clémentine ★★★ (2km NW,
D916 then D32 L)
☎ 04 66 86 54 84
Open April–mid-September
238

Nîmes
Camping Domaine de la Bastide
★★★

B&Bs
Barre-des-Cévennes
Boissier
Le Mazeldan, 48400 Barre-des-
Cévennes
☎ 04 66 45 07 18

Le Pompidou
Causse
48110 Le Pompidou
☎ 04 66 60 31 82
j.m.causse@libertysurf.fr

Anduze
Anfosso
Le Cornadel, 30140 Anduze
☎ 04 66 61 79 44
anfosso@cornadel.fr
www.cornadel.fr

St Christol-les-Alès
Sallieres
Boujac Les Micocouliers, 128 chemin
des Brusques, 30380 St Christol-les-
Alès
☎ 04 66 60 71 94

Alès
Delaporte
Mas de Rochebelle, 44 chemin Sainte
Marie, 30100 Alès
☎ 04 66 30 57 03
masderochebelle@aol.com
www.masderochebelle.net

Hotels
St Jean-du-Gard
La Corniche des Cévennes, Quartier
le Razet, 30270 St Jean-du-Gard
☎ 04 66 85 06 99
barthelemy70752@aol.com

Anduze
Porte des Cévennes, 2300, route de
Saint Jean-du-Gard, 30140 Anduze
☎ 04 66 61 99 44
reception@porte-cevennes.com

Alès
Hotel Durand, 3 Boulevard Anatole-
France, 30100 Alès
☎ 04 66 86 28 94

Hotel Orly, 10 rue d'Avéjan, 30100
Alès
☎ 04 66 91 30 00

For further information on
accommodation, see Appendix B

APPENDIX A
Glossary: Bicycle Parts and other useful Cycling Terms

to adjust	*régler*	cycle lane	*bande cyclable*
adjustable spanner	*clef anglaise*	cycle path	*piste cyclable*
adjusting barrel	*tendeur de gaine*	down tube	*tube diagonal*
allen bolt	*vis à 6 pans*	dropout	*patte*
allen key/wrench	*clé allen/clé*	fork	*fourche*
	BTR/clé male	gears	*vitesses*
axle (bottom bracket)	*axe de pédalier*	gear shifter	*manette de vitesse*
axle (hub)	*axe*	glue	*colle*
bike bag	*housse*	grease	*graisse*
ball bearing	*roulement à billes*	hub	*moyeu*
battery	*pile*	inner tube	*chambre à air*
bent	*tordu*	nut	*écrou*
bike lock	*antivol*	oil	*huile*
bike box	*valise de transport*	pliers	*pince*
bolt	*boulon*	puncture/flat (tyre)	*crevaison*
bottom bracket	*boitier de pédalier*	quick release	*blocage rapide*
brake	*frein*	rack	*porte-baggages*
broken	*cassé*	repair kit	*trousse de reparation*
cassette	*cassette (k7)*	screw	*vis*
chainstay	*base*	screwdriver	*tournevis*
chain tool	*dérive chaîne*	seat post	*tige de selle*
cleat	*cale*	seatstay	*hauban*
crankarm	*manivelle*	seat tube	*tube de selle*
crankset	*pédalier*	spanner	*clef à écrous*

APPENDIX A – GLOSSARY: BICYCLE PARTS AND OTHER CYCLING TERMS

spoke key	*clef à rayons*	top tube	*tube horizontal*
spoke nipple	*écrou de rayon*	tyre lever	*démonte-pneu*
spring	*resort*	washer	*rondelle*
sprocket/rear cog	*pignon*	wheel	*roue*
to straighten	*redresser*	worn out	*usé*

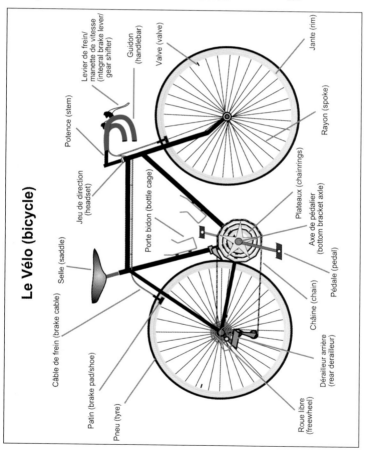

Le Vélo (bicycle)

APPENDIX B

Accommodation

Lists of selected accommodation along or near each route (campsites, B&Bs, hotels), within each stage, are given at the end of each route description. There are other accommodation possibilities, including youth hostels and motel chains. Keen hostellers should visit **www.fuaj.fr** for information on hostelling in France; FUAJ stands for Fédération Unie des Auberges de Jeunesse. Motel chains include Ibis (**www.ibishotel.com**), Novotel (**www.novotel.fr**) and Formule 1 (**www.hotelformule1.com**), amongst others.

To book a room at a B&B or hotel in advance from outside France first dial your international access code (00 from the UK, 011 from the US/Canada, 0011 from Australia), then the country code (33), then the required number given in the accommodation lists *minus* the first 0. Include the first 0 only if calling within France (you will dial 10 digits in all).

Campsites

If you like camping, you'll love France! There are literally thousands of campsites peppered all over the country, ranging from the small camping municipal sites which are cheap and run by the local *communes* to the grand four-star sites usually found along the coasts and near tourist hotspots. The *camping municipal* sites are often little gems, sometimes tucked away in beautiful, quiet surroundings, and can cost as little as 6 euros a night (two people and tent). Don't be surprised if the office is closed when you arrive – it usually only opens early morning and early evening, and sometimes not at all during the spring and autumn. On some sites the person in charge who works for the *commune* will actually come to you for payment, then give you a receipt. The showers sometimes require a *jeton* (token) that you can get at the campsite office.

Most campsites are open from May to the end of September or sometimes mid-October; some are open by early April; quite a few are open all year (*permanent*). Two-star campsites are normally privately owned (8–12 euros on average), and three-star campsites usually have a games room and sometimes an on-site bar or restaurant. A pitch for the night costs 10–18 euros (two people and tent). Four-star sites will normally cost more than 15 euros (especially if the owners are in the process of building an aqua-slide for the swimming pool), but these sites are fully equipped for all your needs. Selected campsites are listed according to the *commune* they come under, which means they could be located several kilo-metres from the village or town stipulated.

Camping à la ferme (camping on the farm) can often be found in rural areas and are yet another cheap option, although some do not have facilities. Michelin's *Camping Caravanning le guide* is published annually and is a very useful guide to over 3000 campsites in France. Camping rough is not advisable, but if you do get stuck in the middle of nowhere try to find out where the local farmer or landowner lives as they will probably let you camp in a corner of a field for the night.

Bed & Breakfast

B&B establishments (*chambres d'hôtes*) can be found all over France, especially in rural areas. You pay for a room in a privately owned house or farm, sometimes even a château. A double-bed or twin-bed room will usually cost around 40–80 euros per night (mostly *en suite*), and includes breakfast. Some offer an evening meal (*table d'hôte*), which may mean you actually dine with the owners. This is a great way of getting to meet local people who know the area, and to eat good food often typical of the region. Most of the proprietors speak English well; some may even be English, having moved to the area after falling in love with it. If dinner is not available at a *chambre d'hôtes* the owners will happily suggest a good restaurant locally.

B&Bs have fewer rooms than hotels, so it might be wise to book in advance, especially if touring in July and August. Contact details for selected B&Bs are given at the end of each route description, or visit **www.gites-de-france.com**, a useful website through which you can often contact many of the proprietors. The AA has published a superb guide to over 4000 *chambres d'hôtes* in France that have been inspected and approved by Gîtes de France, whose green and yellow signs adorn the façades of so many B&Bs (**www.theAA.com/bookshop** and **www.gites-de-france.fr**). You may see roadside signs indicating that there is a *chambre d'hôtes* nearby, especially on the Provence tour. Some *chambres d'hôtes* accept credit cards and even travellers' cheques, but many will require payment in cash, especially in rural areas.

Hotels

French hotels are graded from one to five stars. A standard double-bed room in a one-star hotel should not cost more than 35 euros per night, but city prices may be higher, especially Paris. A two-star hotel should cost around 35–60 euros per night, and a three-star 60–90 euros. A very cheap hotel room may only have a washbasin, while showers and toilets could be communal. A communal shower may be free or may require a token (*jeton*), available at reception. You should be able to get a room with its own bath or shower (but possibly not a toilet) for about 40–45 euros a night. If you want a room with a toilet as well then ask for *une chambre avec une salle de bain*, which should only cost 5–10 euros more. A double room will either have a double bed or twin beds, and costs only slightly more than a single room.

Hotel meals are another consideration. Breakfast (*petit déjeuner*) is usually optional, costing about 5–10 euros per person. Some hotels, especially in tourist areas, will charge half-board (*démi-pension*) which means you are paying for a room, breakfast, and either lunch or dinner. Check the hotel's price list – which should be displayed near the entrance – before booking in.

If you are visiting during the busy summer months and most hotels are full (*complet*) then visit the local tourist office to find accommodation brochures for the area (or phone to book accommodation well in advance). The French Tourist Office also produces a yearly guide to mostly family-run hotels that collectively make up the 4000 or so *Logis et Auberges de France*. These offer value-for-money accommodation and good service (**www.logis-de-france.fr**). If you prefer luxury hotels with character then the more expensive Châteaux & Hôtels de France (**www.chateauxhotels.com**) and Relais du Silence (**www.silencehotel.com**) will be to your liking.

APPENDIX C
Further Reading

There are plenty of useful guidebooks on France and her most popular regions, notably The Green Guides by Michelin, The Rough Guide series, the Lonely Planet series, Cadogan Guides and DK Eyewitness Travel Guides.

Other interesting reads include:

Walking Through France by Robin Neillands (Collins, 1988)
Le Lot by Helen Martin (Columbus Books, 1988)
French Revolutions by Tim Moore (Vintage, 2002)
23 Days in July by John Wilcockson (John Murray, 2004)
Memories of the Peleton by Bernard Hinault (Springfield Books, 1989)
Travellers' Nature Guides France by Bob Gibbons (Oxford University Press, 2003)
The French Pyrenees by John Sturrock (Faber & Faber, 1988)
South to Gascony by Michael Brown (Hamish Hamilton, 1989)
Village France (AA Publishing, 1996)
Villages of France by Joanna Sullam, Charlie Waite and John Ardagh (Weidenfeld & Nicolson, 1988)
The Dordogne by David Gallant and Simon Cobley (Guild Publishing, 1990)

APPENDIX D
Regional Specialities
and Wines of France

Listed below, in alphabetical order, are brief descriptions of the **regional specialities** marked on the map. Although, for example, a *galette* will probably taste better in a Breton restaurant than elsewhere in France – it is a speciality of Brittany – you should be able to eat good variants of some of the selected dishes at any fine restaurant in the country. A wide variety of cheeses from many regions can be found in most large supermarkets, so you won't have to travel halfway across the country to sample Brie or Camembert, for example!

Boeuf à la bourguignonne	Burgundian speciality, beef cooked slowly in a sauce that includes red wine from the region, mushrooms and onions.
Bouillabaisse	This traditionally Mediterranean dish is a chunky soup of various fish.
Brie	A creamy, often slightly runny, soft cheese. If you can find it, try Brie de Meaux, which is produced on farms east of Paris.
Camembert	Another cheese famous worldwide: soft, round, and encased in a white rind. Camembert is a village in Normandy.
Canard rouennais	Roast duck from the Rouen area.
Cassoulet	Traditionally a dish from Languedoc, it includes white haricot beans, pork, unsmoked bacon, sausage, lamb, goose and garlic.
Choucroute garnie	Sauerkraut (shredded cabbage), sausage and pork is a speciality of Alsace.
Clafoutis	A baked cherry pudding from the Limousin region.
Coq au vin	Chicken flamed in brandy then cooked in a red wine sauce that includes butter, mushrooms and shallots; another speciality of Burgundy.

SOME REGIONAL SPECIALITIES OF FRANCE

Cuisses de grenouilles

Canard rouennais

Maroilles

Sole normande

PARIS ◯ Brie

Quiche Lorraine

Camembert

Choucroute garnie

Homard à l'armoricaine

Galette

Boeuf à la bourguignonne

Coq au vin

Valençay

Pithiviers

NANTES

Clafoutis

GENEVA

Truffado

Fondue

Friand sanflorain

Foie gras

Labuiole

BORDEAUX

Roquefort

Salade Niçoise

Soupe au pistou

Cassoulet

Bouillabaisse

Croustade

Pipérade

MARSEILLE

SPAIN

CORSICA

Hot food stall at a market in Brittany

Croustade	An apple pie or pastry. The Ariège (Pyrénées) *croustade* is a sugary apple or pear pie. In Gers, north of the Pyrénées, the *croustade* is made of rolled layers of pastry and apple soaked in Armagnac.
Cuisses de grenouilles	Frogs' legs garnished with garlic or accompanied by a cream sauce.
Foie gras	Goose liver, most popular as a pâté, from the Dordogne and Landes areas.
Fondue	A cheese sauce made up of Gruyère cheese, white wine and kirsch into which you dip strips of bread traditionally; an Alpine dish.
Friand sanflorain	Pork from the Auvergne region mixed with herbs and wrapped in pastry, a speciality from St Flour.
Galette	A Breton speciality, this buckwheat pancake is traditionally topped with a cooked egg and ham, and rolled up.
Homard à l'armoricaine	Lobster in a white wine, brandy, onion and tomato sauce.
Labuiole	A cheese made from cows' milk from the high, rugged Aubrac countryside where thyme is commonly found.
Maroilles	A spicy, strong-smelling cheese from the Ardennes.

Pipérade	Scrambled-egg omelette with red peppers, often with bacon, ham or potato chunks added to make a hearty mountain meal; a Basque speciality.
Pithiviers	An almond- and rum-flavoured gâteau named after a town near Orléans and the River Loire.
Quiche Lorraine	A well-known tart made of eggs and ham.
Roquefort	One of France's great cheeses; made from ewes' milk in the rugged Cévennes and matured for months in the deep caves of Roquefort near St Affrique; a flaky, blue-veined cheese.
Salade Niçoise	Mediterranean salad made up of eggs, olives, anchovies, tuna, tomato, peppers and beans.
Sole normande	Sole, oysters and mussels in a rich cream sauce.
Soupe au pistou	A basil-based vegetable soup from Nice.
Truffado	Potatoes fried with cheese, bacon and garlic; a popular dish in the Auvergne.
Valençay	A pyramidal-shaped goats'-milk cheese from the Loire Valley.

Here are brief descriptions of the typical **wines** to be found in the nine regions marked on the map.

Loire Valley Crisp, white Muscadet wine of Nantes, and Sauvignon wines of Sancerre and Pouilly Fumé north of Nevers. Light, soft, red wine of Chinon, Saumur and Bourgueil. Chenin blanc, sparkling and still wines of Vouvray. Rosé d'Anjou of Angers.

Champagne Three grape varieties – the Chardonnay, Pinot Noir and Pinot Meunier – are grown in this part of northern France, producing the only sparkling wine in Europe that may be called Champagne. High percentage of Pinot Meunier in the fruity wine of the Marne Valley. White Chardonnay vineyards south of Epernay are perhaps the most famous of the Champagne areas. High percentage of Pinot Noir present in the aromatic wine produced between Epernay and Reims to the north. Also Sézanne and the Aube vineyards further south.

Alsace Almost entirely fruity white wines produced from French or German grape varieties such as Reisling.

Burgundy Classic, white wine of Chablis near Auxerre, dominated by the Chardonnay grape. Between Dijon and Lyon the famous red wines of the Côte

Vineyards near Caromb

d'Or (Côte de Nuits, Hautes-Côtes de Nuits and Beaune) and fruity red of Beaujolais, south of Mâcon. Try the wonderful Morgon and Fleurie reds.

Jura and Savoie *Vins jaune,* the golden-coloured white wine of the Jura, and sparkling wines of the Savoie between Lake Geneva and Grenoble.

Rhône Valley and Provence Strong red wines of the Rhône Valley; Châteauneuf-du-Pape is probably the best known. Côtes-du-Rhône-Villages is a good choice. The better *domaines* of rosé wine of Côtes du Ventoux, named after the landmark mountain, Mont Ventoux (northeast of Avignon), and Cotes du Luberon are worth sampling; also Tavel (northwest of Avignon). Rosé accounts for 60 percent of all Provencal wine, but the lesser-known good reds are very good.

Languedoc-Roussillon The largest wine-producing region in France and famous for its *vins de pays* – red, white and rosé – that represent the rural, quaffing wines of the south.

Sud-Ouest The southwest of France, excluding Bordeaux, is home to a number of different wines, notably the dark and fruity, blackcurrant red from the vineyards of Cahors along the River Lot, and the ruby-coloured Bergerac along the River Dordogne. The red, white and rosé wines of Gaillac along the River Tarn have become very popular of late. Worth trying are the earthy reds of Irouléguy in the Pyrénées.

Bordeaux Surely the most famous wine-producing area in the world: the renowned reds of Graves, Médoc, Pomerol and St Emilion, as well as the great whites of Sauternes, to mention but a few. Famous château labels include the *premier crûs* red wines of Lafite, Margaux, Latour and Haut-Brion, and *premier crû supérieur* white of Yquem.

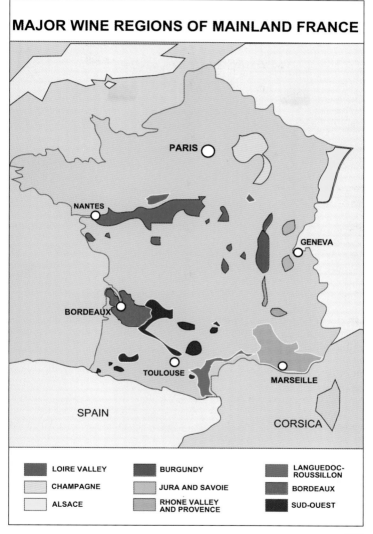

MAJOR WINE REGIONS OF MAINLAND FRANCE

PARIS

NANTES

GENEVA

BORDEAUX

TOULOUSE

MARSEILLE

SPAIN

CORSICA

■ LOIRE VALLEY	■ BURGUNDY	■ LANGUEDOC-ROUSSILLON
■ CHAMPAGNE	■ JURA AND SAVOIE	■ BORDEAUX
■ ALSACE	■ RHONE VALLEY AND PROVENCE	■ SUD-OUEST

APPENDIX E

Information Centres

The following *Offices de Tourisme* and *Syndicats d'Initiative* are the principal information centres to be found along each route, and are listed according to the suggested route descriptions.

Route 1

Morlaix
Place des Otages, BP 135, 29203 Morlaix
☎ 02 98 62 14 94; Txt 940 696

Carantec
4 rue Pasteur, BP 62 Carantec
☎ 02 98 67 00 43
carantec.tourisme@wanadoo.fr

Roscoff
46 rue Gambetta, BP 58, Roscoff
☎ 02 98 61 12 13

Plouguerneau
Place de l'Europe, BP 23 Plouguerneau
☎ 02 98 04 70 93
ot.plouguerneau@wanadoo.fr

Lannilis
1 place de l'Eglise, 29870 Lannilis
☎ 02 98 04 05 43
office@abers-tourisme.com

Ploudalmezeau
Place Chanoine Grall, BP 31 Ploudalmezeau

☎ 02 98 48 12 88
oct.ploudalmezeau@wanadoo.fr

Le Conquet
Parc de Beauséjour, 29217 Le Conquet
☎ 02 98 89 11 31

Plougonvelin
L'Hippocampe, Bd de la Mer, 29217 Plougonvelin
☎ 02 98 48 30 18
omt.plougonvelin@wanadoo.fr

Brest
Place de la Liberté
☎ 02 98 44 24 96
Office.de.Tourisme.Brest@wanadoo.fr

Lanvéoc
Mairie
☎ 02 98 27 59 04
Le Faou
10 rue du Gal de Gaulle, 29590 Le Faou
☎ 02 98 81 06 85

Brasparts
Place des Monts d'Arrée
☎ 02 98 81 47 06

Huelgoat
Moulin du Chaos, BP 22, 29690
Huelgoat
☎ 02 98 99 72 32

Route 2
Lizy-s-Ourcq
Mairie, 5 rue Jean Jaurès
☎ 01 60 01 70 35

Charly-sur-Marne
20 Place du Général de Gaulle,
02310 Charly-sur-Marne
☎ 03 23 82 07 49
otsi@tourismecharlysurmarne.com
www.tourismecharlysurmarne.com

Château-Thierry
11 rue Vallée
☎ 03 23 83 10 14/03 23 83 51 14
otsi-chateau-thierry@wanadoo.fr
www.otsichateau-thierry.com

Dormans
Château de Dormans, Avenue des
Victoires, 51700 Dormans
☎ 03 26 53 35 86

Fèrè-en-Tardenois
18 rue Etienne-Moreau-Nelaton
☎ 03 23 82 31 57
fere-en-tardenois@com02.com
www.fere-en-tardenois.com02.com

Villers-Cotterêts
6 place Aristide Briand, 02600 Villers-

Cotterêts
☎ 03 23 96 55 10
ot.villerscotterets@wanadoo.fr
www.tourisme.cc-villers-cotterets.fr

Pierrefonds
Place de l'Hôtel de Ville
☎ 03 44 42 81 44
ot.pierrefonds@wanadoo.fr

Compiègne
Place de l'Hôtel de Ville, BP 9
Compiègne
☎ 03 44 40 01 00
otsi@mairie-compiegne.fr

Route 3
Colmar
4 rue des Unterlinden
☎ 03 89 20 68 92
info@ot-colmar.fr

Ribeauvillé
1 Grand' Rue, 68150 Ribeauvillé
☎ 03 89 73 62 22
info@ribeauville-riquewihr.com

Châtenois – Scherwiller
2 rue Clemenceau, 67730 Châtenois
☎ 03 88 82 75 00
otchatenoischerwiller@fnac.net

Dambach-la-Ville
Mairie
☎ 03 88 92 61 00
otdlv@netcourrier.com

Itterswiller
Mairie
☎ 03 88 85 50 12/03 88 57 80 25

Barr
Place de l'Hôtel de Ville
☎ 03 88 08 66 65
mairie.barr.ot@wanadoo.fr

Oberhaslach
Mairie, 22 rue du Nideck
☎ 03 88 50 90 15

Wangenbourg
14 rue de la République
☎ 03 88 87 32 44

Saverne
Zone piétonne, 37 Grand Rue
☎ 03 88 91 80 47
info@ot-saverne.fr

Ingwiller
68 rue du Gal Goureau
☎ 03 88 89 23 45
tourisme@pays-de-hanau.com

Niederbronn-les-Bains
6 Place de l'Hôtel de Ville
☎ 03 88 80 89 70
office@niederbronn.com

Lembach
23 Route de Bitche
☎ 03 88 94 43 16
info@ot.lembach.com

Haguenau
Place de la Gare
☎ 03 88 93 70 00

Strasbourg
17 Place de la Cathédrale
☎ 03 88 52 28 28

otsr@strasbourg.com

Route 4
La Roche-sur-Foron
Place Andrevetan, 74800 La Roche-sur-Foron
☎ 04 50 03 36 68
info@larochesurforon.com

Bonneville
63 Boulevard des Allobroges
☎ 04 50 97 38 37
officetourismebonneville@wanadoo.fr

St Jean-de-Sixt
Maison des Aravis
☎ 04 50 02 70 14
infos@saintjeandesixt.com;
infos@aravis.com

Thones
Place Avet
☎ 04 50 02 00 26
thones.tourisme@wanadoo.fr

Faverges
Place Marcel Piquand
☎ 04 50 44 60 24
ot.faverges@wanadoo.fr

Albertville
Place de l'Europe, BP 174, 73204 Albertville
☎ 04 79 32 04 22

La Chambre
Résidence Les Charmettes, 73130 La Chambre
☎ 04 79 56 33 58

St Jean-de-Maurienne
Ancien Evêché, Place de la Cathédrale, 73300 Saint Jean-de-Maurienne
☎ 04 79 83 51 51
St Jean-d'Arves

Les Chambons, 73530 Saint Jean-d'Arves
☎ 04 79 59 72 97

Allemont
☎ 04 76 80 71 60
info@allemont.com

Le Bourg d'Oisans
Quai Girard, 38520 Le Bourg d'Oisans
☎ 04 76 80 03 25
otbo@free.fr

Alpe d'Huez
Place Paganon, 38750 Alpe d'Huez
☎ 04 76 11 44 44
info@alpedhuez.com

Vizille
Place du Château
☎ 04 76 68 15 16
vizille.ot@wanadoo.fr

Grenoble
14 rue de la République, BP 227
☎ 04 76 42 41 41
info@grenoble-isere-tourisme.com

Route 5
Arles
Boulevard des Lices
☎ 04 90 18 41 20; Administration: 04

90 18 41 21
ot.administration@arles.org

Fontvieille
5 rue Marcel Honorat
☎ 04 90 54 67 49

St Rémy-de-Provence
Place Jean Jaurès, 13210 Saint Rémy-de-Provence
☎ 04 90 92 05 22

Cavaillon
Place François Tourel, BP 176 Cavaillon
☎ 04 90 71 32 01
O.T.CAVAILLON@wanadoo.fr

Gordes
Le Château
☎ 04 90 72 02 75

Mazan
83 Place du 8 Mai
☎ 04 90 69 74 27

Caromb
Place du Cabaret
☎ 04 90 62 36 21
Buis-les-Baronnies
Boulevard Michel Eysseric, BP 18
☎ 04 75 28 04 59

Sault
Avenue de la Promenade, 84390 Sault
☎ 04 90 64 01 21
ot-sault@axit.fr

Monieux
Place Léon Doux, 84390 Monieux
☎ 04 60 64 14 14
mairie-de-monieux@wanadoo.fr

Pernes-les-Fontaines
Place Gabriel Moutte
☎ 04 90 61 31 04/04 90 66 47 27

L'Isle-sur-la-Sorgue
Place de la Liberté
☎ 04 90 38 04 78
office-tourisme.islesur-
sorgue@wanadoo.fr

Avignon
41 cours Jean Jaurès
☎ 04 32 74 32 74
information@ot-avignon.fr

Route 6
Toulouse
Donjon du Capitole, BP 0801
Toulouse
☎ 05 61 11 02 22

Foix
29 rue Delcassé, BP 20, 09001 Foix
☎ 05 61 65 12 12

Le Mas d'Azil
Place de l'Eglise, 09290 Le Mas d'Azil
☎ 05 61 69 99 90

Audinac-les-Bains
Mairie, 09200 Montjoie-en-
Couserans
☎ 05 61 66 21 58

St Girons
Place Alphonse Sentein
☎ 05 61 96 26 60
otcouserans@wanadoo.fr

St Lizier
Place de l'Eglise
☎ 05 61 96 77 77

Aspet
Rue Armand Latour
☎ 05 61 94 86 51

St Bertrand-de-Comminges
Les Olivetains, Parvis de la Cathédrale
☎ 05 61 95 44 44

Arreau
Château des Nestes, BP 20 – 65240
Arreau
☎ 05 62 98 63 15

Campan
☎ 05 62 91 70 36
officedetourismedecampan@wanadoo.fr
www.campan-pyrenees.com

Lourdes
Place Peyramale, BP 17, 65101 Lourdes
☎ 05 62 42 77 40
lourdes@sudfr.com

Pierrefitte-Nestalas
Avenue Jean Moulin
☎ 05 62 92 71 31

Argelès-Gazost
Place de la République, BP 35, 65400
Argelès-Gazost
☎ 05 62 97 00 25

Route 7
Brive-la-Gaillarde
Place du 14 Juillet
☎ 05 55 24 08 80
tourisme.brive@wanadoo.fr

Turenne
Le Bourg
☎ 05 55 85 94 38

Carennac
☎ 05 65 10 97 01
ot.intercom.carennac@wanadoo.fr

St Céré
Pavillon du Tourisme, Place de la République
BP 29, 46400 Saint-Céré
☎ 05 65 38 11 85
saint-cere@wanadoo.fr

Figeac
Hôtel de la Monnaie, place Vival, BP 60
☎ 05 65 34 06 25
figeac@wanadoo.fr

Cahors
Place François Mitterrand
☎ 05 65 53 20 65
cahors@wanadoo.fr

Luzech
Maison des Consuls, rue de la Ville
☎ 05 65 20 17 27
office.de.tourisme.de.luzech@wanadoo.fr

Prayssac
Place d'Istrie
☎ 05 65 22 40 57

Lacapelle-Biron
Au Bourg, 47150 Lacapelle-Biron
☎ 05 53 36 55 45

Monpazier
Place des Cornières
☎ 05 53 22 68 59

Belvès
1 rue des Filhols
☎ 05 53 29 10 20

Siorac-en-Périgord
Mairie, Place de Siorac
☎ 05 53 31 63 51

Beynac-et-Cazenac
Parking de La Balme
☎ 05 53 29 43 08

Domme
Place de la Halle
☎ 05 53 31 71 00

Souillac
Boulevard Louis-Jean Malvy, BP 99
☎ 05 65 37 81 56
souillac@wanadoo.fr

Route 8
Meymac
Place de la Fontaine
☎ 05 55 95 18 43/05 55 46 19 90

Bort-les-Orgues
Place Marmontel
☎ 05 55 96 02 49
contact@bort-artense.com

Riom-ès-Montagnes
Place Charles-de-Gaulle
☎ 04 71 78 07 37

Murat
2 rue du fbg Notre-Dame
☎ 04 71 20 09 47

St Flour
Cours Spy des Ternes
BP93
☎ 04 71 60 22 50
off.tourisme@wanadoo.fr

St Chély d'Apcher
Place du 19 Mars 1962, 48200 Saint
Chély d'Apcher
☎ 04 66 31 03 67

Marvejols
Porte du Soubeyran
☎ 04 66 32 02 14

Chanac
Quartier de la Vignogue
☎ 04 66 48 29 28
chanac.tourisme@libertysurf.fr

Ispagnac
Place Jules Loget
☎ 04 66 44 20 89

Florac
Av J. Monestier
☎ 04 66 45 01 14
otsi@ville-florac.fr

St Jean-du-Gard
Place Rabaut St Etienne, BP 02
☎ 04 66 85 32 11
otsistjean@aol.com

Anduze
Plan de Brie, BP.6
☎ 04 66 61 98 17
anduze@ot-anduze.fr

APPENDIX F:

Embassies and Consulates

Embassy and Consulate addresses and websites, and relevant information regarding visas, passports, emergencies and so on while in France.

UK

French Embassy
58 Knightsbridge
London SW1X 7JT
☎ (44) 207 073 1000

General Consulat
21 Cromwell Road
London SW7 2EN
☎ (44) 207 073 1200/Fax: (44) 207 073 1201
Opening hours: Mon–Thurs 08.45–12.00; Friday 8.45–11.30
www.consulfrance-londres.org

USA

Embassy of France
4101 Reservoir Road
NW Washington, DC 20007
☎ (202) 944-6000/Fax: (202) 944-6166
www.info-france-usa.org

Consulates in the United States
www.consulfrance-atlanta.org
www.consulfrance-boston.org
www.consulfrance-chicago.org
www.consulfrance-houston.org
www.consulfrance-losangeles.org
www.consulfrance-miami.org
www.consulfrance-newyork.org
www.consulfrance-nouvelleorleans.org
www.consulfrance-sanfrancisco.org
www.consulfrance.washington.org

CANADA

Visit **www.ambafrance-ca.org**
If you need to apply for a visa, contact your nearest consulate directly.

Consulate Général of France in Toronto
2 Bloor Street East
Suite 2200
Toronto
ON M4W 1A8
Business hours: Mon–Fri, 09.00–12.30 by appointment only. The visa section can only be contacted via the Internet at:
info@consulfrance-toronto.org.
www.consulfrance-toronto.org

Consulate Général of France in Montréal
1 Place Ville Marie
Bureau 2601
Montréal
QC H3B 4S3
Business hours: Mon–Fri, 08/30–12.00
Switchboard (08.30–16.30): 514-878.4385
www.consulfrance-montreal.org
info@consulfrance-montreal.org

Consulat Général of France in Vancouver
Suite # 1100
1130 West Pender Street
Vancouver, BC
V6E 4A4
www.consulfrance-vancouver.org
info@consulfrance-vancouver.org

Consulat Général of France in Québec
25 rue Saint-Louis
Québec (Qc) G1R 3Y8
☎ (418) 694-2294 Fax: (418) 694-1678
Business hours: Mon–Fri, 08.30–12.00, 1400–17.00 by appointment only
www.consulfrance-quebec.org

Consulat Général of France in Moncton
777 rue Main
Suite 800
Moncton NB E1C 1E9
☎ (506) 857-4191/Fax: (506) 858-8169
Business hours: Mon–Fri, 09.00–13.00; afternoons by appointment only
www.consulfrance-moncton.org
info@consulfrance-moncton.org

AUSTRALIA

Embassy of France
6 Perth Avenue
Yarralumla ACT 2600
☎ (02) 6216 0100
Business hours: Mon–Thurs, 09.00–13.00, 14.00–17.45; Fri 09.00–13.00, 14.00–16.00
www.ambafrance-au.org
embassy@ambafrance-au.org
Visa Section (French Consulate-General, Sydney):
visas.Sydney@diplomatie.gouv.fr

NEW ZEALAND

Visit **www.ambafrance-nz.org**

Listed below are Embassies, Consulates and 'American Presence Posts' in France.

UK

The British Embassy
Rue du Faubourg-St.Honoré
75008 Paris
☎ 01 44 51 31 00/Fax: 01 44 51 31 27
www.britishembassy.gov.uk

The five British Consulates General in France are situated in Paris, Bordeaux, Lille, Lyon and Marseille. The British Consulate General in Paris provides full consular services including full passport and visa services. Those in Bordeaux, Lille, Lyon and Marseille provide general consular assistance to British nationals.

The aim of Consular staff is to look after the interests of British nationals visiting France.

Consulate hours open to the public are generally 09.00–12.00 and 14.00–17.00.

Paris 18bis rue d'Anjou, 75008 Paris
☎ 01 44 51 31 00 or 01 44 51 31 02/Fax: 01 44 51 31 27
consulare-mailpavis.consulare-mailpavis2@fco.gov.uk

Lille 1 square Dutilleul, 59800 Lille
☎ 03 20 12 82 72/Fax: 03 20 54 88 16
consular.lille@fco.gov.uk

Bordeaux 353 Boulevard du president Wilson, 33073 Bordeaux Cedex
☎ 05 57 22 21 10/Fax: 05 56 08 33 12
postmaster.bordeaux@fco.gov.uk

Lyon 24 rue Childebert, 69002 Lyon
☎ + 33 (0) 4 72 77 81 70/Fax: + 33 (0) 4 72 77 81 79

Marseille 24 Avenue du Prado, 13006 Marseille
☎ 04 91 15 72 10/Fax: 04 91 37 47 06
MarseilleConsular.marseille@fco.gov.uk

Out-of-hours emergency service
In the event of a serious consular problem, such as a serious illness or accident, a death, or an arrest, contact the Duty Officer on:

Paris Area: 01 44 51 31 00
Bordeaux Area: 05 57 22 21 10
Lille Area: 03 20 54 79 82
Lyon Area: 04 72 77 81 78
Marseille Area: 04 91 15 72 10

If you have lost your passport (or if your passport is out-of-date) and you need to travel urgently, please contact the out-of-hours emergency telephone numbers above. They will explain how to replace your passport or what other documents you may be able to travel on.

UNITED STATES

American Consulates and American Presence Posts in France and their jurisdiction.

The Consular offices in Bordeaux, Lille, Lyon, Nice, Rennes, Strasbourg and Toulouse are not authorised to provide visa services but do provide assistance to American citizens (passport renewals, registrations, notarial services, and so on) in liaison with the US Embassy's Office of American Services.

American Embassy, Paris
2 avenue Gabriel
75382 Paris Cedex 08
Switchboard: +33 1 43 12 22 22/Fax: +33 1 42 66 97 83

Consulate in Paris
Visa Services

Those calling to discuss scheduling appointments are strongly advised to first consult the website or the automated recorded Visa Information Line on 08 92 23 84 72 (fee charged) to be familiar with the information you need when talking with an agent. If you still have unanswered questions or believe that you need to schedule an appointment, then call their Live Service Operators (14,50 Euros per call) at 0 810 26 46 26.

Office of American Services
2 rue Saint-Florentin
75382 Paris Cedex 08
(nearest Métro station Concorde)
☎ 01 43 12 22 22/Fax: 01 42 96 28 39 (passport section)
www.amb-usa.fr
citizeninfo@state.gov

Bordeaux (American Presence Post)
10 place de la Bourse, BP 77
33076 Bordeaux
☎ 05 56 48 63 80/Fax: 05 56 51 61 97
www.amb-usa.fr/bordeaux/default.htm
usabordeaux@state.gov

Lille (American Presence Post)
107 rue Royale
59000 Lille
☎ 03 28 04 25 00/Fax: 03 20 74 88 23

www.amb-usa.fr/lille/default.htm
usalille@state.gov

Lyon (American Presence Post)
1 quai Jules Courmont
69002 Lyon
☎ 04 78 38 33 03/Fax: 04 72 41 71 81
usalyon@state.gov
www.amb-usa.fr/lyon/default.htm

Rennes (American Presence Post)
30 quai Duguay-Trouin
35000 Rennes
☎ 02 23 44 09 60/Fax: 02 99 35 00 92
usarennes@state.gov
www.amb-usa.fr/rennes/default.htm

Strasbourg (Consulate General)
15 avenue d'Alsace
67082 Strasbourg
☎ 03 88 35 31 04/Fax: 03 88 24 06 95
www.amb-usa.fr/strasbourg/default.htm

Marseille (Consulate General)
Place Varian Fry
13086 Marseille Cedex 06
☎ 04 91 54 92 00/Fax: 04 91 55 09 47
www.amb-usa.fr/marseille/default.htm

Nice (Consular Agency)
7 avenue Gustave V
3rd floor
06000 Nice
☎ 04 93 88 89 55/Fax: 04 93 87 07 38
www.amb-usa.fr/marseille/nice.htm

Toulouse (American Presence Post)
25 Allée Jean-Jaurès
31000 Toulouse
☎ 05 34 41 36 50 / Fax: 05 34 41 16 19

usconsulate-tlse@wanadoo.fr
http://www.amb-usa.fr/toulouse/default.htm

CANADA

Canadian Embassy in France
Ambassade du Canada
35 Avenue Montaigne
75008 Paris
Switchboard: (011 33 1) 44 43 29 00/Fax: (011 33 1) 44 43 29 99
(nearest Metro station Franklin D. Roosevelt or Alma Marceau)
Opening hours: Mon–Fri, 09.00–12.00, 14.00–17.00
www.amb-canada.fr

AUSTRALIA

Australian Embassy in France
The Consular Section
Australian Embassy
4 rue Jean Rey
75724 PARIS Cedex 15,
☎ 33 (0)1 40 59 35 40/41/42/Fax: 01 40 59 33 15
www.france.embassy.gov.au

For location of all Embassies in France visit:
www.embassyworld.com/embassy/directory.htm

NOTES